The Ross, Monmouth, & Pontypool Road Line

by

Stanley C. Jenkins MA

THE OAKWOOD PRESS

British Library Cataloguing in Publication Data
A Record for this book is available from the British Library
ISBN 978 0 85361 692 4

First Edition 2002
Second Revised Edition 2009

Typeset by Oakwood Graphics.
Repro by PKmediaworks, Cranborne, Dorset.
Printed by Cambrian Printers, Aberystwyth, Ceredigion.

Front cover: A commercial postcard view of the beautifully situated railway station at Symond's Yat. This card was posted in July 1910, the sender writes 'Rather chilly here, but very nice. The rain kept off. Splendid scenery'. *Oakwood Collection*

Rear cover: The auto-train from Ross is propelled into Monmouth (May Hill) by a '14XX' class 0-4-2T. *Derek Chaplin*

Published by The Oakwood Press (Usk), P.O. Box 13, Usk, Mon., NP15 1YS.
E-mail: sales@oakwoodpress.co.uk
Website: www.oakwoodpress.co.uk

Contents

A commercial postcard of Symond's Yat which clearly shows the railway station.

A general view of Usk station looking east towards Usk tunnel in 1955. Notice the railway delivery lorry standing on the station forecourt. *Derek Chaplin*

Introduction

Monmouthshire is in many ways a microcosm of the Welsh borderlands. Here, in a comparatively small geographical area, rival cultures met in a violent, but ultimately productive conflict. In Romano-British times, this border area was occupied by a warlike Celtic tribe known as the Silures, who had resisted the Romans under their famous leader Caractacus. In later years, they offered similar resistance to the Anglo-Saxons, though in the 11th century the rapacious Norman conquerors were able to subdue the borders by a ruthless campaign of occupation and castle-building.

The turbulent history of the South Wales borderlands produced a romantic and picturesque landscape of castles and villages. In Victorian times, this attractive, Anglo-Celtic district contained a network of local branch lines, which opened-up the area to tourists and visitors from England and elsewhere. These railways, most of which have now been closed, became integral parts of the communities through which they ran, and their stories are an important aspect of local history that is only now being properly appreciated.

The single-track cross-country branch lines from Ross-on-Wye to Monmouth, and from Monmouth to Little Mill Junction (near Pontypool) were interesting, but relatively little-known rural lines that have received curiously little attention from railway enthusiasts or local historians. They were, nevertheless, classic Great Western rural lines that deserve to be much better known, and it is hoped that this new addition to the Oakwood Press will go some way towards redressing the balance.

Historically, the route from Ross-on-Wye to Pontypool Road was built by two entirely separate companies, the Ross & Monmouth Railway being responsible for the eastern section of the line, while the western portion from Monmouth to Little Mill Junction, near Pontypool Road, was built by the Coleford, Monmouth, Usk & Pontypool Railway. The Great Western Railway, which absorbed both undertakings, regarded the Ross-on-Wye to Little Mill Junction line as a continuous route, and it would seem sensible to treat them as one line for the purposes of this present study.

The Wye Valley Railway, which impinged on the Ross-on-Wye to Little Mill Junction route at Monmouth (Troy), is the subject of a companion volume in the Oakwood range, and for this reason it will not be necessary to cover the Wye Valley branch in any detail. On the other hand, there must be at least some mention of this connecting line, which was also a part of the railway history of Monmouth. For the same reason, it will be necessary to mention a number of abortive schemes, notably the Monmouth & Hereford Railway and the Worcester, Dean Forest & Monmouth Railway, both of which featured in the pre-history of the local railway system.

In fact, there were a bewildering number of abortive lines in the Monmouthshire district during the hectic periods of speculation in the mid-1840s and mid-1860s. Many of these failed to gain Parliamentary approval, while others obtained their Acts of Incorporation but were unable to raise sufficient capital. Space precludes a detailed consideration of all of these failed schemes, though it would be impossible to ignore them altogether, as they form an integral part of the story of the Ross to Pontypool Road cross-country route.

Bridge Street, Usk in the 1950s. *Bert Perrott Collection*

The text falls logically into six parts, Chapters One and Two being purely historical chapters that tell the stories of the Ross & Monmouth and Coleford, Monmouth, Usk & Pontypool railways respectively, while Chapter Three deals with the operation of the line under Great Western auspices. The next chapters describe the stations and infrastructure of the two lines in greater detail, and again, it would seem sensible to treat the route as two distinct sections. Finally, Chapter Six completes the historical narrative by recounting the decline of the railway after World War II.

Special thanks are due to Chris Turner, who very kindly allowed me to consult various original books and documents in his collection, and also to Roger Carpenter, Jane Kennedy, R.M. Casserley and the late John Smith, for help in locating photographs of the stations between Ross-on-Wye and Pontypool Road. Chris Potts supplied copies of the line's closure details held in the BR Records Office. It is intended that all Western Region 'closure files' will eventually be transferred to the Wiltshire County Records Office at Trowbridge.

Stanley C. Jenkins
Witney
Oxon
2002

Pubisher's Note: Since publication of the First Edition, the WR Closure files have been transferred to Trowbridge.

Chapter One

The Ross & Monmouth Railway

The Ross to Pontypool Road line was a true 'border route' in that it commenced at Ross-on-Wye on the English side of the border, and ran through parts of Herefordshire and Gloucestershire before entering Monmouthshire beyond Symond's Yat. Westwards, branch trains continued through Welsh territory to their ultimate destination at Pontypool Road. As three-quarters of the 31 mile line was in Monmouthshire, the line could legitimately be described as a 'Welsh' route, although as we shall see, the Ross & Monmouth Railway was formed by a small group of Herefordshire-based promoters.

The Setting

In Roman times the indigenous Celtic and Pre-Celtic people of the South Wales district were known as the Silures, while their neighbours on the east side of the River Severn were the Dubunni. These early Britons were primarily farmers, though the Silures were evidently a warlike people who, under their tribal leader Caractacus, offered strenuous resistance to the Roman invaders. The Romans had occupied southern Britain in 43 AD, but the power of the Silures was not broken until 75 AD.

As far as can be ascertained there were few large settlements in the area during the Roman period, the most important township being *Venta Silurum*, the 'capital' of the Silures. The Roman countryside was probably covered by a patchwork of country estates, each of which had a large house or villa at its centre, though very few of these villa estates have yet been discovered in South Wales. There were also a number of Roman forts or military stations, including a major stronghold at *Isca* (Caerleon), which served as the headquarters of *Legio II* - the second, or 'Augustan' Legion of the Roman Army. Smaller military sites existed at Usk, Monmouth, Abergavenny, Cardiff and elsewhere.

The end of Roman rule in 410 AD was followed by a period of turmoil known as the Dark Ages. In those years, urban life was abandoned, while the great fort at *Isca* fell into decay. Scientific evidence points to a period of climatic change that resulted in a series of catastrophic harvest failures and other calamities - not only in Britain but also around the World. This great calamity hastened the end of Roman civilisation in Britain, and much of the land that had been adapted for cultivation throughout the preceding centuries may have reverted to nature. (The cause of this natural disaster has been much debated, though it may have been caused by a meteorite striking the earth.)

In spite of this enormous setback, the Dark Ages witnessed the birth of the English state, as southern Britain was colonized by settlers from Europe such as the Angles and Saxons. The number of invaders must have been relatively small, but the newcomers were able to settle among the Britons and impose their Germanic language, law and customs upon the earlier Celtic population.

The existing Romano-British inhabitants of the districts east of the River Severn may have been killed or driven away, but it is perhaps more likely that they married and intermingled with the Saxon settlers to produce a mixed Anglo-Celtic population along the Welsh borders.

It was, for many years, considered that the Anglo-Saxons were Germanic conquerors who exterminated the native British population or drove them into Wales and the far West. However, in more recent years historians have concluded that the numbers of Anglo-Saxon settlers were relatively small, while DNA testing has positively demonstrated that people descended from the Ancient Celtic Britons are still abundant in supposedly 'Saxon' areas. On the other hand, the Anglo-Saxon settlement created linguistic and cultural differences between the 'English' and the 'Welsh' people further west, and a political division thereby developed between England and Wales.

The development of Saxon England was disrupted by conflict between the rival kingdoms of Wessex and Mercia, although the South Wales area was largely unaffected by these purely English rivalries. For this reason it is believed that Roman traditions persisted for many years in parts of South Wales. The border, meanwhile, remained ill-defined and flexible in its nature, until, in the reign of King Offa of Mercia (757-96), the great linear earthwork known as 'Offa's Dyke' was constructed. Extending from Chepstow in Monmouthshire, to Gop Hill (near Newmarket) in Flintshire, this impressive feat of engineering effectively delineated the boundary between Wales and Mercia.

The Midland kingdom of Mercia was at its peak during the 8th century, and much of the Welsh borderland was under Mercian control by that time. Hereford, for instance, was an important ecclesiastical centre by 679, while the English County of Herefordshire was brought into existence at a relatively early date, together with the neighbouring counties of Worcestershire and Gloucestershire. In October 1055 Hereford was sacked by a combined Welsh-Irish force, but in the following year Harold Godwinson, the future King of England, raised an avenging army and by tradition built Hereford Castle as a defensive stronghold against further Welsh incursions.

Late Saxon England was undoubtedly one of the richest countries in Europe, and it was perhaps for this reason that it fell victim to William the Conqueror and his followers from Normandy. However, William I had at least some claim to the throne, and he was clever enough to adapt the existing laws and institutions of England to his own needs. For this reason, as far as England was concerned, the Norman Conquest did not mark any great break with the past, and the existing system of manors, parishes and shires was retained as the basis of Anglo-Norman rule on the English side of the border.

Wales had, until this time, enjoyed a large measure of independence, the Welsh princes being content to acknowledge the kings of Wessex as their nominal overlords, in return for help and protection against the marauding Vikings. This comparatively amicable arrangement was overturned by the Norman Conquest, the new rulers of England being grasping empire-builders who saw Wales as ripe for conquest. The Norman invasion of South Wales was led by William Fitz Osbern, Earl of Hereford, who built the first castles at Chepstow, Monmouth and Raglan, and seized the fertile land between the rivers Wye and Usk. This campaign of occupation and fortress building was soon repeated all over South Wales and the borders.

Realising that the turbulent Welsh borderlands presented a major security threat, the Anglo-Norman kings established a network of quasi-independent princedoms known as the Marcher Lordships. Each of these lordships had a fortress as its headquarters, while the Marcher Lords themselves were granted extraordinary powers within their allotted spheres of influence. In this way the indigenous population was subdued, and towns and villages sprung up in the shadow of the Marcher castles. There were, in all, 140 Marcher Lordships, and they extended from the Severn Estuary in the South to the River Dee in the North.

Although castles were soon established at various key points such as Monmouth, Chepstow and Abergavenny, the area between the rivers Wye and Usk was not organized into an English-style 'county' until the Tudor period. To the Welsh, this attractive border district was known as Gwent, a name which was derived from *Venta Silurum*, the tribal capital of the Silures during the Romano-British era.

The distinctive status of the Lords Marchers was finally ended in 1535, when the Marches were 'incorporated, united and annexed to and with this Realm of England' by Henry VIII. Thereafter, Wales and the Marches were administered on the English system, the new counties of Denbigh, Montgomery, Brecon, Radnor and Monmouthshire being established in place of the Marcher Lordships. English law and the English language were imposed on the local population, but in return the Welsh were granted equal citizenship within the unified Tudor state - which was of course ruled by a Welsh dynasty.

Arguably, the Union heralded a 'golden age' in which Wales experienced a national revival, and Welshmen exerted an influence on British life out of all proportion to their numbers. Medieval society was replaced by a new economic and social order that facilitated the growth of commercial agriculture, and ultimately paved the way for large scale industrial development in the 18th and 19th centuries. In particular, South Wales became important as a coal-mining region, and this, in turn, led to the appearance of early tramways and railways in Monmouthshire and the neighbouring Forest of Dean.

An engraving of Usk Castle which was published in the Great Western Railway's book *Castles*, published in 1926.

Early Railway Schemes

The first railways in the South Wales border areas were horse-worked tramways, which were constructed in connection with coal mines or other industrial activities. There were, for example, three such tramways between Abergavenny and Hereford, including the Llanvihangel Railway from Llanwenarth to Llanvihangel Crucorney, and the Grosmont Railway from Llanvihangel Crucorney to Monmouth Cap; these early lines dated from 1811 and 1812 respectively. In 1826 the Hereford Railway was formed to extend the Grosmont Railway north-eastwards to Hereford.

To the east of the Llanvihangel and Grosmont lines, a tramway known as The Monmouth Railway had been incorporated as early as 24th March, 1810 with powers for the construction of a railway or tramway from Howler Slade, in the Forest of Dean, to Monmouth May Hill. This pioneering line, which ran via Coleford and Redbrook, was open by 1817, and it could therefore claim to be the very first railway to reach Monmouth. Confusingly, there was also a company known as the Monmouthshire Railway & Canal Company, which had been incorporated in 1792 to link the ironworks around Blaenavon with Pontypool and Newport by means of a system of tramways and waterways.

There was a similar network of horse-worked railways or tramways in the Forest of Dean, which was at that time an important coal mining and industrial area. Several of these Forest of Dean lines were in existence in the early 19th century, about 30 miles of track being in operation by the 1820s. Interestingly, many of these early lines were built to a gauge of 3 ft 8 in., which seems to have been adopted as the local 'standard' gauge. Lines of this type were essentially products of the canal age, which functioned as adjuncts to the local waterway system. They were rapidly superseded following the introduction of efficient steam locomotives during the 1830s and 1840s.

Railways were then a new and revolutionary form of transport, but the obvious success of lines such as the Liverpool & Manchester Railway seemed to guarantee that the new form of transport was safe, speedy and efficient, and there were soon demands for new railways throughout the British Isles.

One of the schemes promoted at this time was the Cheltenham & Great Western Union Railway which, as its name suggests, was intended to form a connecting link between the town of Cheltenham, the City of Gloucester, and the Great Western Railway main line at Swindon. The Cheltenham project was supported by the GWR, and with Isambard Kingdom Brunel (1806-59) as its Engineer, the railway would be built as a 7 ft broad gauge route. The Cheltenham & Western Union Railway Bill received the Royal Assent on 21st June, 1836, and the resulting Act provided consent for railways from Cheltenham to Gloucester, and from Gloucester to a junction with the GWR main line at Swindon.

Meanwhile, further to the south, an entirely separate company known as the Bristol & Gloucestershire Railway had obtained an Act for construction of a short line from Bristol to collieries near Coalpit Heath. This line was opened, as a horse-worked route, on 6th August, 1835, and on 1st July, 1839 the company obtained a new Act permitting a 22 mile extension to Gloucester; by this same Act, the company shortened its name, the undertaking being henceforth known as the Bristol & Gloucester Railway (B&GR).

At this stage the Bristol & Gloucester Railway was still an independent concern, but logic dictated that the B&GR should move towards closer association with the Cheltenham & Great Western Union Railway. As the Cheltenham company was itself an ally of the GWR (it was purchased outright in 1843), the Bristol & Gloucester Railway was brought firmly into the Great Western sphere of influence. Brunel had already been appointed Engineer to the Bristol & Gloucester company, and it was agreed that the line would be built as a broad gauge route in conjunction with the Cheltenham & Great Western Union Railway.

The Bristol & Gloucester line was opened throughout between Bristol and Gloucester on 6th July, 1844, on which day special trains were arranged for the benefit of the Directors and their guests. Public services began two days later, a temporary station having been erected at Gloucester. There was, as yet, no Great Western station at Gloucester, as the Cheltenham & Great Western Union line had not been completed. However, a 7 mile 30 chain section of the Cheltenham & Great Western Union line between Gloucester and a point known as Standish Junction had been constructed and opened in connection with the Bristol & Gloucester Railway, by arrangement between the two companies.

The Monmouth & Hereford Railway

The Cheltenham & Great Western Union Railway was opened between Swindon and Kemble on 31st May, 1841, and completed throughout from Kemble to Standish Junction on Whit Monday, 12th May, 1845. This new line from Swindon to Gloucester formed an obvious starting point for an undertaking known as the South Wales Railway, which was formed in 1844 with the aim of completing a rail link between London, Pembroke and Fishguard. The South Wales Railway would be built as a broad gauge route, with I.K. Brunel as its Engineer.

Various other schemes for extensions beyond the existing Great Western terminus at Gloucester were suggested during the Railway Mania years of the 1840s. At that time of hectic speculation, ambitious entrepreneurs promoted a whole system of inter-connecting lines between Gloucester, Hereford, Ross-on-Wye and Monmouth. One of these lines was the Monmouth & Hereford Railway (M&HR) which, as proposed in 1844, would have run north-westwards from Standish Junction, on the Cheltenham & Great Western Union Railway, and crossed the River Severn by means of a bridge between Framilode and Westbury-on-Severn.

Having crossed the River Severn, the Monmouth & Hereford main line would have run generally northwards via Walford, Ross-on-Wye and Holme Lacy to Hereford, with a branch from Walford to Monmouth. At Monmouth, the suggested line would form a connection with a proposed branch of the South Wales Railway which would run from Newport to Monmouth via Caerleon and Usk. There was considerable public support for these schemes which, if successfully implemented, would provide an entire system of broad gauge lines in and around Monmouth.

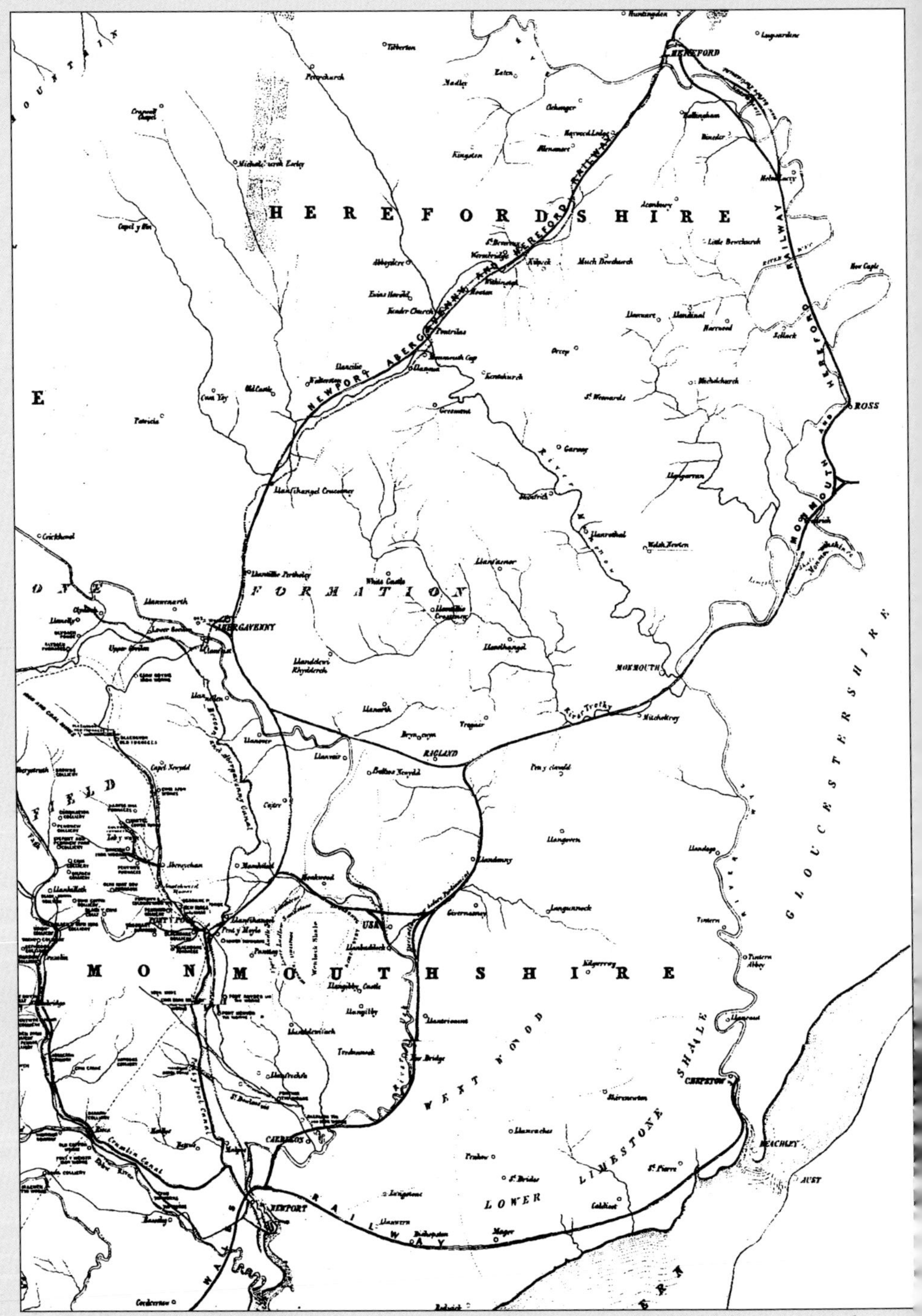

Map of proposals for the Monmouth & Hereford Railway in 1846. Note also a proposed line to connect the M&HR with Abergavenny and the abrupt ending of the South Wales Railway at Chepstow.

A Bill seeking consent for the construction of a railway from Standish Junction to Hereford and Monmouth was submitted to Parliament in the following year, and with the full support of the Great Western Railway the scheme seemed destined for success. On 4th August, 1845 the Monmouth & Hereford Railway Bill received the Royal Assent, although Parliament refused to sanction the proposed bridge across the River Severn. Despite this initial setback, the promoters were keen to proceed with the major part of their scheme for a line between Hereford and Monmouth.

The South Wales Railway had, in the meantime, obtained its Act of Incorporation on 4th August, 1845. The South Wales Railway was, by any definition, a major project, which was designed from its inception as a line between England and Ireland. As such, the proposed railway would form a vital link between two disparate parts of the United Kingdom, with many perceived benefits in terms of mutual trading opportunities and (hopefully) greater political integration. The South Wales Railway was thus seen as a 'great national undertaking to connect the South of Ireland as well as South Wales and the Metropolis'. Its authorized capital was no less than £2,500,000 - an enormous sum by early Victorian standards.

As originally proposed the South Wales Railway would have left the Cheltenham & Great Western Union line at Standish Junction and crossed the River Severn by means of a bridge between Fretherne and Awre. The new main line would have passed well to the south of Monmouth and Gloucester, and for this reason the traders and residents of the Gloucester and East Monmouthshire areas had opposed the scheme. There was also opposition from the Admiralty on the grounds that the proposed Severn Bridge would be an impediment to navigation. Parliament therefore refused to sanction the eastern end of the route, and the authorized railway would now commence at Chepstow rather than Standish Junction.

This unexpected problem was mitigated by the fact that a line known as the Gloucester & Dean Forest Railway had been proposed as a 15 mile connecting link between the Great Western at Gloucester, the Monmouth & Hereford line at Westbury-on-Severn, and the South Wales Railway at Hagloe Farm, near Awre. Royal Assent for the Gloucester & Dean Forest scheme was obtained on 27th July, 1846. This new company was intimately connected with the GWR and its broad gauge allies, and both the Great Western and the South Wales railways had agreed to subscribe capital to the new scheme.

Construction was soon under way on all of these lines, but wet weather and a series of failed harvests in 1845, 1846 and 1848 brought an abrupt end to the railway construction boom. At a time when most of the nation's surplus capital was tied up in new railway schemes, the Victorian stock market collapsed, and in these melancholy circumstances many of the grandiose projects promoted during the Railway Mania failed in their entirety, while other projects were severely impeded as their hapless promoters struggled to raise sufficient capital. By 1848, there was revolution in Europe and mass starvation in Ireland.

One of the casualties of this severe economic crisis was the Monmouth & Hereford Railway. The successful promotion of the Gloucester & Dean Forest Railway had been a source of considerable encouragement for the Monmouth

& Hereford supporters, and having secured this vital link to Gloucester and the rest of the national railway system, the promoters had commenced work on their authorized line. The route was soon marked out for most of its length, and construction began on some of the tunnels and earthworks. Sadly, the works were abandoned in 1847, after £59,000 had been spent on the abortive scheme.

Little progress had been made with the South Wales Railway or the Gloucester & Dean Forest schemes, the underlying social and economic crisis having severely retarded the work of construction. At length, it was agreed that the Dean Forest Railway would be reduced to just 7 miles 36 chains of line between the Great Western at Gloucester and the site of the proposed junction with the Monmouth & Hereford line at Grange Court, near Westbury-on-Severn. The remaining section from Grange Court to Awre would be built by the South Wales company, while both the South Wales and Dean Forest lines would be leased and worked by the Great Western Railway, when completed, as part of the broad gauge system.

The Dean Forest line was substantially completed by 1850, although the need to cross two branches of the River Severn at the Gloucester end delayed completion until the following year. The line from Gloucester to Grange Court was belatedly opened on 19th September, 1851, together with the intervening portion of the South Wales Railway between Grange Court and Chepstow East. The South Wales Railway main line from Gloucester South Wales was finally opened throughout on 19th July, 1852, following completion of the Wye Bridge at Chepstow. An important broad gauge main line was therefore brought into full use as a principal means of communication between London, South Wales and the South of Ireland.

The Hereford, Ross & Gloucester Railway

The failure of the Monmouth & Hereford Railway had caused great disappointment in the district between Grange Court and Hereford, but in the 1850s a similar scheme was resurrected by local interests. The revised proposals were welcomed by the Great Western, and on 5th June, 1851 the Hereford, Ross & Gloucester Railway was incorporated by Act of Parliament, with powers for the construction and maintenance of a broad gauge railway commencing at Grange Court and terminating by a junction with the Shrewsbury & Hereford Railway at Hereford. The authorized capital was £275,000, of which £25,000 had been subscribed by the Great Western Railway.

This new line from Grange Court to Ross-on-Wye and Hereford was, in essence, a revival of the earlier Monmouth & Hereford proposal, which would have followed a similar route through Longhope, Ross-on-Wye and Holme Lacy. On the other hand, the line authorized in 1851 did not include the expensive and controversial bridge across the Severn at Framilode. Instead, the route would commence by a junction with the Gloucester & Dean Forest Railway at Grange Court.

Having obtained their Act of Incorporation, the supporters of the Hereford, Ross & Gloucester Railway began construction of their 22 mile line without further delay, and the southern end of the route was well advanced by the following Spring. In engineering terms the route presented many problems. From its junction at Grange Court the authorized line pursued a circuitous course through an outlying part of the Forest of Dean, a 782 yds-long tunnel being necessary at Lea, near the summit of the route. Descending towards Ross-on-Wye, the chosen route then crossed the River Wye three times within as many miles, beyond which three further tunnels and another viaduct were needed between Ross and Hereford.

Building work continued apace on this new line, and the first section was ready for opening on 11th July, 1853, when trains began running between Grange Court and a temporary terminus at Hopesbrook, a distance of 5 miles 5 chains. The railway was completed throughout to Hereford on 1st June, 1855, all services being provided by the GWR. In 1862 the Hereford, Ross & Gloucester company was fully amalgamated with the GWR under the terms of a Great Western Act obtained on 29th July in that same year. At first, trains ran to and from Grange Court, where connection was made with the main line, but Gloucester later became the terminus for most services to and from Hereford.

Formation of the Ross & Monmouth Railway

A comprehensive system of main lines and connecting branches had been brought into existence in and around the east Monmouthshire area by the late 1850s. In theory, the farmers and traders of the district should have been well satisfied with this new transport system, which provided them with useful railheads at places such as Chepstow on the South Wales route, and Ross-on-Wye on the Hereford, Ross & Gloucester line. It was felt, however, that towns and villages such as Monmouth, Raglan and Usk were important enough to have their own rail links, and for this reason local investors were prepared to support a variety of new branch line schemes.

In this context, there was a further flurry of promotional activity during the 1860s, when several lines were proposed in the Monmouth area. As mentioned earlier, the town had first been served by rail in 1816, but the original Monmouth Railway was merely an isolated tram line. In the next few years, there were a number of proposals for lines to Monmouth, including the abortive Monmouth & Hereford Railway and the Coleford, Monmouth, Usk & Pontypool Railway, which will be dealt with in the following chapter. Another scheme projected at this time was the Worcester, Dean Forest & Monmouth Railway, which would have provided a cross-country link between Monmouth, Coleford and Great Malvern.

The Worcester, Dean Forest & Monmouth Railway obtained Parliamentary sanction on 21st July, 1863, but this project failed to get off the ground. The Ross & Monmouth Railway, in contrast, was an ultimately successful company. The Ross & Monmouth Railway was intended to form a link between the Hereford, Ross & Gloucester Railway and the Coleford, Monmouth, Usk & Pontypool line. There would also have been a junction with the abortive Worcester, Dean Forest & Monmouth line, while another connecting railway would have run southwards from Monmouth to Chepstow, via Tintern and the lower Wye Valley.

The Ross & Monmouth Railway was formed during the 'Second Railway Mania' of the mid-1860s, when a small group of landowners and entrepreneurs sought powers for the construction and maintenance of a railway commencing at Ross-on-Wye by a junction with the Hereford, Ross & Gloucester line, and terminating at Monmouth on the Coleford, Monmouth, Usk & Pontypool Railway.

Like the Hereford, Ross & Gloucester Railway, the Ross & Monmouth scheme was in many ways a lineal descendent of the abortive Monmouth & Hereford Railway, which would have covered roughly the same ground with its proposed branch from Walford to Monmouth. There was, nevertheless, an important difference between the Monmouth & Hereford and Ross & Monmouth schemes, in that the original proposals had envisaged an expensive, broad gauge main line which would form part of a network of connecting routes. The Ross & Monmouth scheme, in contrast, was a more modest proposal, which would be constructed and opened as a standard gauge branch rather than a broad gauge main line.

Although the proposed Ross & Monmouth line was in theory merely a 13 mile branch, it would be a cross-country line rather than a dead-end route, and a such it provided scope for further extensions to east and west. The presence of the Coleford, Monmouth, Usk & Pontypool Railway at the Monmouth end would allow access to the South Wales coal field, while at the eastern end of the Ross & Monmouth route there were various possible extensions and connecting lines towards the Northamptonshire iron ore area. (One of these lines was the Northampton & Banbury Junction Railway, which will be mentioned in further detail below.)

The principal supporters of the Ross & Monmouth scheme included Colonel A.W.H. Meyrick, Colonel H. Morgan Clifford, John Partridge, Henry Richard Luckes and Lieutenant Colonel John Francis Vaughan. As far as can be ascertained these gentlemen were all members of the local landowning or business communities, and they had no obvious connections with the GWR or other main line companies. It would appear, therefore, that the Ross & Monmouth Railway was a predominantly local venture, that was intended to bring railway communication to an otherwise isolated rural area.

All of the leading promoters lived locally, most of them having houses or country estates in or around Ross-on-Wye. Colonel Meyrick, for example, resided at Goodrich Court, about three miles to the south-west of Ross, while Lt-Colonel Vaughan lived at Courtfield, near Kerne Bridge. Colonel H. Morgan Clifford, in contrast, lived at Llantilio House, near Abergavenny, but John Partridge and Henry Luckes were both based in or near Ross-on-Wye. It is likely that these gentlemen would have known each other socially, and it is easy to imagine them meeting behind the closed doors of their country houses during the early stages of promotion.

As in other areas, the decision to build the railway seems to have been taken by members of the landowning class, who alone would have had the financial resources to embark upon such a venture. In the case of the Ross & Monmouth Railway, the most prestigious supporters of the scheme were probably Colonel

Meyrick and Lt-Colonel Vaughan, both of whom belonged to long-established county families. In theory at least, the presence of such illustrious individuals on the provisional Board of Directors should have guaranteed a successful promotion, and indeed, it does appear that the project made very good progress during the preliminary stages of the scheme.

Having obtained encouraging support within the local community, the promoters prepared a Parliamentary Bill for submission to Parliament in the 1865 session. This course of action was necessary so that the company could be properly incorporated, but more importantly, an Act of Parliament would, if necessary, allow the company to obtain land by powers of compulsory purchase, and run its trains over the lines of connecting companies at Ross-on-Wye and Monmouth.

In the latter context, the 1865 Bill sought Parliamentary consent for the construction of a railway from Ross-on-Wye to Monmouth, with powers to run trains over portions of the Coleford, Monmouth, Usk & Pontypool Railway, the Hereford, Ross & Gloucester Railway, and the Worcester, Dean Forest & Monmouth Railway. It was also felt to be desirable that there should be only one station at Monmouth, and for this reason the Bill sought consent for the construction of a joint station that would be shared by trains from the Ross-on-Wye, Pontypool Road and Great Malvern lines.

The proposed Ross & Monmouth Railway had a relatively easy passage through Parliament and this modest scheme received the Royal Assent on 5th July, 1865. The resulting Act (28 & 29 Vict. cap. 312) provided Parliamentary consent for the construction of a 13 mile standard gauge line commencing at Ross-on-Wye and terminating at Monmouth. The Act provided consent for the necessary working arrangements with neighbouring companies, while further provisions allowed the promoters to organize themselves into a properly-constituted Board of five (later six) Directors. The quorum would be three, and the qualification for Board membership was set at £500.

To pay for their scheme, the Directors were authorized to raise capital of £120,000, with a further £40,000 by loans. Lt-Colonel Vaughan, Colonel Meyrick, Colonel Morgan Clifford, John Partridge and Henry Luckes became the first Directors, while Charles Liddell and Edward Richards, of 24 Abingdon Street, Westminster, were appointed as Engineers. Charles Liddell was one of the foremost engineers of his day; he had already carried out much work in the area, having been Engineer of the Newport, Abergavenny & Hereford, Worcester & Hereford, and Monmouthshire Railway & Canal lines.

Having obtained their Act of Incorporation, the Ross & Monmouth (R&M) Directors seem to have experienced second thoughts in respect of the course of the proposed railway. The steep-sided Wye Valley provided an obvious route for the new line, but in 1866 it was decided that 'it would be more beneficial to have a railway on the left side of the river', and the R&M Directors therefore resolved that they would proceed with a deviation Bill, which would allow them to construct the line on the south bank of the Wye.

At the same time, they agreed that there should be better provision for connecting links to other lines, and a Bill seeking Parliamentary consent for deviations in lieu of the old line, and a branch to Lydbrook, was lodged in the

1867 session. The new proposals were sanctioned on 31st May, 1867, and the resulting Act (30 & 31 Vict. cap. 67) also permitted the Ross & Monmouth Railway to increase its capital to £160,000 in shares and £53,000 by loans. Construction work had not yet commenced but meanwhile, further to the east, other interests envisaged that the Ross & Monmouth line might form part of a major trunk route between the Northamptonshire iron producing area and the South Wales coalfield.

The Midland Counties & South Wales Proposals

On 28th July, 1863 a company known as the Northampton & Banbury Junction Railway had obtained an Act for construction of an 18 mile line between Blisworth and Cockley Brake Junction, near Banbury. From its inception, this obscure undertaking was intended to form part of a main line to South Wales, and in 1865 the Northampton & Banbury Junction promoters obtained further powers for extensions to Blockley and elsewhere. In the following year, the company deposited another Bill seeking consent for a line from Blockley to Ross-on-Wye; here, connection would be made with the Ross & Monmouth Railway, by means of which through trains would be able to continue westwards over the Coleford, Monmouth, Usk & Pontypool Railway.

This grandiose scheme received the Royal Assent in 1866. The resulting Act (29 & 30 Vict. cap. 310) provided consent for a 34 mile railway between Blockley and Ross-on-Wye, which would form an integral part of a 96 mile main line between Ross-on-Wye and Northamptonshire. The 1866 Act granted running powers over the Ross & Monmouth Railway and other lines while, in view of the magnitude of their projected scheme, the Northampton & Banbury Junction promoters were permitted to change the name of their undertaking - 'The Midland Counties & South Wales Railway' being deemed a suitably expansive title for the enlarged undertaking!

Having obtained their Acts of Incorporation, the supporters of these railways were faced with serious financial and other problems following the failure of bankers Overend, Gurney & Co. on 10th May, 1866. The results were catastrophic, and with the bank rate standing at 10 per cent the Victorian financial system was plunged into chaos. New companies such as the Ross & Monmouth Railway were unable to raise their authorised capital, while the so-called Midland Counties & South Wales Railway became a laughing stock, its authorized main line being reduced to just four miles of line between Blisworth and Towcester!

At length, a gradual improvement of the underlying economic situation enabled the supporters of these diverse schemes to make belated progress. The Midland Counties & South Wales company eventually managed to open a line from Towcester to Cockley Brake Junction on 1st June, 1872, and having resumed its former identity as The Northampton & Banbury Junction Railway, this Northamptonshire line settled down to eke out an impecunious existence as a country branch line. Meanwhile, in similar fashion, the Ross & Monmouth Directors were able to proceed with their own scheme, Charles Liddell and Edward Richards being the Engineers for both lines.

Construction of the Ross & Monmouth Line

The 1866 economic crisis had retarded the Ross & Monmouth project, but in August 1868 the Directors were able to report that 'the subscriptions, with few exceptions, had been satisfactorily paid up'. It was announced that construction of the railway would shortly be commenced, the necessary contract having been let to Joseph Firbank (1819-1886), a well-known civil engineering contractor. The son of a Durham miner, Joseph Firbank was a classic self-made man, who had carried out much work on lines throughout the country, and eventually became Deputy-Lieutenant of Monmouthshire, with a large house on the outskirts of Newport.

Perhaps significantly, Mr Firbank was well-known to Charles Liddell, having worked with him on the Monmouthshire Railway & Canal Company, and on the Midland Railway London extension contract between Kentish Town and Brent. Although his character and demeanour was said to have been that of a rough and uncultivated Geordie, Joseph Firbank was generally regarded as one of the best railway contractors of his day; he paid his navvies good wages, and supplied them with water and oatmeal gruel in an attempt to dissuade them from consuming excessive amounts of whiskey and ale.

In engineering terms the proposed route was relatively easy, in that the Wye Valley would provide a convenient path through the most difficult terrain between Kerne Bridge and Monmouth. On the other hand, the serpentine nature of the river would entail the construction of an extremely circuitous route which meandered for almost 13 miles between two towns that were barely eight miles apart. The most important engineering features would be three viaducts across the River Wye, two of these being at Kerne Bridge, while the third would be at Monmouth. Elsewhere, there would be numerous cuttings and earthworks along the route, together with tunnels at Symond's Yat and Lydbrook.

The major earthworks were well under way by the summer of 1869. The half-year report for the period ending 30th June, 1869 revealed that £19,688 had been expended, of which £17,668 had been met from share subscriptions, leaving a balance against the account of £2,420. The Directors report stated that 'satisfactory progress had been made in the construction of the line'. The company had 'sufficient uncalled and unspent capital available to complete the line to Kerne Bridge, as well as to make considerable progress with the construction of the tunnels'. It was anticipated that there would be enough money to complete the railway without further delay.

The Directors added that they were trying to make arrangements for the immediate commencement of Symond's Yat tunnel, while on an optimistic note, they referred to the impending change of gauge on the Hereford, Ross & Gloucester Railway, which the Great Western intended to convert to standard gauge. This would obviously be in the interests of the Ross & Monmouth Railway, which would be placed in direct communication with standard gauge lines at each end. 'Looking at the lines with which the railway would be connected', continued the Directors, 'both at Ross and at Monmouth, and the internal traffic which must flow over it, the undertaking would turn out to be remunerative'.

In the event, the Ross & Monmouth scheme was still unable to proceed as well as its promoters would have wished. Approximately four miles of permanent way was in place by 1870, and it was reported that this first section of line, between Ross-on-Wye and Kerne Bridge, was ready for opening. Little progress had been made on the more difficult section between Kerne Bridge and Monmouth, although it was reported that the company was 'in possession of nearly all of the land' that would be required. There had, furthermore, been unspecified problems at Ross-on-Wye, where the junction with the Great Western Railway was still not ready.

The accounts for the period ending June 1870 showed that £51,323 had been expended on the line till that time, while by June 1871 the expenditure had reached £60,652, leaving a balance against the company of £5,447. On the other hand, the Ross & Monmouth Directors were able to report that the necessary funds had been obtained to complete the line, and an agreement had been made on favourable terms with the Great Western Railway. Taking all things into consideration, the Directors had 'every reason to hope that the entire line would be ready for traffic by the middle of 1872'.

The Ross & Monmouth Railway Company was still an independent undertaking with its own Chairman and Board of Directors, though there were at one time suggestions that this entirely localized scheme might be taken up and brought to a successful conclusion by the Midland Railway. However, having obtained a further Act of Parliament in 1872, the supporters of the Ross & Monmouth scheme eventually came to an agreement with the Great Western Railway whereby the line from Ross-on-Wye to Monmouth would by worked by the GWR for 50 per cent of the gross receipts. Thus, with Great Western support, the Ross & Monmouth scheme approached fruition after eight years of effort, and many bitter disappointments.

The heavily-engineered section of line between Kerne Bridge and Monmouth began to take shape in 1872, over £176,000 having been spent on the project by June of that year. Work was still in progress at the beginning of 1873, and the accounts for the half-year ending 30th June reveal that expenditure had reached £201,650. These figures indicate that the major works between Ross and Monmouth must have been tackled around 1872, after the Great Western had started to display a greater interest in the scheme. By 30th June, 1873, the railway was virtually complete between Ross-on-Wye and the east side of the River Wye at Monmouth.

Opening of the Line

The Ross & Monmouth Directors initially hoped that the railway could be opened between Ross-on-Wye and a temporary terminus at Monmouth (May Hill) on Friday 1st August, 1873. Posters and timetables were displayed in Monmouth and the surrounding area, and it was anticipated that the customary celebrations would take place on the appointed day. Unfortunately, unforeseen problems arose as a result of the compulsory Board of Trade inspection, which was undertaken by Colonel Francis Rich RE.

As usual, the newly-completed railway was subjected to minute scrutiny, and it is easy to imagine the government inspector proceeding slowly along the line in company with a somewhat apprehensive Colonel Vaughan. The inspector was accompanied by Thomas T. Firbank (1850-1910) the contractor's son, and various Great Western officials including Joseph Armstrong (1816-77), the locomotive superintendent, and William Owen, the company's Chief Engineer.

The inspector travelled on foot through the tunnels, while the bridges and viaducts were carefully examined for deflection, each bridge being tested at maximum weight as the inspection train was driven backwards and forwards across each structure. The Inspection Report, dated 3rd August, 1873, reveals that there were seven overbridges and 11 underbridges between Ross and Monmouth (May Hill), together with two viaducts over the River Wye. One of the overbridges was of stone construction but the remaining six had stone abutments and cast- or wrought-iron girders. Seven of the underbridges incorporated stone abutments and what were described as 'wooden tops', while four had stone abutments and cast iron girders.

The masonry had 'settled and cracked in many of the bridges, but more particularly in the underbridge at 56 chains', but as these bridges had been built for some time there was 'no reason to apprehend further settlement'. The tunnels had been lined throughout and there were no public level crossings. The steepest gradient was at 1 in 100, while the sharpest curve had a minimum radius of 14 chains.

In general, Colonel Rich was well-satisfied with the strength and stability of the new works, although he identified several minor defects, including unsatisfactory platform arrangements at Monmouth (May Hill) and an inadequate junction layout at Lydbrook. Similarly, at Ross, the Board of Trade Inspector stipulated that 'sprung buffers should be provided at the end of the branch bay platform', while the 'points at the end of the loop line ... would have to be taken out until the locking of points and signals had been properly completed'.

The inspector added that the GWR representatives present at the time of the inspection had agreed to rectify these deficiencies but, unfortunately, there was a last-minute misunderstanding concerning the way in which the railway was to be operated. There was no turntable at the Monmouth end of the route because it was anticipated that, when the connection at Monmouth was completed, trains would run through to Pontypool Road. The Board of Trade inspector therefore stipulated, quite reasonably, that a tank engine would have to be used to work the section of line between Ross and Monmouth (May Hill), in order to obviate the need for tender-first running.

Incredibly, this appears to have caused a temporary problem, the likeliest explanation being that the Great Western could not find a suitable tank locomotive with which to operate the line. The Friday opening was therefore postponed, although this disappointing news did not reach the ordinary people of the district - many of whom turned up at the stations hoping to ride on the first public services. At length, it was agreed that the Ross & Monmouth line would be worked only by tank locomotives, and having received this assurance, Colonel Rich immediately gave permission for the railway to be opened for the carriage of passengers on Monday 4th August, 1873.

The Ross & Monmouth Railway was therefore opened on that day, when public trains began running between Ross-on-Wye and a temporary platform at Monmouth (May Hill). All services were provided by the GWR as previously agreed, and the new railway was, in effect, an integral part of the Great Western system. Although there had been insufficient time to arrange a proper opening ceremony, many people turned up to see the first trains, while others eagerly awaited their chance to ride on the new railway. The first day of operation was described in detail in the pages of *The Ross Gazette* on 7th August, 1873, and this interesting first-hand account of the occasion is worth quoting in some length:

> It is with much pleasure that we have to chronicle the opening of the Ross & Monmouth Railway, which took place on Monday last, and in so doing we have to congratulate the promoters of the line and all those who have aided it towards its present state of completion . . . On Saturday, it was reported that the line would really be open on Monday morning in accordance with the timetables issued, and to re-assure the public, the Town-Crier was sent round early on Monday morning with the sweeping confirmation of the report.
>
> About seven minutes behind time, a well-filled train, consisting of eight carriages, steamed out of the station in the tamest manner, not even a drum was heard, nor a flag unfurled to mark the auspicious event. If it was tame, it was soon shown that there was business meant, and the officials at the stations *en route* were civil, prompt and energetic. Long may this be so! The travelling was remarkably easy and smooth . . . The line, we are informed, is twelve and a half miles in length from the station at Ross to Wye Bridge, Monmouth.
>
> It was commenced in the Autumn of 1868, on the Ross side, and the operations were confined to the portion of the line between this town and Kerne Bridge for the first two years. Then there was an interval of a year in which there was a cessation of work; consequently the line as far as completed will have been nearly four years in hand. There are two tunnels, the principal of which is at Coppet Wood and is of 628 yards in length. The second tunnel runs under Symond's Yat, is cut through solid rock, and is a quarter of a mile in extent. The time occupied in the boring of the tunnels was eighteen months.
>
> At the Coppet Cutting the operation was commenced at each end, and the boring parties met at the centre of the tunnel within an inch - a very considerable feat of engineering skill. At each end of the tunnels, as may be supposed, there is some heavy open cutting, and beyond this the groundwork has been of an ordinary character. Three bridges, however, will span the Wye in connection with the line. Two of these, of elegant construction, form part of the route completed, one being at Kerne Bridge, and the other at Stowfield. The former is 330 feet, has a centre span of 150 feet, and a span on each side of 62 feet.
>
> Of stations there are four, including that at Wye Bridge - viz., Symond's Yat, the Severn & Wye Valley Junction at Lydbrook, and Kerne Bridge. The permanent stations are built of Old Red Sandstone obtained from Tudorville, and have a neat and substantial appearance.
>
> At the Kerne Bridge, a diversion of the turnpike road, as at Monmouth, had to be made, and a great deal more work has had to be performed than had been anticipated in the original scheme in this kind of work. The line of railway runs by the side of the River Wye nearly all the way, and thus the advantages of the 'Wye Tour' are partially secured to the railway passengers . . . The journey ends at Wye Bridge, where a temporary station has been erected. It is the intention of the company to complete the line in the course of a short time as far as Troy. This will necessitate the completion of a third bridge across the river.

Persons journeying from the temporary station for South Wales, and vice-versa, can be conveyed through the town, from one station to the other, by omnibus for about the same fare as that charged from the Troy terminus at present into Monmouth, whilst visitors to the town will have only a few yards to walk to be in the centre of it.

On the occasion of our visit, the Monmouth folks appeared to be smarting under the disappointment of the previous Friday, and little or no notice having been given that there was to be no mistake this time, they were unaware for the most part that trains were really to run on Monday. It was the tale of the wolf over again. Consequently there was but a small number of passengers travelling on the return journey to Ross. Many passengers, however, were picked up at the intervening stations.

There was no demonstration or attempt at anything of the kind if we except a flag hung out at Kerne Bridge station, and a cheer raised by some boys in the train when at Lydbrook. It may be a simple matter to record, but we may as well mention it in the absence of events of greater moment - our townsman Mr Joseph Turnock was fortunate in securing the first 1st Class ticket from Ross to Monmouth and the first from Monmouth to Ross. These tickets he will be allowed to keep as relics of the day.

We should add that the stations at Kerne Bridge and Symond's Yat are very convenient - that at the latter place being constructed with an idea of the probable greater influx of visitors that will occasionally occur. We cannot conclude our notice without expressing our earnest hope for the success and prosperity of the line, both on account of the benefit it will confer on the town, and to the reward, the pluck and perseverance of the original promoters. That the railway may enjoy a long and safe career of usefulness, adding its strong yet ornate link to the chain of important commercial enterprise, is the sincere wish of *The Ross Gazette*.

Colonel Rich returned to the R&MR line in the following January in order to carry out an inspection of the short section of line between Monmouth (May Hill) and Monmouth (Troy) stations. He discovered that the necessary improvements at May Hill station had not been fully implemented while, more seriously, the triple-span bow string girder bridge across the River Wye appeared to be unstable. His inspection report, dated 9th January, 1873, explained the problems as follows:

The lattice bars of the 150 ft bow string girders should be fitted, so as to prevent the loud clapping noise which they make when a train is passing along the viaduct, and a cross beam should be fixed at the top and centre of these girders to prevent their straining inwards when loaded. This viaduct has a considerable lateral motion when a train is passing over it, which I attribute to the height of the iron columns, the very short distance between columns laterally, no stays between them and want of struts up and down stream at each side, so as to give the bridge supports a wider base.

These iron columns were intended to be vertical; the two at the east side of the river are reported to have been placed over a rock which was levelled to carry them, but the two at the west side were placed on marl and one of them subsequently sank until it is supposed it reached the rock. In sinking it got a cant of some few inches to the south and pulled the adjacent column with it, so that neither are upright, and the nature of the foundation on which they rest is doubtful. I believe it to be hard, and possibly rock, but it is not level.

In view of these problems, Colonel Rich was unable to 'pass' the line for public traffic. However, some four months later, on Friday 1st May, 1874, the railway was belatedly extended south-westwards for three-quarters of a mile from its original terminus at Monmouth (May Hill) to the Coleford, Monmouth, Usk & Pontypool station at Monmouth Troy, the viaduct that carried the single line across the intervening River Wye having finally passed its Board of Trade inspection. Figures published shortly after the completion of the R&MR line reveal that the railway had been built at a cost of £15,846 per mile - total expenditure to June 1875 having reached £206,554.

Some Details of the Line

The line was a 13 mile 10 chain single-track branch, with intermediate stations at Kerne Bridge, Lydbrook, Symond's Yat and Monmouth (May Hill). Trains travelling northwards to Ross-on-Wye (then known as 'Ross') were designated up workings, while those proceeding in the opposite direction were regarded as down services. Crossing loops were provided at Kerne Bridge, Lydbrook and Symond's Yat, all three stations being equipped with two platforms for up and down traffic. Lydbrook became a junction in August 1874 (although not renamed as such until January 1899), when a branch of the Severn & Wye Railway was opened for mineral traffic from Serridge Junction, on the Severn & Wye route from Lydney to Cinderford.

The principal engineering features included the 433 yds-long tunnel at Symond's Yat, a 630 yds-long tunnel between Kerne Bridge and Lydbrook, and bridges across the River Wye at Monmouth, Lydbrook and Kerne Bridge. Kerne Bridge and Lydbrook stations had attractive stone station buildings, while Symond's Yat was equipped with a timber-framed building of similar external appearance. Monmouth (May Hill), in contrast, had a timber building of no architectural pretension. Public goods facilities were available at Kerne Bridge and Lydbrook, but not at Symond's Yat or Monmouth (May Hill).

At Ross-on-Wye, trains ran into and out of the Great Western station, but at Monmouth (Troy) a new joint station was constructed to deal with traffic from the Ross & Monmouth, Wye Valley and Coleford, Monmouth, Usk & Pontypool lines. The permanent way was laid in conventional fashion with transverse wooden sleepers, while the minor over and underbridges were soundly constructed. The line was signalled with lower quadrant semaphores, the signalling equipment having been supplied by Messrs McKenzie & Holland.

The new railway was soon carrying modest levels of passenger and freight traffic. The accounts for the period ending 31st December, 1874 showed that rent from the GWR, when added to £5 received as transfer fees, produced gross receipts of £3,743 for the local company. These figures were fairly constant for the first years of operation, the gross receipts for the period ending 30th June, 1875 being £3,116. The revenue received from the Great Western for the half-year ending 31st December, 1875, when added to transfer fees and income tax recouped, amounted to £3,990, while gross income for the following half-year ending 30th June, 1876 was £3,860.

Chapter Two

The Monmouth to Pontypool Road Line

As mentioned above, the Ross & Monmouth Railway was designed, not as a dead-end branch from Ross-on-Wye, but as part of a cross-country route which would form a junction with the existing Coleford, Monmouth, Usk & Pontypool Railway at Monmouth (Troy). Chronologically, the latter railway was somewhat older than the Ross & Monmouth company, and when opened throughout to Monmouth on 12th October, 1857, it became the second railway to serve this historic border town (the first being the Monmouth Railway's much earlier horse-worked tramway).

Origins of the Coleford, Monmouth, Usk & Pontypool Railway

As in so many other cases, the origins of the line between Monmouth and Pontypool Road can be traced back to the Railway Mania years of the 1840s, when ambitious promoters had projected a variety of routes in all corners of the land - often with little or no regard for overall planning or co-ordination. On 3rd August, 1846 a company known as The Newport, Abergavenny & Hereford Railway was incorporated by Act of Parliament, with powers for the construction and maintenance of a railway commencing at Hereford and terminating 'by a junction with the intended Newport & Pontypool Railway' at Ceodygric Farm, about one mile from Pontypool.

At first, the Newport, Abergavenny & Hereford scheme made very little progress, the project having been severely hindered by the economic crisis that had developed in 1846. Eventually, with help and assistance from the London & North Western Railway, the Newport, Abergavenny & Hereford promoters were able to implement their scheme. Charles Liddell was appointed as Engineer in 1851, and the works were in full progress by the following year.

The Newport, Abergavenny & Hereford Railway was opened on 2nd January, 1854, Newport (Mill Street) station being reached by means of the Newport to Pontypool line of the Monmouthshire Railway, which had been opened in 1852. In the meantime, the Newport, Abergavenny & Hereford Railway had obtained powers for an extension running westwards from the main line at Pontypool Road to a junction with the Taff Vale Railway at Quakers Yard. The total length of the Newport, Abergavenny & Hereford Railway was 40 miles, and the projected Taff Vale Extension would add another 12 miles to this total.

The completed Newport, Abergavenny & Hereford Railway ran south-westwards from Hereford via Pontrilas and Abergavenny, and then continued southwards to its junction with the Monmouthshire Railway near Pontypool. This new main line route passed well to the south of the fertile agricultural districts around Usk and Raglan, and there were, as a result, suggestions that a modest branch line scheme might be promoted to fill this hitherto railwayless area. The Newport, Abergavenny & Hereford Directors were in favour of such

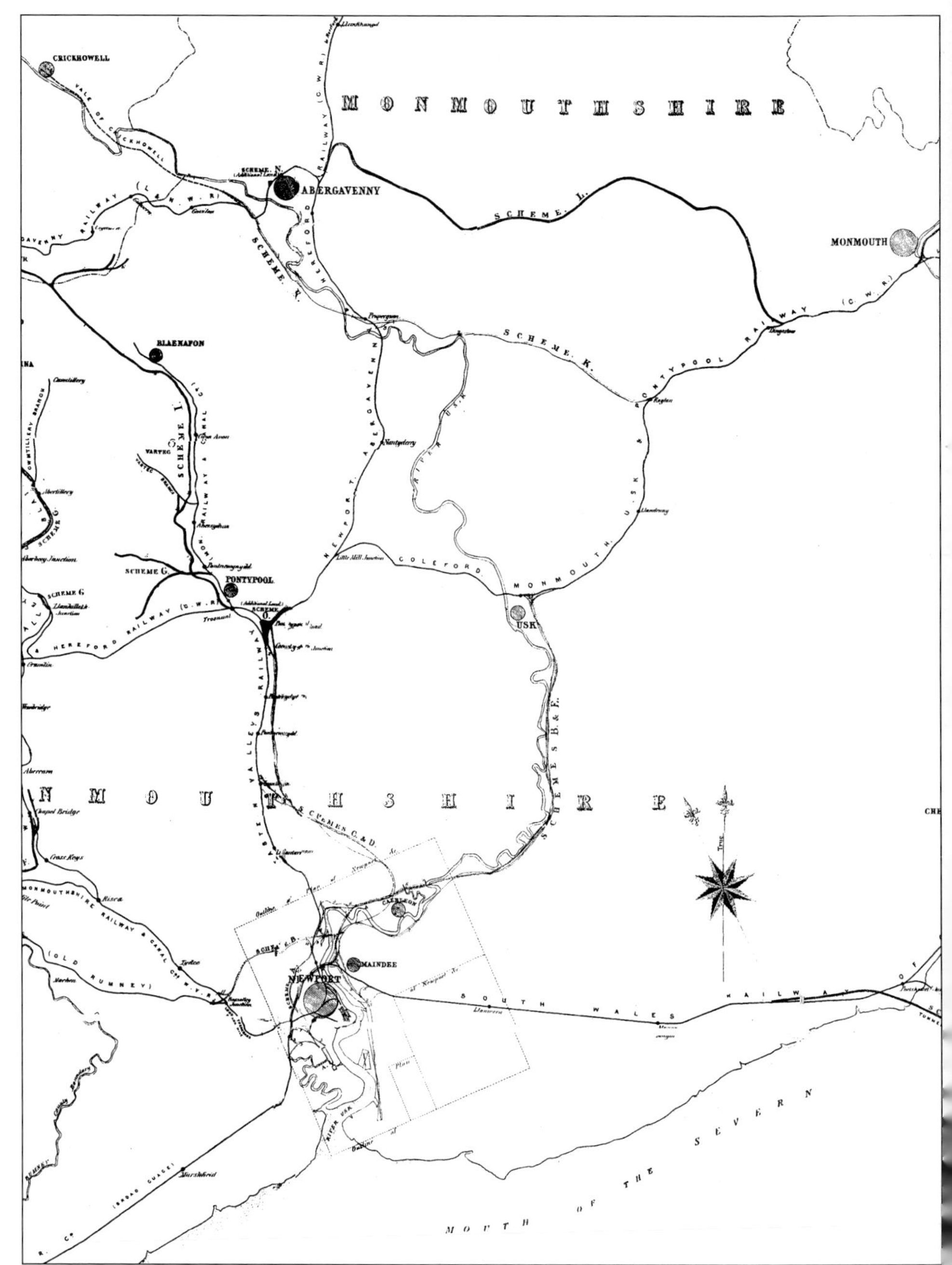

Plan of the Coleford, Monmouth, Usk & Pontypool Railway in 1865. Note also the proposed connections from Dingestow to Abergavenny, Raglan to Crickhowell and Usk to Caerleon.

a line being built, and a company known as The Coleford, Monmouth, Usk & Pontypool Railway was therefore formed to construct the hoped-for branch line to Usk and Monmouth.

The supporters of the proposed railway were primarily local men, many of whom had interests in the local coal and iron industries. The leading promoters included Crawshay Bailey (1789-1872) of Nantyglo House, Monmouthshire; Osmond Wyatt of Troy House, Monmouth; Greenshaw Relph of Usk; Thomas Brown of Chepstow and Henry Dyke of Monmouth, together with George Cave, George Relph and Thomas Gratrix. None of these gentlemen were Directors or leading promoters of the Ross & Monmouth Railway, although Osmond Wyatt and George Relf would subsequently emerge as leading supporters of the unsuccessful Abergavenny & Monmouth scheme.

Crawshay Bailey was involved with numerous other railway schemes. Indeed, with his brother Joseph Bailey, this Yorkshire-born industrialist was one of the most prolific railway promoters in South Wales. He was intimately connected with companies such as the Monmouthshire Railway & Canal Company and the Merthyr, Tredegar & Abergavenny Railway, and the Coleford, Monmouth, Usk & Pontypool project was clearly seen as one more piece in a sophisticated jigsaw of mineral-carrying lines that would facilitate the development of local iron and coal resources.

Before proceeding with their scheme, the supporters of the proposed Coleford, Monmouth, Usk & Pontypool line held a series of public meetings in the area through which the railway would be built. One of the most important of these meetings took place in the Town Hall at Usk on Friday 1st October, 1852 with the aim of considering 'the propriety of forming a railway from the Forest of Dean by way of Coleford, Monmouth and Usk to Pontypool'. At that meeting, it was stated the promoters hoped to 'unite, by a direct line, the iron works of South Wales with the valuable iron ores of the Forest of Dean'.

Such a line, which would commence at Coleford and extend through Monmouth and Usk to a junction with the Newport, Abergavenny & Hereford main line, would form a connection with Pontypool, Newport and the highly populous mining districts around Merthyr. It was pointed out that this thriving industrial district contained a population of between 250,000 and 300,000, while the proposed railway would also offer the 'most direct route' for coal traffic between London and South Wales.

It was agreed that the Coleford branch would commence at a point known as Little Mill on the Newport, Abergavenny & Hereford Railway some two miles to the north of Pontypool Road. From there, the route would proceed generally eastwards across easy terrain to its terminus at Coleford. It was envisaged that the earlier Monmouth Railway would be incorporated into the new line, the tramway being upgraded for the carriage of passengers between Wyesham and Coleford. The estimated cost of this line through central Monmouthshire would be £160,000.

A Bill seeking consent for the proposed railway was sent up to Parliament for the 1853 session, and having successfully passed each stage of the complex Parliamentary process, the Coleford, Monmouth, Usk & Pontypool Railway scheme received the Royal Assent on 20th August, 1853. The resulting Act (16

& 17 Vict. cap. 217) empowered the promoters to construct a railway which, if completed in its entirety, would connect the South Wales coalfield with the industrial district around Lydbrook and Coleford.

The Act allowed the Coleford, Monmouth, Usk & Pontypool company to purchase the earlier Monmouth Railway, which would be needed in connection with the authorized route between Monmouth and Coleford. Further provisions dealt with the formation of the Board of Directors, which would have no less than 12 members, although the quorum would be just four. Perhaps inevitably, the energetic Crawshay Bailey was confirmed as Chairman of the Coleford, Monmouth, Usk & Pontypool company.

The first ordinary meeting of the newly-constituted company was held on 12th September, 1853, and at that meeting the Chairman announced that the railway could be built at a cost of only £5,000 per mile. On an optimistic note, he suggested that the line was expected to be complete 'by 1st December 1854'. The total length from Coleford to the junction with the Newport, Abergavenny & Hereford Railway at Little Mill would be 22 miles. Hinting at a roseate future for the proposed railway, Crawshay Bailey added that the bridges and other works would be 'suitable for a double track as necessary' - the implication being that large amounts of goods and mineral traffic would soon be flowing over the route.

Cutting the First Sod

Having obtained their Act of Incorporation, the promoters of the Coleford, Monmouth, Usk & Pontypool Railway were understandably keen to begin construction, but before work actually began the Directors decided that a ceremony should be held to celebrate the cutting of the first sod. Accordingly, on Wednesday 11th April, 1855 the Coleford, Monmouth Usk & Pontypool Directors arranged for a variety of public entertainments to be held in a field on Rhadyr Farm. It was agreed that the day's festivities would include a coracle race on the River Usk, mule and donkey races, climbing the slippery pole, pig-chasing 'and other rural and laughter-provoking amusements'.

Although it was published many years after the event, J.H. Clark's account of the 'First Sod' ceremony, in his book *Usk Past & Present* (1891), captures the flavour of the proceedings. Having briefly outlined the origins of the Coleford, Monmouth, Usk & Pontypool company, he described the festivities as follows:

> At about ten o'clock Mr David Jones, the engineer, Messrs Richards, Giles and Gaskill, the contractors, with numerous other gentlemen, proceeded from Usk to the Rhadyr Farm, where the spot was marked out, on which to commence operations. Here, in one of the most picturesque and lovely valleys of the Usk, and at a point where the intended line across meadows, stream and river will permit the splendid panorama of the Monmouthshire scenery, the initiatory steps were taken to accomplish the new roadway of the iron horse.
>
> A large number of persons had assembled on the ground; on one side were the sturdy navvies, eager to commence operations; on another, hosts of anxious spectators. In the centre a group of ladies, the contractors Messrs Richards, Giles & Gaskill, and some of

their men, were prepared with spade, wheelbarrow and plank to receive from the sod-turner, Mrs J.H. Clark of Usk, the newly-cut turf; and at half past-past one o'clock the ceremony was performed, amidst enthusiastic cheering, led off by the stentorian voice of Mr Miles of Little Mill.

The first sod having been placed in the wheelbarrow and taken along the plank, the corks from the champagne fled out in rapid succession, and 'Success to the Railway!' was drunk amidst renewed cheering. The sports of the day then commenced - boy races for small stakes were followed by man races for larger prizes; and a steeple chase, and a hurdle and flat race, were admirably contested for by some fleet runners from Abergavenny, Usk and the neighbourhood.

The climbing of the greased pole induced shouts of laughter; but the climbers had no success - they could not reach the height of their ambition; the pig chase was a failure - the fat and lazy animal being little inclined to run hard; and so, getting withdrawn, had the pleasure of saving his bacon; but the 'Jerusalem pony' race was the best fun of all, and might fairly be described as a fair and honest competition. The chief prize being borne off by a Raglan donkey, amidst repeated huzzas.

The dinner afterwards took place at the Three Salmons Hotel, which was numerously attended, and presided over by Mr William Treharne Rees . . . the cloths having been removed, the Chairman gave the usual loyal toasts which were fervently pledged. The Chairman then called upon the company to fill a bumper. He knew that they would all cordially respond to the toast which he was about to give them - 'The Directors of the Railway', the first sod of which had that day been cut. The Directors were men who did not promise to do a thing, and afterwards leave it undone. When he had first heard them named he was perfectly satisfied the work would be thoroughly and well carried out.

He was sure the railway would remunerate those who had embarked their capital in it. He begged to couple the name of their excellent Secretary of the Company, Mr Waddington, with the toast; a more efficient and trustworthy gentleman than whom could not be found to carry out the duties devolving on him. Mr T.P. Williams led the 'honours', and the toast of the Directors and Secretary, and others connected with the undertaking, and who had officiated that day, were pledged in bumpers with three times three.

The initial section of line between Little Mill Junction and the town of Usk, a distance of four miles, was virtually complete by the summer of 1855, and the Coleford, Monmouth, Usk & Pontypool Directors were able to report that the works on the remaining portion of the route between Usk and Monmouth, a distance of 12 miles, were 'considerably advanced', although little work had yet been attempted on the tunnel that would be necessary on the east side of the station at Usk. On the other hand, considerable progress had taken place on the west side of the station site, where a large viaduct was taking tangible shape in the pleasant Monmouthshire landscape.

The partially-constructed bridge was pressed into use as a dance floor on Wednesday 1st August, 1855, when a 'quadrille party' was held on one of the completed spans. This unusual event was staged to raise money for William Watkins, the driver of the Usk omnibus who, in the words of *The Usk Observer*, had broken his leg 'while conveying passengers from the Little Mill Station to Usk on the 11th instant'. Tickets were advertised at one shilling, and the public were also invited to make donations for the benefit of the injured horse-bus driver. Dancing commenced at 5 o'clock in the evening, while refreshments were also available on the bridge.

The Usk viaduct having been completed, the Coleford, Monmouth Usk & Pontypool Directors recommended that the line from Usk to the junction with the Newport, Abergavenny & Hereford main line should be opened for public traffic as soon as the sanction of the Board of Trade could be obtained.

In engineering terms, the line from Little Mill Junction to Usk had presented comparatively few problems, and this first section of the route was opened on Monday 2nd June, 1856, all services being worked by the Newport, Abergavenny & Hereford Railway under the terms of an operating agreement. As usual in those days, Opening Day was treated as a public holiday, although the scale of the celebrations was somewhat muted in comparison to the lavish festivities that had surrounded the earlier sod-cutting ceremony.

The inaugural train was welcomed on arrival at Usk by a procession of townsfolk and, accompanied by bands and streaming banners, the Coleford, Monmouth, Usk & Pontypool Directors and their invited guests were escorted through the town to the usual reception. The shops and houses were specially decorated as part of the Opening Day celebrations, flags being displayed on nearly every building in Bridge Street, while floral wreaths and triumphal arches of evergreens had been erected across the roadway in several places.

The Coleford, Monmouth, Usk & Pontypool Directors were of the opinion that their new railway would be 'of great public utility', and when extended into the Forest of Dean industrial districts it 'would be very remunerative, providing an excellent investment for capital'. On a critical note, they expressed disappointment that the project had not been 'better supported by the gentlemen of the district, notwithstanding the undoubted benefits' that their estates and businesses would receive from the completed line.

In 1857, *Bradshaw's Shareholders' Guide* opined that the weekly traffic returns were 'as favourable as could be expected' in relation to the Little Mill Junction to Usk section, while the portion of line between Usk and Monmouth was 'in a forward state', and would soon be ready for public opening. The eastern part of the line was slightly more difficult than the western extremity of the Coleford, Monmouth, Usk & Pontypool route, and its largest engineering features included tunnels at Usk and Monmouth, together with a large river viaduct at the Monmouth end of the line.

Extension to Monmouth

Construction work on the 12 mile 4 chain line between Usk and Monmouth was, meanwhile, in full progress. The tunnel at Usk was undoubtedly the most troublesome engineering feature on the entire line, and its construction delayed the completion of the railway for several months. There was at least one major earthfall, which caused several injuries and left a gaping hole in the fields above the tunnel.

Notwithstanding their difficulties at Usk, the railway builders were, in general, making commendable progress. The remaining part of the route traversed an area of gently rolling farmland, and with few physical obstacles to impede the work of construction, the railway was completed throughout to Monmouth on 12th October, 1857. The total length of the railway from Little

Mill Junction to Monmouth was 16 miles 19 chains. The Coleford, Monmouth, Usk & Pontypool Railway took over the working of the line on its opening to Monmouth, two locomotives being hired for that purpose from the Newport, Abergavenny & Hereford Railway.

The newly opened railway was single track throughout, with intermediate stations at Usk, Llandenny and Dingestow. The major engineering features included the viaducts across the river at Usk, and over the River Trothy at Monmouth, together with smaller bridges over the Brethin Brook between Little Mill Junction and Usk. There were two tunnels, that at Usk having a length of 256 yards, whereas Monmouth tunnel was somewhat shorter, with a length of 148 yards. Both of these tunnels had been built with sufficient room for a second line of rails in accordance with the Chairman's wishes that the Coleford, Monmouth, Usk & Pontypool route would be suitable for doubling at some future date.

The idea of a continuation to Coleford was quietly dropped, although on 1st July, 1861 a short extension was built across the river to an interchange with the Monmouth Railway's tramway at Wyesham Wharf. This served as a connection, of sorts, with the Coleford area, but there were still plans for a direct railway link between Monmouth and Coleford - this being one of the aims of the Worcester, Dean Forest & Monmouth proposal (*see below*).

As originally built, the Little Mill Junction to Monmouth line was a very modest branch line with sparse facilities at its three intermediate stopping places. These were all single-platform stations with utterly simple, single-storey buildings and basic goods accommodation; Usk station was equipped with an engine shed and a turntable for the branch locomotive. A small junction station was provided at Little Mill, but this was closed in 1861 and not re-opened for several years. At Monmouth, the railway terminated in a small station on the east side of the River Wye at Troy House.

There was, at first, no formal station at Raglan, though it appears that trains called at a place known as 'Raglan Footpath', to the east of Raglan village from an early date. It also became the practice for trains to stop at Raglan Road level crossing, and although the term 'halt' did not appear until the Edwardian period, it would seem that these obscure stopping places were simple, halt-like stations, with minimal facilities for the convenience of occasional travellers. A contemporary press report, dated 3rd October, 1863, suggests that Raglan Footpath was sited about half a mile from Raglan Castle, while its facilities included what was described as 'a small station house' (*see Chapter Five*). The infrastructure at Raglan Footpath was considerably enhanced in 1867, when a short platform was constructed on the up side of the line.

The Formation of the West Midland Railway

The Newport, Abergavenny & Hereford line was originally worked by the London & North Western Railway (LNWR), but the operating agreement with the latter was terminated following a disagreement about through traffic. Having broken away from its former allegiances, the Abergavenny company had to find a new eastern outlet for its South Wales coal traffic, and in 1858 the Newport,

Abergavenny & Hereford Railway (NA&HR) joined forces with the Oxford Worcester & Wolverhampton Railway (OW&WR) in order to complete the Worcester & Hereford Railway. The latter company had been authorized in 1853 as a link between Worcester, Great Malvern and Hereford, but little progress was made until 1856, when the NA&HR injected money and new life into the scheme.

Although the Newport, Abergavenny & Hereford Railway was prepared to support the Worcester & Hereford scheme, the Abergavenny company was a struggling local railway with few capital resources. The Oxford Worcester & Wolverhampton Railway, on the other hand, was comparatively well-off by the late 1850s, and the new partnership between the NA&HR and OW&WR companies was in effect an Oxford Worcester & Wolverhampton takeover. It was agreed that the two railways would be merged into a new undertaking, to be known as the West Midland Railway (WMR), which would also include the Worcester & Hereford Railway. These arrangements were formalized by the provisions of an Act of Parliament obtained on 1st July, 1860.

By this Act, the Newport, Abergavenny & Hereford and the Worcester & Hereford railway companies were dissolved and merged with the Oxford Worcester & Wolverhampton Railway under its new name. Sixteen OW&WR Directors were joined by five from the NA&HR and two from the Worcester & Hereford Railway to form an enlarged Board, based at Worcester. The then Chairman of the Oxford Worcester & Wolverhampton Railway, William Fenton, became Chairman of the West Midland Railway, while W.P. Price, the former Chairman of the Newport, Abergavenny & Hereford Railway, became Deputy Chairman of the West Midland Railway Company.

The formation of the WMR was a development of considerable significance for the Coleford, Monmouth, Usk & Pontypool Railway. The creation of this enlarged undertaking offered greater opportunities for traffic development and future investment, and it was therefore agreed that the local company would be transferred to the WMR under a somewhat complex leasing arrangement. The necessary Parliamentary sanction was obtained under an Act passed on 22nd July, 1861 (24 & 25 Vict. cap. 197), and the Coleford, Monmouth, Usk & Pontypool Railway was then leased to the West Midland company at a rent of £4,680 for the first year.

The rental would increase to £5,616 in the second year of the lease, rising to £7,020 for the third, fourth, fifth and sixth years, and £8,190 in the seventh year. The annual rental would continue rising to £9,360 in year eight, £10,062 in year nine, and £10,764 per annum thereafter. In this way, it was hoped that both companies would benefit from improved receipts as the West Midland developed the line's hitherto meagre traffic potential.

The Worcester, Dean Forest & Monmouth Railway

The Coleford, Monmouth, Usk & Pontypool Railway was originally proposed as a local branch line that would serve an additional purpose by providing a useful link between the industrial districts of South Wales and the Forest of Dean. In practice, the line from Little Mill Junction to Monmouth was of purely local importance, though in the 1860s, at the height of the 'Second Railway Mania', the Monmouth branch featured in a number of speculative schemes, some of which have already been mentioned in connection with the Ross & Monmouth line.

The passing of the Ross & Monmouth Act of Incorporation on 5th July, 1865 heralded a whole series of speculative schemes for connecting lines between the Coleford, Monmouth, Usk & Pontypool Railway at Monmouth, and various places further to the North and East. Although the Ross & Monmouth company was primarily a localized concern that was intended to bring railway communication to the Upper Wye Valley, it also presented tempting opportunities for those seeking to build competitive rail links to the South Wales coalfield. The Worcester, Dean Forest & Monmouth Railway was one of the more ambitious proposals put forward at this time.

The Worcester, Dean Forest & Monmouth Railway was incorporated by Act of Parliament on 21st July, 1863 (26 & 27 Vict. cap. 185), with a capital of £456,000 in shares and a further £150,000 by loan. This proposal, which was mentioned briefly in Chapter One, envisaged a line running eastwards from Monmouth to Coleford, and thence northwards through the Forest of Dean to Newent, from where the route would have continued to a junction with the Worcester & Hereford line at Great Malvern. The main line would have been about 37 miles long, and on 29th July, 1864 the company obtained further powers for a branch line running south-eastwards from Newent to Gloucester.

The Worcester, Dean Forest & Monmouth line was supported by industrialists such as Abraham Darby of Ebbw Vale, but it also enjoyed considerable support among the landowners and businessmen of Worcester, Newport and Monmouth. The promoters of the scheme also included Peter Hardy of Worcester, Richard Wood of Worcester and Frederick Levick of Newport, together with Osmond A. Wyatt and George Relph from the Board of the Coleford, Monmouth, Usk & Pontypool Railway.

In the event, the supporters of these railways and other diverse schemes were faced with serious financial and other problems following the sudden failure of bankers Overend, Gurney & Co. on 10th May, 1866. New companies such as the Worcester, Dean Forest & Monmouth Railway were unable to raise their authorized capital, and against this background of financial crisis the scheme could not be implemented. In 1868 the project was reduced to a short section between Monmouth and Coleford only, the main line to Great Malvern being abandoned in its entirety.

Despite the total failure of the Worcester, Dean Forest & Monmouth Railway scheme, ambitious local interests were still willing to support such a line, and in the early 1860s a new company, known as the Ledbury & Gloucester Railway, was formed to construct the hoped-for rail link. In essence, the new proposals were a revival of an earlier scheme for conversion of the Herefordshire & Gloucestershire Canal. The Ledbury & Gloucester project was fully supported by the West Midland Railway, which had temporarily severed most of its links with the parent Great Western company, and was eager to promote rival standard gauge lines which would penetrate deep into GWR broad gauge territory.

For a time, the West Midland system was indeed able to expand in several directions, but as pro-Great Western interests among the WMR Directors asserted themselves, the West Midland Railway returned to the Great Western fold. In 1861 it was announced that the GWR would lease the West Midland system, and two years later the Great Western and West Midland railways were fully amalgamated. These momentous developments meant that the West Midland-backed scheme for a line between Gloucester and Ledbury was not immediately implemented, although the idea of a railway that would bring rail communication to small towns such as Newent and Dymock was never entirely abandoned.

A substantially-similar project was floated during the next decade. Once again, the proposed route would follow the Herefordshire & Gloucestershire Canal for much of its length between Gloucester and Ledbury, and if implemented in its entirety the scheme would also include the construction of a branch from Dymock to Ross-on-Wye. The promoters decided that their application to Parliament would be made in two parts, and two Bills were therefore prepared for submission in the 1873 session. One of these sought Parliamentary consent for the construction and maintenance of a railway connecting Ross, Dymock and Ledbury, while the other proposed a line from Dymock to the GWR at near Gloucester.

Meanwhile, a separate scheme known as the Ross, Ledbury & Gloucester Railway had been promoted by rival interests. This proposal envisaged the construction of a line from Gloucester to Ross and Ledbury, with a bridge over the River Severn at Over. In the event, Parliament rejected the latter scheme on the grounds that the proposed Severn bridge would hinder navigation. On the other hand, the Bill authorizing the Ross & Ledbury Railway received the Royal Assent on 28th July, 1873, and on 5th August, 1873 a second Act of Parliament incorporated the Newent Railway Company, with powers for the construction of a connecting line between Dymock, Newent and the Great Western Railway at Over, near Gloucester.

The Great Western Railway Directors eventually decided that there would be some advantage in having a new through route between Gloucester and Ledbury, and in May 1876 the GWR agreed to subscribe to both the Ross & Ledbury and the Newent railways. However, as a corollary of Great Western involvement, it was agreed that the proposed line between Dymock and Ross-on-Wye would be abandoned. Thus, when opened throughout on 27th July, 1885, the Gloucester to Ledbury line had no direct connections to the Ross & Monmouth route, all thoughts of extension beyond Ross having been abandoned as a result of Great Western disapproval.

The Wye Valley Railway

The Wye Valley Railway was another line promoted during the Second Railway Mania of the mid-1860s, when a small group of landowners and entrepreneurs sought powers for the construction and maintenance of a railway commencing near Chepstow by a junction with the South Wales Railway main line, and terminating near Monmouth by a junction with the Coleford, Monmouth, Usk & Pontypool Railway. The Wye Valley Railway scheme was sanctioned by Act of Parliament on 10th August, 1866, though the scheme was not implemented for several years - the 1866 economic crisis having intervened.

The supporters of the Wye Valley scheme included local people such as Osmond Wyatt of Monmouth, and London-based investors such as Captain Robert O'Brian Jameson and Joseph Cary. In due course, the Board seems to have been taken over by other interests, and by the 1870s the Directors included William Hawes, Lord Alexander Gordon Lennox, Isaac W. Home, Hugh Dalrymple and James Goodson. The Engineers were S.H. Yockney & Sons of Westminster, and the contract for construction was awarded to Messrs Reed Bros & Co. of London.

Construction of the Wye Valley line was in progress by 1874, and the 13 mile line was opened on 1st November, 1876. Like the Ross & Monmouth and Coleford, Monmouth, Usk & Pontypool railways, the Wye Valley route was worked by the GWR under the terms of an operating agreement.

The new line was single track throughout, with intermediate stations at Tidenham, Tintern, Bigsweir and Redbrook. Northbound trains travelling from Chepstow to Monmouth (Troy) were regarded as up workings, while those proceeding in the opposite direction were regarded as down services. The principal engineering works included the 101 yds-long Redbrook viaduct, a similar viaduct with a length of 69 yards at Tintern, and the tunnels at Tintern and Tidenham.

At its northern end, the new railway joined the Coleford, Monmouth, Usk & Pontypool line at Wyesham to the east of Monmouth (Troy) station, and Wye Valley trains ran over the Coleford, Monmouth, Usk & Pontypool route for a short distance in order to reach Monmouth (Troy) station.

The Abergavenny & Monmouth Railway

In addition to these speculative projects, there were other proposals for lines running south-eastwards and north-westwards from the Coleford, Monmouth, Usk & Pontypool route. For example, on 5th July, 1865 the Abergavenny & Monmouth Railway was empowered to construct a line from Abergavenny to a junction with the Coleford, Monmouth, Usk & Pontypool line at Dingestow. The proposed route would have been about 12 miles long, and its authorized capital was £150,000 in shares and a further £49,000 by loan.

Proponents of the scheme included Abraham Darby and Crawshay Bailey, while the Engineer was John Gardner. If completed, the Abergavenny & Monmouth line would have formed a western outlet for the Worcester, Dean Forest & Monmouth line, enabling trains to run through from The Forest of Dean to Abergavenny, from where the Merthyr, Tredegar & Abergavenny Railway (MT&AR) would have provided a convenient means of access to the industrial areas of South Wales. Significantly, the MT&AR had also been promoted by Crawshay Bailey and other industrialists, who were clearly intending to create a direct route for heavy freight and mineral traffic between South Wales, the Forest of Dean and the industrial Midlands.

In connection with this scheme, another line was proposed along the Monnow Valley from Monmouth to Pontrilas, utilizing portions of the Coleford,

Monmouth, Usk & Pontypool line and the GWR. The proposed route would cross the River Monnow in five places, and there would also be two tunnels, one of which, at Skenfrith, would have a length of 475 yards. It was suggested that there might be a joint station at Monmouth, for which purpose the Monnow Valley promoters announced that they would seek to make arrangements with the GWR, Coleford, Monmouth, Usk & Pontypool, Ross & Monmouth, Abergavenny & Monmouth and Worcester, Dean Forest & Monmouth companies.

As might be expected, the Abergavenny & Monmouth Railway did not survive the great financial panic of 1866 and, like so many other lines projected during the Second Railway Mania, the project was a total failure. Despite these unsuccessful schemes, the 1860s nevertheless saw the creation of a large number of branch lines and secondary routes. As far as the Monmouth area was concerned, the largely speculative ventures of the 1860s had eventually produced an interesting network of local railways, the station at Monmouth (Troy) becoming a junction at the meeting point of three distinct branch line routes.

It will be noted that, as a result of the shifting sands of railway politics, the minor railways of the Herefordshire, Monmouthshire and West Gloucestershire districts tended to fall, one by one, into Great Western hands. Reverting, briefly, to the Coleford, Monmouth, Usk & Pontypool line, it should be mentioned that when the West Midland Railway was amalgamated with the GWR in 1863, the line from Little Mill Junction to Monmouth inevitably passed into Great Western hands - the GWR having inherited the West Midland lease.

Further Growth of the System

In theory, the traders and businessmen of the Monmouthshire district should have been satisfied with the network of lines which, by 1872, formed part of a useful system of interconnecting routes. There were, however, persistent demands for further lines in the coal-producing areas of the Forest of Dean, and in particular, Richard Thomas, the proprietor of Lydbrook Tinplate Works, was keen to see the establishment of a northern extension of the Severn & Wye Railway, in order to form a link with the Ross & Monmouth Railway at Lydbrook Junction. Work on this extension began in 1872, and the line was opened for mineral traffic on Wednesday 26th August, 1874.

This new line joined the Severn & Wye 'main line' at an isolated point known as Serridge Junction. As the line from Lydney fell steeply at 1 in 40, it was necessary for the junction to face northwards - a reversal being necessary for trains proceeding between Lydbrook Junction and Lydney. The principal engineering work on the extension was Lydbrook viaduct, which included three wrought-iron spans resting on stone piers, and a number of approach arches.

Passenger services were introduced in September 1875, and trains initially ran between Lydney and Lydbrook Junction, with an intermediate reversal at Drybrook Road, about one mile to the north of Serridge Junction.

A further line was opened in the Monmouth area in the following decade, when the Coleford Railway was belatedly completed between Wyesham Junction and Coleford, a distance of 5 miles 6 chains. This modest undertaking had been incorporated in 1872, but the single-track branch was not opened until 1st September, 1883. The completed line formed a connecting link between Monmouth and the Coleford branch of the Severn & Wye Joint Railway at Coleford. The Coleford Railway Company was worked by the Great Western, and fully absorbed by the larger company in 1884. There was just one intermediate station, at Newland, and the branch was steeply-graded.

It is interesting to reflect that the promoters of the Coleford, Monmouth, Usk & Pontypool Railway had hoped to reach Coleford as long ago as 1853, but their line had stopped short at Wyesham. Later, in 1863, the Worcester, Dean Forest & Monmouth Railway had similarly aspired to serve Coleford with its line to Great Malvern, but these aims had also been thwarted by events. The opening of the Coleford branch was, therefore, the culmination of several years of effort, though in reality this five mile line carried little traffic, and can hardly have been described as a successful venture.

The Coleford Railway was the last line to be constructed in the Monmouth area, although there were, for many years, suggestions that an additional cross-country route might be brought into use between Pontrilas, on the Newport, Abergavenny & Hereford main line, Monmouth and the Bristol Channel. As we have seen, a line along the Monnow Valley had first been suggested in the 1860s, and the idea that a rail link might one day be constructed between Monmouth and Pontrilas was strangely persistent. On 21st October, 1876, for instance, *The Monmouthshire Beacon* reported that there was 'every probability' that the proposed Monnow Valley Railway from Monmouth to Pontrilas would be carried out.

Meetings in support of the proposed railway had been held in the neighbourhood, and as 'a highly influential number of gentlemen' had shown an interest in the project, the paper saw no reason why the scheme 'should be much longer delayed'. The course of the proposed Monnow Valley line would have run north-westwards from Monmouth via Blackwood, Tregate Bridge, Llanrothal, Skenfrith, Garway Hill, Trevorney, Lower Duffryn and Great Corras to its junction with the former Newport-Abergavenny main line at Pontrilas.

In 1883, new plans were deposited for a line running south-eastwards from Pontrilas to Monmouth, and north-westwards from Dorstone to a junction with the Midland Railway at Hay-on-Wye. The Dorstone to Hay line was authorized by Parliament in 1884, and this northwards extension of the Golden Valley Railway was opened for passenger traffic on 27th May, 1889. The planned southwards extension to Monmouth, on the other hand, was not pursued, the Great Western having objected strongly to this competitive line which could have brought the rival Midland Railway into GWR territory.

Developments in the Victorian Era

Having seen their railway opened through to Wyesham, the supporters of the Coleford, Monmouth, Usk & Pontypool Railway had no wish to control or manage the line indefinitely, and with services being successfully worked by the Great Western, the Directors agreed that the best course of action would be an outright sale to the GWR. In this respect the history of the company was similar to that of many other minor lines - the local company being formed mainly to get the railway built, with a longer term intention to sell out a larger company that would have the resources to develop the line once it was in operation.

Accordingly, the Coleford, Monmouth, Usk & Pontypool Railway Company was vested in the GWR on 1st January, 1887, this arrangement being formalized under the terms of a Great Western Act obtained in 1881. The Wye Valley Railway, meanwhile, was worked as a branch of the GWR until 1906 when it, too, was fully and finally absorbed by the larger company. The Ross & Monmouth Railway Company, in contrast, retained its nominal independence for many more years, and it was not fully absorbed into the Great Western until 1st July, 1922, when it became part of the latter company under the provisions of the Railways Act of 1921.

Local travellers had anticipated that the Great Western takeover would herald a noticeable improvement in public transport facilities, but in reality these expectations were not immediately realized. There were numerous complaints about the infrequent train service provided on the Coleford, Monmouth, Usk & Pontypool line, while the inadequate accommodation at Usk station was a source of constant irritation. In 1891, J.H. Clarke complained that 'the miserable hut called a station, without waiting rooms and with very little protection from the inclemency of the weather', had remained in use for over three decades.

The Great Western management was also criticised for its system of accounting, which treated the local branch lines in isolation from the main line system, and made them appear less remunerative than they actually were. In particular, the range of through tickets available from stations such as Usk and Raglan was severely limited, and for this reason travellers wishing to reach destinations such as Bristol or Paddington were obliged to re-book at Pontypool Road. This was in itself an inconvenience for the passengers concerned, but on a more insidious level it distorted the traffic receipts at Usk station, which was not credited with many long distance bookings beyond the junction.

In truth, the Little Mill Junction to Monmouth line was never a particularly remunerative route, although it seems to have entered a period of modest prosperity after the completion of the Ross & Monmouth line in 1874. There were some considerable changes during the later Victorian period, most of these being introduced by the GWR in an attempt to bring the branch up to acceptable standards. The somewhat obscure wayside stopping places in the vicinity of Raglan were closed, and in their place an improved station was opened at Raglan in March 1876.

Twenty years later, after the Great Western had fully absorbed the local company, the original station at Usk was swept away. In its place, the GWR erected one of its standard late-Victorian stations, with up and down platforms and neat brick buildings. The new works were authorized on 10th May, 1893 and completed by 15th January, 1897. At around the same time, the Monmouth to Little Mill Junction section was re-signalled, with new signal boxes at Dingestow, Raglan and Usk.

Chapter Three

The Railway in Operation

The Ross-on-Wye to Pontypool Road line served a largely rural area that offered very few opportunities for large scale traffic development. In these circumstances the route was unable to rise above local branch line status, and its train services were modest in the extreme. There were, in general, no more than four or five passenger workings each way between Ross-on-Wye and Pontypool Road, together with one or two shorter distance workings between Ross-on-Wye and Lydbrook Junction, and Pontypool Road and Usk.

Passenger Services in the GWR Era

In the Victorian period, there were usually around five passenger trains in each direction on the eastern section of the line between Ross-on-Wye and Monmouth, together with one or two shorter distance services between Ross-on-Wye and Lydbrook Junction. In 1876, for example, the Great Western public timetable showed a basic pattern of five trains each way, with most services running through from Ross-on-Wye to Pontypool Road, a distance of 31 miles 14 chains.

A generally-similar level of service was maintained on the western section of line between Monmouth and Pontypool Road, most of the workings on this section being through services from the Ross & Monmouth branch, though a few trains worked between Pontypool Road and Monmouth (Troy). This basic pattern of operation was to persist for many years, the line between Ross-on-Wye and Pontypool Road being treated as a continuous east-to-west cross-country route.

Trains that did not run through between Ross-on-Wye and Pontypool Road generally connected with each other at Monmouth (Troy), where the three lines from Ross, Chepstow and Pontypool Road converged in a single station. Connections were available to and from Chepstow via the Wye Valley route - although there was little attempt to arrange through workings to and from the last-mentioned line, which was normally worked as a self-contained branch between Monmouth (Troy) and Chepstow. Connecting services were also available on the Monmouth to Coleford branch, which was typically served by four trains in each direction.

The original train service was maintained, with only minor alterations, for many years, and by April 1902 there were still just five trains each way between Ross and Monmouth, with four working to or from Pontypool Road. There was, however, a considerable amount of summer excursion traffic during the Edwardian period - the Wye Valley area being regarded as an important tourist destination in its own right.

The May 1903 working timetable shows four up and four down passenger trains between Ross-on-Wye and Pontypool Road, with a few short distance workings between Ross and Monmouth, and Monmouth and Pontypool Road.

ROSS, MONMOUTH,

Down Trains.

Distance from Ross. M	C	Single Line between Ross and Little Mill Junction. Worked by Train Staff and Ticket and Block Telegraph. STATIONS.		1 A Light Engine. (Wednesdays only.)	2 A Passenger.	3	4 A Passenger.	5 D Goods. (To run when the 11.20 a.m. Goods from Pontypool Road starts at 8.55 a.m.)	6 A Passenger to Monmouth, Mixed beyond.	7 D Goods.	8	9 D Goods. N	10 D Cattle and Goods. TO (Second and fourth Monday in each month.)	11 D Hereford and Monmouth Goods. S. T. 3 & 356	12
				A.M.	A.M.		A.M.	A.M.	A.M.	P.M.		P.M.	P.M.	P.M.	
		Ross	dep.	6 45	**7 2**	....	**8 17**		**10 35**	....	....	....		1X10	....
4	10	Kerne	arr.	—	—	..	—		—	..	..	..		1 25	..
		Bridge ..	dep.	6 56	7 11	....	8 27		10 46	....	....	....		1 40	....
5	40	Lydbrook Jct	arr.	—	—	..	—		—	..	..	..		1X45	..
			dep.	7 1	7 16	....	8 32		10 52	....	....	....		2 25	....
7	50	Symonds'	arr.	—	—	..	—		—	..	..	..		—	..
		Yat ..	dep.	7 6	7 21	....	8 37		10 59	....	....	....		2 35	....
8	41	Slaughter Siding	,,	—	—	..	—		—	..	..	..		CR	..
11	3	Hadnock Siding	,,	—	—	....	—		—	....	....	....		CR	....
12	31	**Monmouth**	arr.	7 17	**7 31**	..	**8 48**		**11 11**	**RR**	..	..		2 55	..
		(May Hill)	dep.	7 18	**7 33**	....	**8 50**		**11 14**	12 55	....	....		2 56	....
13	10	**Monmouth**	arr.	7 20	**7X35**	..	**8 52**		**11 17**	1 0	..	..		3 0	..
		(Troy)	dep.		**7 38**	..	**9 35**		X **12 45**	..	..	1 30	3X5	..	..
16	43	Dingestow	,,		7 46	....	9 42		12 54	....	....	—	—	....	....
19	44	Raglan	,,		7 54	..	9 49		1 2	..	..	1 57	3 30	..	..
21	63	Llandenny	,,		7 59	....	9 55		1 8	....	....	—	—	....	....
24	63	Davies' Siding	dep.		—	..	—	10 55	—	..	..	2 20	—	..	..
25	14	**Usk**	arr.		**8 6**	....	**10 2**	11 0	**1 17**	....	....	2 25	3 45	....	....
			dep.		**8X8**	..	X **10 4**	RR	**1 19**	..	..	●X 5 0	3 55	..	..
29	31	Little Mill	arr.		8 17	....	10 12	....	1 30	....	....	5 15	4 10	....	....
		Junction	dep.	..	8 20	..	10 14	..	1 33	..	..	5 30	4 40	..	..
31	14	**Pontypool Rd.**	arr.	....	**8 25**	....	**10 18**	....	**1 38**	....	....	5 40	4 50	....	....

Up Trains.

Distance from Pontypool Road. M	C	Single Line between Little Mill Junction and Ross. Worked by Train Staff and Ticket and Block Telegraph. STATIONS.		1 A Passenger. (Wednesdays only.)	2 A Passenger.	3 A Passenger.	4 D RR Goods. T.O.	5	6 D Goods and S. T. Truck. Nos. 212, 389, 407A, and 414.	7 D Goods. (To run when the 11.20 a.m. Goods ex Pontypool Road starts at 8.55 a.m.)	8 A Passenger.	9	10	11 D Goods. N	12
				A.M.	A.M.	A.M.	A.M.		A.M.	A.M.	A.M.			A.M.	
		Pontypool Rd.	dep.	....	**7 40**	**8 45**	8 55	..	9 5	..	**11 5**	....	....	11 20	....
1	63	Little Mill	arr.	..	7 44	8 49	—	....	9 12	....	11 9	..	..	—	..
		Junction	dep.	....	7 45	8 50	9 2	..	9 30	..	11 10	....	....	11 27	....
6	0	**Usk**	arr.	..	**7 53**	**8 58**	9 15	....	9 45	RR	**11 18**	..	..	11 40	..
			dep.		X **8 20**	**8 59**	●X 11 55	....	X 10 10	10 35	**11 20**	..	..	11 55	..
6	31	Davies' Siding	dep.		—	—	—	..	—	10 40	—	....	....	12 5	....
9	31	Llandenny	,,		8 27	9 5	—	....	10 30		11 27	..	..	—	..
11	50	Raglan ..	,,		8 33	9 11	—	..	10 50		11 33	....	....	—	....
14	51	Dingestow	arr.		8 40	9 16	—	....	11 5		11 40	..	..	—	..
			dep.		8 43	9 18	—	..	11 10		11 43	....	....	—	....
18	4	**Monmouth**	arr.		**8 50**	**9 25**	12 35	....	11 25		**11 50**	..	..	12X35	..
		(Troy)	dep.	7X36	....	— **9 30**	X 1 5	....	....		X **12 30**	....	....	....	....
18	63	**Monmouth**	arr.	7 38	..	**9 32**	1 9	..	..		**12 32**	..	..	..	..
		(May Hill)	dep.	7 39	....	**9 34**	1 10	....	....		**12 34**	....	....	....	....
20	11	Hadnock Siding	,,	—	..	—	—	..	..		—	..	..	..	..
22	53	Slaughter Siding	,,	—	....	—	—	....	....		—	....	....	....	....
23	44	Symonds'	arr.	--	..	9 45	1 23	..	..		12 45	..	..	..	..
		Yat	dep.	7 49	....	9 46	1 25	....	....		12 46	....	....	....	....
25	54	Lydbrook Jct.	,,	7 54	..	9 53	1X45	.	..		12 53	..	..	..	..
27	4	Kerne Bridge	,,	7 59	....	9 58	—	....	....		12 58	....	....	....	....
31	14	**Ross** ..	,,	8 7	..	**10 8**	2 5	..	..		**1X8**	..	..	..	..

Working timetable for the Ross, Monmouth & Pontypool Road line, October 1899.

AND PONTYPOOL ROAD.

Week Days only.

Single Line between Ross and Little Mill Junction. Worked by Train Staff and Ticket and Block Telegraph.	13	14	15	16	17	18	19	20	21	22	23	24	25
	A			B	A	D	A	D	A	A	A	D	D
STATIONS.	Mixed to Monmouth, Passenger beyond.			RR Goods. T.O.	Passenger.	RR Goods.	Passenger.	Goods and S.T. Nos. 33 & 356.	Passenger.	Passenger.	Passenger.	RR Engine & Van.	Goods.
	P.M.			P.M.	P.M.	P.M.	P.M.	P.M.	P.M.	P.M.	P.M.	P.M.	P.M.
Ross .... dep.	**2 55**	Does not convey Goods traffic Ross to Monmouth on Wednesdays.	..	3 20	....	4 30	4 55	Thursdays excepted during October.	Thursdays excepted during October.	**7 10**	Thursdays only, and during October only.	**8 5**	..
Kerne Bridge arr.	—		....	—	..	—	—			—		—	....
Kerne Bridge .. dep.	3 6		..	—	....	—	5 7			7 21		—	..
Lydbrook Jct arr.	—		....	3 35	..	4X 45	—			7 27		**8 15**	....
Lydbrook Jct dep.	3 12		..	3X58	....		5X13			7 29			..
Symonds Yat arr.	—		....	—	..	..	—			—		..	....
Symonds Yat .. dep.	3 19		..	4 5	....	....	5 20			7X35		....	..
Slaughter Siding ,,	—		....	—	..	Suspended during October.	—			—		..	Thursdays only, and during October only.
Hadnock Siding ,,	—		..	—	....		—			—		....	
Monmouth (May Hill) arr.	**3 30**		....	4 18	..		5 31			**7 46**		..	
Monmouth (May Hill) dep.	**3 33**		..	4 19	....		5 33	..	..	**7 48**		....	
Monmouth (Troy) arr.	**3 35**		....	4 21	..		5 35	....	....	**7 50**		..	
	X			X									
Monmouth (Troy) dep.	**3 55**	..	....	4 35	**5 10**			7X35	..	Runs as a Mixed Train on Wednesdays.	8 0	..	
Dingestow .... ,,	4 3	....	..	—	5 17		Runs during October only.	7 55	....		8 7	....	
Raglan .. .. ,,	4 11	..	....	CR	5 24			8 15	..		8 14	..	
Llandenny .... ,,	4 16	....	..	CR	5 30			8 30	....		8 20	....	
Davies' Siding dep.	—	..	....	—	—	..		—	..		—	..	
Usk .. .. arr.	**4 23**	....	..	5 10	**5 38**	....		8 40	....		8 28	....	
			....					X			X		
Usk dep.	**4 25**	..	..	5 50	**5 40**	..		8 55	**8 30**		8 30	..	9 15
Little Mill Junction arr.	4 34	....	....	6 5	5 49	....		—	8 39		8 39	....	—
Little Mill Junction dep.	4 36	..	..	6 15	5 51	..		9 13	8 41		8 41	..	9 30
Pontypool Rd. arr.	**4 41**	....	....	6 25	**5 55**	....		9 20	**8 45**		8 45	....	9 40

Week Days only.

Single Line between Little Mill Junction and Ross. Worked by Train Staff and Ticket and Block Telegraph.	13	14	15	16	17	18		19	20	21	22	23	24
	D		A		D	D		A		A	A	D	A
STATIONS.	May Hill and Troy Goods.		Passenger.		RR Goods.	Monmouth and Hereford **Goods** S. T. Nos. 407 and 414.		Passenger.		Mixed Passenger and **Goods.**	Passenger.	RR Goods.	Passenger.
	P.M.		P.M.		P.M.	arr.	dep.	P.M.		P.M.	P.M.	P.M.	P.M.
Pontypool Rd. dep.	**RR**	....	**2 15**	..	Suspended during October.			Runs during October only.	....	**6 15**	**8 10**	....	....
Little Mill Junction arr.	..	..	2 19	....		P.M.	P.M.		..	—	8 14	..	..
Little Mill Junction dep.	....	....	2 20	..		....	....		....	6 20	8 15	....	....
Usk .... arr.	..	..	**2 28**	....		..	..		..	**6 29**	**8 X 23**	..	..
			X										
Usk dep.	..	..	**2 30**	..		..	..		..	**6 31**	....	..	..
Davies' Siding dep.	....	....	—	....		....	....		...	—	..	....	....
Llandenny.... ,,	..	..	2 37	..		..	..		..	6 40	....	..	..
Raglan .. ,,	....	....	2 43	....		....	....		....	6 46	..	....	....
Dingestow arr.	..	..	2 50	..		..	..		..	6 54		..	..
Dingestow dep.	....	....	2 53	....	..	....	....		....	6 56		....	....
Monmouth (Troy) arr.	..	..	**3 0**	....	....	..	..		..	**7 5**	* Arrive at Lydbrook at 7.42 p.m.	..	..
			X							X			
Monmouth (Troy) dep.	12 35	....	**3 38**	..	....	—	X4 12	6 5	....	**7 17**		....	**8 15**
Monmouth (May Hill) arr.	12 40	..	**3 40**	....	..	—	—	6 7	..	**7 19**		..	**8 18**
Monmouth (May Hill) dep.		....	**3 42**	..	....	4 16	4 17	6 9	....	**7 20**		....	**8 20**
Hadnock Siding ,,	..	..	—	....	..	CR		—	..	—		..	—
Slaughter Siding ,,	....	....	—	..	....	CR		—	....	—		....	—
Symonds' Yat .... arr.	..	..	3 51	....	..	—	—	6 20	..	7 31		..	8 32
Symonds' Yat .... dep.	....	....	3X52	..	....	4 40	4 41	6 21	....	7X36		....	8 33
Lydbrook Jct. ,,	..	..	3 58	....	4 55	4 50	X5 15	6 28	..	*7 45		8 25	8 40
Kerne Bridge ,,	....	....	4 3	..	—	5 25	5 30	6 33	....	7 50		—	8 45
Ross .. arr.	..	..	**4 12**	....	5 15	5 45	7 10	6 43	..	**8 0**		8 40	**8 55**

Working timetable for the Ross, Monmouth & Pontypool Road line, October 1899.

The ambulance class pose on the platform at Ross-on-Wye in 1898. *C.G. Maggs Collection*

A station staff portrait outside the booking office at Ross-on-Wye in 1900. *C.G. Maggs Collection*

The Royal Train stands at Ross-on-Wye on 29th October, 1900. The Duke and Duchess of York are *en route* to Monmouth. *C.G. Maggs Collection*

Ross-on-Wye station, view looking north *c*.1905. A train awaits departure in the Monmouth platform. *C.G. Maggs Collection*

Monmouth (Troy) station on the occasion of the funeral of Charles Stewart Rolls in 1910. His earliest experience in engineering was at the London & North Western Railway's Crewe works. He became a motor dealer in 1902 and in 1906 had founded Rolls-Royce with Henry Royce. He lost his life in an aviation accident in Bournemouth. *The Nelson Museum, Monmouth*

Believed to be another view of the same occasion. The funeral cortège stands outside the Monmouth (Troy) up side buildings. *Lens of Sutton Collection*

'3521' class 4-4-0 No. 3545 at Symond's Yat with an engineer's inspection saloon. *A.G. Ellis*

Permanent way staff at work in the early part of the 20th century.

A general view of Symond's Yat station around 1912, looking north-west towards the River Wye. The small waiting shelter on the up platform was identical to those found at Witney and Bampton, on the East Gloucestershire line. *Lens of Sutton Collection*

Symond's Yat station early in the 20th century showing a saddle tank with its train in the down platform. Railway staff pose for the photographer. *Monmouthshire County Council Museum*

An unidentified '517' class 0-4-2T departs from Kerne Bridge with a six-coach local train; the formation consists of four third class or composite vehicles, with a passenger brake van at each end. This *circa* 1912 view shows the station after the removal of signalling and the closure of the passing loop; the left-hand platform line was merely a siding, entered from the south end.

Lens of Sutton Collection

A poor quality postcard view showing severe flooding at Monmouth (May Hill) station, *circa* 1912. The locomotive appears to be a '517' class 0-4-2T. *Lens of Sutton Collection*

An unidentified '517' class 0-4-2T crosses the river as it arrives at Usk with a train from Pontypool Road in 1908. Note the cattle dock in the foreground and the footbridge which was removed at an early date.

Symond's Yat, looking north towards Ross-on-Wye during the early years of the 20th century.
Lens of Sutton Collection

In the up direction, eastbound workings left Pontypool Road at 8.45, 11.05 am, 2.20, and 6.20 pm, arriving at Ross-on-Wye at 10.08 am, 1.10, 4.12 and 8.00 pm respectively. At 7.45 am, a service left Pontypool Road for Monmouth (Troy), and at 8.15 pm, an evening up train left Monmouth (Troy) *en route* for Ross-on-Wye. These two workings were of little use for through travellers, as there were no connecting services at Monmouth.

There were usually around four or five connecting passenger trains in each direction on the Wye Valley line between Chepstow and Monmouth (Troy), together with one pick-up freight service in each direction. In the 1880s, for example, the Great Western public timetable showed a daily service of four trains each way, and this same basic pattern of operation persisted for many years. At the end of the Victorian period, there were still just four up and four down trains between Monmouth and Chepstow, most of these services being extended over the South Wales main line to Severn Tunnel Junction.

The 1903 GWR public timetable provides a glimpse of the Wye Valley line in operation in the years before World War I. In the up (northbound) direction, trains left Severn Tunnel Junction at 6.59, 10.38 am, 3.26 and 6.15 pm, while at 7.20 pm an additional short distance working ran as far as Tintern. In the down direction, corresponding southbound workings departed from Monmouth (Troy) at 9.00 am, 12.20, 4.00 and 6.00 pm; there were no Sunday services. The number of daily trains on the Wye Valley route had increased to five workings each way by the 1930s, and this level of service was maintained until the British Railways period.

The May 1914 working timetable reveals a pattern of operation that was, in most respects, similar to the mode of operation in 1903. The Ross-on-Wye to Pontypool Road line was still worked as a continuous 30 mile cross-country route, with a basic service of four through trains each way. Up workings left Pontypool Road at 7.45, 8.45, 11.05 am, 2.20, and 6.20 pm, the first up service being a short-distance working that terminated at Monmouth (Troy), while the remaining services worked through to Ross-on-Wye. The 6.20 pm evening train was advertised as a 'mixed' passenger and goods working and there were also one or two short-distance services between Monmouth and Ross-on-Wye.

Balancing down workings departed from Ross-on-Wye at 6.55, 8.13, 10.38 am, 2.57 pm, and arrived at Pontypool Road at 8.20, 10.18 am, 1.10 and 4.46 pm respectively. Short-distance services left Ross-on-Wye for Lydbrook Junction at 12.00 noon, and at 1.35, 5.00 and 7.05 pm for Monmouth (Troy) - all of these services being worked by a steam railmotor car. At 5.15 and 8.05 pm, trains left Monmouth (Troy) for Pontypool Road; the 2.57 pm service from Ross-on-Wye and the 8.05 pm train from Monmouth were both 'mixed' services that conveyed goods vehicles as well as passenger stock. There were no advertised Sunday services at that time.

After World War I, there was an important change in the way in which the line was worked, the Ross to Pontypool Road through services being largely replaced by separate Ross-on-Wye to Monmouth, and Monmouth to Pontypool Road services. In conjunction with this new mode of operation, push-pull 'auto-trains' began working most of the branch services, motive power for the Ross & Monmouth line being supplied mainly from Ross-on-Wye shed, while

Down Trains. ROSS, MONMOUTH,

Single Line between Ross and Little Mill Junction. Worked by Electric Train Staff between Ross (South) and Symonds Yat, and Train Staff and Ticket and Block Telegraph between Symonds Yat and Little Mill Junction.

Distance from Ross M	C	STATIONS.		1	2	3	4	5	6	7	8	9	10	11
				G	B	B	B	B	K	K	K	K	B	
				Light Engine.	Passenger.	Pasesnger.	Passenger.	Passenger.	Goods.	Goods.	RR Goods. T	Hereford and Monmouth Goods.	Mixed Passenger and Goods.	
				A.M.	A.M.	A.M.	A.M.	A.M.	P.M.	P.M.	P.M.	P.M.	P.M.	
		Ross	dep.	6 45	7 0	....	8 18	10 35	....		....	1x12	2 55	
4	10	Kerne Bridge	arr.	—	—	..	—	—	..		..	1 25	—	
			dep.	6 56	7 9	....	8 27	10 46	....		....	2 5	3 6	
5	39	Lydbrook Jct	arr.	—	—	..	—	—	..		..	2x10	—	
			dep.	7 1	7 14	....	8 32	10 52	....		1 50	2 40	3 12	
7	49	Symonds' Yat	arr.	—	—	..	—	—	..		—	—	—	
			dep.	7 6	7 19	....	8 37	10 59	....		1 55	2 50	3 19	
8	40	Slaughter Siding	,,	—	—	..	—	—	..		—	CR	—	
11	1	Hadnock Siding	,,	—	—	....	—	—	....		—	CR	—	
12	30	**Monmouth** (May Hill)	arr.	7 17	7 29	..	8 48	11 11	RR		—	—	3 30	
			dep.	7 18	7 31	..	8 50	11 14	12 55		2 7	3 6	3 33	
13	9	**Monmouth** (Troy)	arr.	7 20	7x33	..	8 52	11 17	1 0		2 10	3 10	3 35	
						....		x			x		x	
			dep.		7 37	..	9 35	12 40	..	1 30	3 10		3 55	..
16	42	Dingestow	,,		7 45	....	9 42	12 47	....	—	—		4 4	....
19	44	Raglan	,,		7 53	..	9 49	12 54	..	1 57	3 37		4 12	..
21	62	Llandenny	,,		7 59	....	9 55	12 59	....	—	—		4 18	....
24	63	Davies' Siding	dep.		—	.	—	—	..	2 20	—		—	..
25	14	**Usk**	arr.		8 6	....	10 2	1 5	....	2 25	3 55		4 27	....
						..	x	x	..	•x	•x		•	..
			dep.		8x8	9 22	10 4	1 7	....	5 0	6 40		4 29	....
29	31	Little Mill Junction	arr.		8 17	9x29	10 12	1 15	..	5 15	6 55		4 40	..
			dep.	...	8 20	9 31	10 14	1 18	....	5 30	7 10		4 43	....
31	14	**Pontypool Rd.**	arr.	..	8 25	9 35	10 18	1L25	..	5 40	7 20		4 48	..

Column 1: Wednesdays only. Column 7: Not run when 1.50 p.m. from Lydbrook runs. Column 9: S. T. 33, 477 & 514. Column 10: Does not convey Goods traffic Ross to Monmouth on Wednesdays.

Up Trains.

STATIONS.		1	2	3	4	5	6	7	8	9	10	11
		B	B	B	B		K		B		K	K
		Passenger.	Passenger.	Passenger.	Passenger.		Goods and S.T. Truck. Nos. 212, 414 & 548.		Passenger.		Goods.	Goods.
		A.M.	A.M.	A.M.	A.M.		A.M.		A.M.		A.M.	P.M.
Pontypool Road.	dep.	....	7 45	8 45	9 0	....	9 20	....	11 5	....	11 10	RR
Little Mill Junction	arr.	..	7 49	8 49	—	..	9x27	..	11 9	..	11 17	..
	dep.	....	7 50	8 50	C 94 S	....	9 37	....	11 10	....	11 35	....
Usk	arr.	..	7 58	8 58	9 11	..	9 50	..	11 18	..	11 50	..
			x				x					
	dep.		8 20	8 59	..	..	10 10	..	11 20	..	11 55	..
Davies' Siding	dep.		—	—	....	....	—	....	—	....	12 5	....
Llandenny ..	,,		8 27	9 5	..	..	10 30	..	11 27	..	—	..
Raglan	,,		8 33	9 11	....	....	10 50	....	11 33	....	—	....
Dingestow	arr.		8 40	9 16	..	..	11 5	..	11 40	..	—	..
	dep.		8 43	9 18	....	....	11 10	....	11 43	....	—	....
Monmouth (Troy)	arr.		8 50	9 25	..	..	11 25	..	11 50	..	12x35	..
				—					x			
	dep.	7x36	....	9 30	....	....	....	....	12 30	....	....	12 35
Monmouth (May Hill)	arr.	7 38	..	9 32	..	..	..	..	12 32	..	..	12 40
	dep.	7 39	....	9 34	....	....	....	....	12 34	....	....	....
Hadnock Siding ..	,,	—	..	—	..	..	..	..	—	..	..	..
Slaughter Siding	,,	—	....	—	....	....	....	....	—	....	....	....
Symonds' Yat	arr.	—	..	9 45	..	..	..	..	12 45	..	..	..
	dep.	7 49	....	9 46	....	....	....	....	12 46	....	....	....
Lydbrook Junction	,,	7 54	..	9 53	..	..	..	..	12 55	..	..	..
Kerne Bridge ..	,,	7 59	....	10 0	....	....	....	....	1 2	....	....	....
Ross	arr.	8 7	..	10x10	..	..	..	..	1x11	..	..	..

Column 1: Wednesdays only.

Coal Traffic, Lydbrook Junction to Fawley, Holme Lacy, etc.

Preference must be given at Lydbrook Junction by the 4.12 p.m. Goods ex Monmouth to traffic for Fawley, Holme Lacy, Hereford and beyond. When necessary to run the conditional train from Ross to clear out surplus traffic from Lydbrook Junction, the traffic held over should be for Ross as far as possible.

The 4.12 p.m. ex Monmouth to call at Fawley or Holme Lacy to detach the traffic for those stations when necessary.

4.30 p.m. (RR) Ross to Lydbrook Junction and back.
8.15 p.m. (,,) ,, ,, ,,

The maximum load of above Trains worked by Ross Passenger Engines will be 12 ten-ton wagons of coal OR THE EQUIVALENT.

Maximum Loads for Goods and Mineral Trains:

Ross to Monmouth / Monmouth to Ross } Tank Engines. 20 Coal, 30 Goods, 40 Empties.

Coal Traffic Lydbrook Colliery (S. & W. Jt.) to Cheltenham.

Loaded and empty wagons to travel via Lydney instead of Lydbrook. Wagons not to be delayed.

Working timetable for the Ross, Monmouth & Pontypool Road line, February 1907.

AND PONTYPOOL ROAD. Week Days only.

Crossing Places:—Lydbrook Junction, Symonds Yat, Monmouth (Troy), Usk and Little Mill Junction. Monmouth (May Hill), Staff Station only.

STATIONS.		12	13	14	15	16	17	18	19	20	21	22	23
		K	B	F	K			B	K	B	B	K	K
		Goods. P	Passenger.	RR Cattle. Q	RR Goods.			Passenger.	Goods and S.T. Nos. 33, 477 and 514.	Passenger.	Passenger.	RR Engine & Van.	Goods.
		P.M.	P.M.	P.M.	P.M.			P.M.	P.M.	P.M.	P.M.	P.M.	P.M.
Ross	dep.	....	....	4X30	4 30	....	....	....	....	**7 12**	....	8X15	....
Kerne Bridge ..	arr.	..	..	—	—	..	..	..	..	—	..	—	..
	dep.	....	....	—	—	....	....	....	....	7 23	....	—	....
Lydbrook Jct	arr.	Suspended.	..	4 51	4X45	..	..	..	..	7 29	..	8 28	..
	dep.		....	—		....	....	....	....	7 32	....		....
Symonds Yat ..	arr.		..	—	..	..	..	..	..	7 37	..	..	..
	dep.		....	CS	....	....	....	....	....	7X39	Suspended.	....	....
Slaughter Siding	,,		..	—	..	..	..	..	..	—		..	..
Hadnock Siding	,,		....	—	....	....	....	....	....	—		....	....
Monmouth (May Hill)	arr.	..	..	—	..	..	..	..	..	**7 49**		..	..
	dep.	....	....	5 12	....	....	....	....	....	**7 51**		....	....
Monmouth (Troy)	arr.	..	..	5 15	..	..	..	..	..	**7 53**		..	..
	dep.	4 10	**5 10**	5 20	..	..	..	..	7X35	Runs as a Mixed Train on Wednesdays.	8 10	..	
Dingestow	,,	4 30	5 17	—	....	....	....	....	7 55		8 17	....	Suspended.
Raglan	,,	4 50	5 24	—	..	..	..	..	8 20		8 24	..	
Llandenny	,,	5 5	5 30	—	....	....	....	....	8 35		8 30	....	
Davies' Siding	dep.	—	—	—	..	..	..	..	—		—	..	
Usk	arr.	5 15	**5 38**	—	....	....	....	....	8 45		8 36	....	
		X	•										
	dep.	7 35	**5 40**	5 50	....	....	....	**8 40**	9 0		8 40	....	9 0
Little Mill Junction	arr.	7 50	5 48	—	..	..	..	8 49	—		8 49	..	—
	dep.	8 5	5 51	6X0	....	....	....	8 51	9 13		8 51	....	9 13
Pontypool Rd.	arr.	8 15	**5 55**	6 5	..	..	..	**8 55**	9 20		8 55	..	9 20

Week Days only.

STATIONS.		12	13	14	15	16		17	18	19	20	21	22
		K	B		K	K				B	B	K	B
		RR Goods. Q.T.	Passenger		RR Goods.	Monmouth and Hereford **Goods.**				Passenger and Goods.	Passenger.	RR Goods.	Passenger.
		P.M.	P.M.		P.M.	arr.	dep.			P.M.	P.M.	P.M.	P.M.
Pontypool Rd.	dep.	....	**2 20**	....	....			....	....	**6 20**	**8 15**	....	....
Little Mill Junction	arr.	..	—	..	..	P.M.	P.M.	..	..	6 24	8 19	..	..
	dep.	....	2 25	....	....	....	....	....	....	6 25	8 20	....	....
Usk	arr.	..	**2 33**	..	..	..	..	..	..	**6 34**	**8 28**	..	..
			X			S.T. No. 548.				X			
	dep.	..	**2 35**	..	..			..	..	**6 36**		..	..
Davies' Siding	dep.	....	—	....	....	....	....	....	....	—	* Arrive at Lydbrook at 7.45 p.m.	....	....
Llandenny....	,,	..	2 42	..	..	..	..	..	..	6 45		..	..
Raglan ..	,,	....	2 48	....	....	....	....	....	....	6 51		....	....
Dingestow	arr.	..	2 55	..	..	..	..	..	..	6 59		..	..
	dep.	....	2 58	....	....	....	....	....	....	7 1		....	....
Monmouth (Troy)	arr.	..	**3 5**	..	..	..	..	..	..	**7 10**		..	..
			X							X			
	dep.	1X5	**3 38**	..	..	—	X4 12	..	..	**7 23**	..	....	**8 15**
Monmouth (May Hill)	arr.	1 9	**3 40**	....	....	—	—	....	....	**7 25**	....	..	**8 18**
	dep.	1 10	**3 42**	..	..	4 16	4 17	..	..	**7 26**	..	....	**8 20**
Hadnock Siding	,,	—	—	....	....	**C**	**R**	....	....	—	....	..	—
Slaughter Siding	,,	—	—	..	..	**C**	**R**	..	..	—	..	....	—
Symonds' Yat	arr.	1 23	3 51	....	....	—	—	....	....	7 36	....	..	8 32
	dep.	1 25	3 52	..	..	4 40	X4 41	..	..	7X40	..	....	8 33
Lydbrook Jct.	,,	2X10	3 58	....	4 55	4 50	X5 30	....	....	*7 50	....	8 56	8 40
Kerne Bridge	,,	—	4 4	..	—	5 37	5 50	..	..	7 56	..	—	8 46
Ross ..	arr.	2 25	**4X13**	....	5 15	6 5	7 15	....	....	**8X5**	....	9 10	**8 56**

L Time allowed in running for check outside Pontypool Road.

P This Train must shunt Davies' Siding after the 5·10 p.m. Monmouth has passed and before the arrival of the 6.20 p.m. from Pontypool Road.

Q When the 4.30 p.m. from Ross is required to run, the 9.20 a.m. from Pontypool Road must be sent through to Ross, leaving Monmouth (Troy) at 1.5 p.m., taking forward from there traffic for Lydbrook or Ross, if required, and an Engine, Van, and Guard must leave Pontypool Road coupled to the 2.20 p.m. Passenger Train to work from Monmouth to Pontypool Road at 4·10 p.m.

T The 9.20 a.m. Goods from Pontypool Road may be run to Lydbrook Jct. when there are fifteen or more Wagons for Lydbrook Junction or beyond, leaving Monmouth (Troy) at 1.5 p.m., and returning from Lydbrook Jct. at 1.50 p.m. with Engine and Van only to Monmouth. The Station Masters at Monmouth (Troy) and Lydbrook Junction to arrange and advise Staff Stations.

The mixed Trains must be confined to Cattle Traffic only, as between Pontypool Road and Monmouth, but this restriction will not apply between Monmouth and Ross.

Working timetable for the Ross, Monmouth & Pontypool Road line, February 1907.

Down Trains. ROSS, MONMOUTH,

Distance from Ross M	C	STATIONS.		Station No.	1 D	2 B	3 B	4 B	5 B	6	7 B	8	9	10	11
					Empty Coaches.	Passenger.	Passenger.	Passenger.	Motor dep.	Goods. RR	Motor	RR Goods. T	Hereford and Monmouth Goods.	Hereford and Monmouth Goods.	Goods RR
					A.M.	A.M.	A.M.	A.M.	noon.	P.M.	P.M.	P.M.	P.M.	P.M.	P.M.
		Ross	dep.	2618	6 35	6 55	8 18	10 38	12 0	Commencing June 1st.	1X35	....	1X15	1 55	....
4	10	K'rne B'ge	arr.	2625	—	—	—	—	—		—	..	1 27	2 7	..
			dep.		—	7 3	8 27	10 47	12 10		1 47	....	1 52	2 40	....
5	40	Lydbr'k Jc	arr.	2626	—	—	—	—	12 15		—	..	1X57	2 45	..
			dep.		CS	7 7	8 32	10 52	Goods		1 53	1X40	2e45	3e40	....
7	50	Sym'ds Y't	arr.	2627	—	—	—	—	RR		—	—	—	—	..
			dep.		CS	7 12	8 37	10 57		....	2 0	1 45	2 55	3X55	....
8	41	Sl'ughter Sdg.	,,	2628	—	—	—	—	P.M.	..	—	—	CR	CR	..
11	2	Hadnock Sdg.	,,	2629	—	—	—	—	....	....	—	—	CR	CR	....
12	31	M'nm'uth	arr.	2630	7 7	7 22	8 47	11 7	..	..	2 13	—	—	CS	..
		(May Hill)	dep.		7 8	7 25	8 49	11 10	12 55	....	2 14	1 57	CS	—	....
13	10	M'nm'uth (Troy)	arr.	2631	7 10	7X27	8 51	11 13 X	1 0	..	2 17	2 0	3 10	4 10	..
			dep.		..	7 33	9 35	12 30	....	1 30	..	....			1 30
16	42	Dingestow	arr.	2640	....	7 40	—	—	..	—	....	..		..	CR
			dep.		..	7 42	9 42	12 37	....	CR	..	....		....	—
19	44	Raglan ..	arr.	2641	Wednesdays only and during May only.	7 49	—	—	..	1 50	Commencing June 1st.	....	During May only. S.T. 33, 477, 514 & 724.	Commencing June 1st.	1 50
			dep.			7 51	9 49	12 44	....	2 20		..			2 20
21	62	Llandenny	arr.	2642		7 55	—	—	..	2 27		....			—
			dep.			7 57	9 55	12 50	....			..			3X10
24	59	Davies' Sdg.	dep.	2643		—	—	—	..	..		....			3 27
25	14	Usk ..	arr.	2644		8 3	10 2 X	12 56 X	....	....		....			3 30
			dep.			8X6	10 4	12 58	....	....		..			..
29	22	Little Mill Junction	arr.	4539		8 14	10 12	1 5	..	..		..			..
			dep.			8 15	10 13	1 6	..	..	..	..	..	..	....
30	74	P'nty-pool Road	Pass. arr.	4001		8 20	10 18	1 10	....	....	....	....	....	....	..
31	14		Goods arr.	4002					..	..	..	..	..	..	....

Up Trains.

Distances from Pontypool Rd. M.	C.	STATIONS.		1 B	2 B	3 B	4 arr.	4 dep.	5 B	6 B	7	8	9
				Passenger (Motor in June).	Passenger.	Passenger.	Goods. T		Motor.	Passenger.	Goods.	Goods.	RR Goods. Q.T.
				A.M.	A.M.	A.M.	A.M.	A.M.	P.M.	A.M.	A.M.	P.M.	P.M.
—	—	Pontypool Road, Goods	dep.		—	—	—	9 10		—	11 10	RR	..
—	—	Pontypool Road, Passenger	dep.		7 45	8 45	—	—		11 5	—	....	....
1	72	Little Mill Junction	arr.	Wednesdays only in May. Daily from June 1st.	7 49	8 49	—	—	Commencing June 1st.	11 9	11 17	..	..
			dep.		7 50	8 50	9 17	9 22		11 10	11 30	....	....
6	0	Usk	arr.		7 58 X	8 58	—	—		11 18	11 43	..	..
			dep.		8 10	8 59	9 35X	10 5		11 20	11 50	..	..
6	35	Davies' Siding	dep.		—	—	—	—		—	12 0	....	....
9	32	Llandenny ..	,,		8 17	9 5	10 15	10 30		11 27	—	..	..
11	50	Raglan	,,		8 23	9 11	10 40	10 55		11 33	—	....	....
14	52	Dingestow	arr.		8 30	9 16	—	—		11 40	—	..	..
			dep.		8 33	9 18	11 5	11 15		11 43	—	....	....
18	4	Monmouth (Troy)	arr.		8 40	9 25	11 25	—		11 50 X	12X28	..	..
			dep.	7X28	..	9 30	..	..	..	12 25	..	12 35	12X55
18	63	Monmouth (May Hill)	arr.	7 30	....	9 32	....	....	....	12 28	....	12 40	—
			dep.	7 31	..	9 34	..	..	..	12 34	..		1 0
—	—	Hadnock Siding	,,	—	....	—	....	....	....	—	....	....	—
22	53	Slaughter Siding	,,	—	..	—	..	..	..	—	..	..	—
23	44	Symonds' Yat	arr.	—	....	—	....	....	....	—	....	....	CS
			dep.	7 42	..	9 45	..	..	..	12 45	..	..	—
25	14	Lydbrook Junction	,,	7 48	....	9 51	....	....	12 25	12X51	....	....	CS
27	4	Kerne Bridge ..	arr.	7 51	..	9 54	..	..	12 28	12 54	..	..	—
			dep.	7 52	....	9 56	....	....	12 32	12 56	....	....	—
31	14	Ross	arr.	8 1	..	10 5	..	..	12 43	1X 5	..	..	1X35

N Does not convey Goods traffic Ross to Monmouth on Wednesdays.

P This Train must shunt Davies' Siding after the 5.15 p.m. Monmouth has passed and before the arrival of the 6.20 p.m. from Pontypool Road.

Working timetable for the Ross, Monmouth & Pontypool Road line, May 1914.

AND PONTYPOOL ROAD. Week Days only.

STATIONS.		12B	13	14 B	15 F	16	17 B	18 B	19	20 B	21	22
		Mixed Passenger and Goods. N	Goods. P	Passenger.	RR Cattle. Q	RR Goods.	Passenger.	Passenger.	Goods. RR	Mixed Passenger and Goods.	RR Engine & Van.	
		P.M.	P.M.	P.M.	P.M.	P.M.	P.M.	P.M.	P.M.	P.M.	P.M.	
Ross ←⋘	dep.	2 57	....	....	4X20	4 45	5 0	7 5	....	....	8X20	....
Kerne	arr.	—	..	..	—	—	—	—	..	..	W	..
Bridge ..	dep.	3 7	....	....	—	—	5 9	7 14	....	....	—	....
Lydbrook Jct	arr.	—	..	..	CS	5 0	—	—	..	..	8X33	..
	dep.	3 13	....	....	—	SUSPENDED when 5.0 p.m. running.	5 14	7 19	....	....	W Tuesdays excepted.	....
Symonds	arr.	—	..	..	—		—	—	..	..		..
Yat ..	dep.	3 19	....	....	CS		5X19	7 24	....	....		....
Slaughter Siding	,,	—	..	..	—		—	—	..	..		..
Hadnock Siding	,,	—	....	....	—		—	—	....	....		....
Monmouth	arr.	3 30	..	..	—		5 29	7 34	..	..		..
(M.H.) ←⋘	dep.	3 33	....	....	4 57		5 31	7 36	....	....		....
Monmouth	arr.	3 35	..	..	5X 0		5 33	7X38	..	..		..
(Troy)		X	....					Runs as a Mixed Train on Wednesdays.	....	....		....
	dep.	3 55	4 10	5 15	5 25		..		5 25	8 5		..
Dingestow	arr.	—	4 20	—	—		....		5 35	8 13		....
	dep.	4 4	4 30	5 22	—		..		5 40	8 15	Goods. K	..
Raglan ..	arr.	—	4 40	—	—		....		5 50	8 22		....
	dep.	4.12	4 50	5 29	—		..		6 0	8 24		..
Llandenny	arr.	—	4 57	—	—		....		6 7	8 30		....
	dep.	4 18	5 5	5 35	—		..		6 15	8 33		..
Davies' Siding	dep.	—	—	—	—	....	....		—	—		....
Usk	arr.	4 27	5 15	5 42	—	..	..		6 25	8 42		..
		•	X	•		....	....				P.M.	....
	dep.	4 29	7 35	5 45	5 55	..	..		7 35	8 46	10 30	..
Little Mill	arr.	4 40	7 50	5 53	—	....	....		7 50	8 54	—	....
Junction	dep.	4 41	8 5	5 55	6X5	...	..	..	8 5	8 56	10 43	..
Ponty- Pass.	arr.	4 46	—	6 0	—	....	..	....	—	9 0	—	....
p'l Rd. Goods	arr.		8 15		6 10	..	..	..	8 15		10 50	..

V When conveying Goods Traffic, 1 minute extra is allowed in running between Lydbrook Junc. and Kerne Bridge and 2 between Kerne Bridge and Ross.

Week Days only.

STATIONS.		10B	11	12	13	14		15	16A	17B	18B	19B	20
		Passenger	Engine and Van. RR	Engine and Van. RR	RR Goods.	Monmouth and Hereford Goods.		Monmouth & Hereford Goods.	Passenger.	Passenger and Goods.	Passenger.	Passenger.	RR Goods.
		P.M.	P.M.	P.M.	P.M.	arr.	dep.	P.M.	P.M.	P.M.	P.M.	P.M.	P.M.
Ponty- Goods	dep.	—	..	..	..	—	—	..	..	—	—	..	..
p'l Rd. Pass.	dep.	2 20	....	....	....	..	..	....	....	6 20	9 22	....	....
Little Mill	arr.	—	..	..	..	P.M.	P.M.		..	6 24	9 26	..	..
Junction	dep.	2 25	....	....		....	....	Commencing June 1st.	....	6 25	9 27	....	....
Usk	arr.	2 33	..	..		..	..		..	6 34	9 34	..	..
		X	....	....		S.T. No. 548.			....	X			
	dep.	2 35	..	4 30	SUSPENDED When 6.2 p.m. running.				..	6 36	..	..	Tuesdays excepted.
Davies' Siding	dep.	—	....	—		During May only.			....	—	....	....	
Llandenny....	,,	2 42	3 0	—					..	6 45	..	..	
Raglan ..	,,	2 48	—	—					....	6 51	....	....	
Dingestow	arr.	2 55	—	—					..	6 59	..	..	
	dep.	2 58	—	—				..	....	7 1	....	....	
Monmouth	arr.	3 5	3 30	5 0				....	..	7 10	..	..	
(Troy)		X								X			
	dep.	3 38	..	..		—	4X12	5 0	6 2	7 20	..	8 13	
Monmouth	arr.	3 40	....	....		—	—	5 3	6 4	7 42	....	8 18	
(M.H.) ←⋘	dep.	3 42	..	..		4 16	4 17	5 4	6 6	7 43	..	8 20	....
Hadnock Siding	,,	—	....	....		C	R	CR	—	—	....	—	..
Slaughter Siding	,,	—	..	..		C	R	CR	—	V	..	—	....
Symonds'	arr.	—	....	....	....	—	—	5X17	—	—	....	—	..
Yat	dep.	3 53	..	..	..	4 35	4 36	5 20	6 17	7 53	..	8 31	....
Lydbrook Jct.	,,	3 59	....	....	5 10	4 43	X5 30	5 50	6 23	8 0	....	8X37	9 0
Kerne	arr.	4 2	..	..	—	5 36	5 51	—	6 26	8 3	..	8 40	—
Bridge	dep.	4 4	....	....	—	—	—	6 6	6 28	8 5	....	8 42	—
Ross ..	arr.	4X13	..	..	5 30	6 8	X7 30	6 20	6 37	8X14	..	8 51	9 22

T The 9.10 a.m. Goods from Pontypool Road may be run to Lydbrook Junction when there are fifteen or more wagons for Lydbrook Junction or beyond, leaving Monmouth (Troy) at 12.55 p.m., and returning from Lydbrook Junction at 1.35 p.m. with Engine and Van only to Monmouth. The Station Masters at Monmouth (Troy) and Lydbrook Junction to arrange and advise Staff Stations. The mixed trains must be confined to cattle traffic only, as between Pontypool Road and Monmouth, but this restriction will not apply between Monmouth and Ross.

Working timetable for the Ross, Monmouth & Pontypool Road line, May 1914.

A tranquil view of the station at Monmouth (May Hill). *The Nelson Museum, Monmouth*

A view along the up platform at Symond's Yat seen from the train on 5th April, 1931.
H.C. Casserley

Pontypool Road-based locomotives appeared on the western section of the route between Monmouth and Pontypool Road.

The Great Western public timetable for September 1928 illustrates this new method of operation. In the up direction, there were five trains between Pontypool Road and Monmouth, and six between Monmouth and Ross-on-Wye, while in the down direction there were six workings between Ross-on-Wye and Monmouth (Troy), and six between Monmouth (Troy) and Pontypool Road. The number of through trains was cut to one up and three down workings, while additional short-distance services were provided between Pontypool, Usk and the newly-opened (1927) Glascoed Halt. A Sunday service was now advertised, and this consisted of two trains in each direction over the entire length of the line between Ross-on-Wye and Pontypool Road.

The 1938 GWR timetable provides a useful glimpse of the railway in operation in the immediate pre-war period. There were, at that time, five up and six down workings between Pontypool Road and Monmouth, May Hill being shown as the terminal point for most of the up workings, though three of the down services commenced their journeys at Monmouth (Troy). In the up direction, trains left Pontypool Road at 7.42, 8.33, 11.14 am, 2.30 and 6.02 pm. The 2.30 pm service was a through working to Ross-on-Wye, but the other up workings terminated at Monmouth (May Hill).

The Ross & Monmouth section was at that time served by six trains in each direction between Monmouth (Troy) and Ross-on-Wye. In the up direction, there were departures from Monmouth (Troy) at 7.24, 9.46 am, 12.40, 3.51, 6.20 and 8.43 pm, arriving at Ross-on-Wye at 7.55, 10.20 am, 1.12, 4.22 , 6.52 and 9.17 pm respectively. The 3.51 pm service was the above-mentioned through working from Pontypool Road, which had started its journey at 2.30 pm and arrived at Monmouth (Troy) at 3.12 pm, before going forward to Ross-on-Wye 39 minutes later.

In the opposite direction, balancing southbound workings left Ross-on-Wye at 6.40, 8.22, 10.57 am, 3.01, 5.10 and 7.25 pm. The 6.40 and 10.57 am trains ran through to Pontypool Road, where they arrived at 8.11 am and 12.42 pm respectively. This basic service was supplemented by short-distance return trips from Ross-on-Wye to Lydbrook Junction at 7.13 am and 4.13 pm, with a similar out-and-back trip to Symond's Yat at 1.50 pm. The Sunday service consisted of just two trains each way between Pontypool Road and Ross-on-Wye, the up workings leaving Pontypool Road at 1.52 and 5.15 pm, while the down trains departed from Ross-on-Wye at 10.10 am and 7.15 pm.

Other down trains left Monmouth (Troy) at 7.28, 9.25, 11.55 am, 3.51, 5.25 and 8.48 pm - the 7.28 am and 11.55 am services being the advertised through trains from Ross-on-Wye mentioned above. There were, in addition, two up trains and one down working between Pontypool Road and Usk on weekdays, rising to three up and four down workings on Saturdays.

Freight Trains and Traffic

Goods traffic was important on the Ross-on-Wye to Pontypool route, although such traffic was never particularly heavy. Like other rural lines, the railway carried coal and general merchandise inwards, and agricultural traffic outwards. Important customers included Monmouth Gas Works and the Monmouth Steam Saw Mills, both of these lineside industrial concerns being served by private sidings. Another industrial siding served Edison Swan Cables Ltd at Lydbrook Junction, while a brick works siding was provided at Little Mill Junction.

Further private sidings were available on the section of line between Symond's Yat and Monmouth, these being associated mainly with timber and mineral traffic. In the early 1920s the sidings concerned were known as Hadnock Siding, Slaughter Siding, High Meadow Siding and Roberts & Lewis' Siding.

There was normally just one goods train in each direction on the Ross & Monmouth, Monmouth to Pontypool Road and Wye Valley branch lines. In 1876, for instance, the Ross & Monmouth branch was served by a pick-up working from Grange Court to Monmouth, which returned from Monmouth to Ross-on-Wye as an up service and then continued northwards along the Hereford, Ross & Gloucester line to Hereford. There was also a short-distance service from Ross-on-Wye to Lydbrook, which ran on an 'as required' basis.

This pattern of goods train operation had changed little by the end of the Victorian period, and the 1903 working timetable shows just one through goods train in each direction between Hereford and Monmouth, with a connecting service from Ross-on-Wye to Gloucester; other branch goods trains were still operated on an 'as required basis'. Around 1913, the daily goods train left Hereford at 11.15 am, and returned from Monmouth at 4.12 pm. There was, in addition, provision for 'mixed' passenger and goods working, one or two passenger trains being advertised as mixed services that conveyed both passenger and goods vehicles.

The Monmouth to Pontypool Road section was served by two goods trains in each direction in the years before World War I, and in May 1914 these departed from Pontypool Road at 9.10 and 11.10 am, returning later in the day from Monmouth. The Wye Valley branch was typically served by one train in each direction, although there was, at various times, provision for short-distance workings between Monmouth and Redbrook, on the Wye Valley route. Similar short-distance trip workings were provided between Monmouth (Troy) and Monmouth (May Hill) stations - Monmouth (Troy) being used as a convenient exchange and marshalling point between the three local branch lines.

The goods rolling stock used on the line reflected the types of traffic carried, with wooden open wagons being used for many years for both coal and general merchandise traffic. As usual on the Great Western system, domestic coal was normally carried in privately-owned coal merchants' or colliery wagons - the GWR itself having very few coal or mineral-carrying vehicles in its own wagon fleet. Various private owner wagons appeared on the line over the years, among them vehicles belonging to the Monmouth Steam Saw Mills.

Open wagons were employed for timber, sacked goods or other commodities, sheets being used to protect vulnerable consignments. Later, covered vans

A glimpse of wagons in Monmouth(Troy) goods yard on 5th April, 1931. Several different private owner wagons can be seen, together with GWR match truck No. 32484. Match trucks could be used for containers, motor vehicles or similar large loads, but they were not equipped with chains, chocks or other accessories. *H.C. Casserley*

began to appear in increasing numbers for a range of goods including general merchandise and fertilizers, together with specialized vehicles for meat, bananas or other perishables. Contemporary photographs suggest that local Great Western vehicles were predominant, though Midland Railway (later London Midland & Scottish Railway (LMS)) rolling stock was also very common.

Other specialized vehicles that would have been seen on the line included standard Great Western 'Mex' cattle wagons and characteristic GWR 'Siphons' for the carriage of milk churns by passenger or parcels trains. Consignments of felled timber or other long thin loads were conveyed on Great Western 'Macaw' bolster wagons, while machinery or other heavy consignments would have brought 'Loriot' low loading vehicles onto the branch. In the latter context, most (though not all) of the stations on the line were equipped with end-loading docks for agricultural machinery or road vehicles, and Monmouth (Troy), Usk and Ross-on-Wye were equipped with fixed hand cranes.

In 1903, the single line between Ross-on-Wye (South Junction) and Little Mill Junction was worked mainly by Train Staff and Ticket in conjunction with Block Telegraph, although the more advanced Electric Train Staff system had already been introduced at the northern end of the line between Ross-on-Wye and Lydbrook Junction. The Staff and Ticket system was a variant of the 'divisible staff' system whereby a series of up or down trains were able to follow each other through a single line section on the authority of a 'ticket' - the wooden train staff being carried by the last train of an up or down series. This system allowed greater flexibility than the ordinary train staff system of operation.

A general view of Pontypool Road shed from the south in September 1936. The shed consisted of eight roads, one of which continued on through a roundhouse.
W. Potter/Kidderminster Railway Museum

'57XX' class 0-6-0PT No. 9788 is seen in the bay platform at Pontypool Road in August 1936. To the right is 'Bulldog' 4-4-0 No. 3308 which formerly carried the name *Falmouth*, although by that date the nameplate had been removed. *W. Potter/Kidderminster Railway Museum*

The Electric Train Staff system had been installed throughout the line by 1914, the staff sections being: Ross-on-Wye to Lydbrook Junction; Lydbrook Junction to Symond's Yat (introduced 1905); Symond's Yat to Monmouth (May Hill); Monmouth (May Hill) to Monmouth (Troy); Monmouth (Troy) to Dingestow; Dingestow to Llandenny; Llandenny to Usk; and Usk to Little Mill Junction. The main crossing stations were Lydbrook Junction, Symond's Yat, Monmouth (Troy) and Usk. Dingestow was subsequently taken out of use as a block post, though in World War II an additional block post was opened at Glascoed.

Locomotives and Rolling Stock in the Great Western Period

The Ross to Pontypool Road route was classified as a 'Yellow' route under the Great Western system of locomotive weight restrictions, and for this reason it was normally worked by four- or six-coupled tank engines. It is likely that Armstrong '517' class 0-4-2Ts were employed on the line at a comparatively early date, together with various small-wheeled saddle tank classes such as the '2021' class 0-6-0STs - many of which were later rebuilt as pannier tanks.

In 1921, Pontypool Road's allocation included '2021' class tank locomotives Nos. 2066, 2131, 2140 and 2160, these engines being used on local services to Monmouth, Newport and elsewhere. The Armstrong '517' class 0-4-2Ts were also widely used on the line, some typical examples being Nos. 216, 222, 468, 526, 534, 536, 545, 565, 574, 576, 845, 979, 1164, 1422, 1432, 1465 and 1476, all of which were stationed at Ross-on-Wye at various times between 1900 and 1930.

When push-pull operation was introduced on the Ross & Monmouth and Monmouth and Pontypool Road lines, auto-fitted '517' class 0-4-2Ts and 'Metro' class 2-4-0Ts were employed on these duties. The 'Metro' class 2-4-0Ts became associated with the route during the early 1920s, when one or two examples were allocated to Ross-on-Wye shed for use on the Monmouth route. In 1933 auto-fitted 'Metro' 2-4-0T No. 1455 was noted at work on the route.

At the other end of the line, other 'Metro' tanks were also stationed at Pontypool Road for use on local services to and from Monmouth. In 1921, Pontypool Road shed housed several small tank locomotives that would have been suitable for use on the line, including 'Metro' class 2-4-0Ts Nos. 632 and 1462 and various small tank engines such as '850' class 0-6-0PT No. 1915, and 0-6-0 saddle tanks Nos. 1966 and 1984.

The Collett '48XX' (later '14XX') class 0-4-2Ts were introduced in 1932 as replacements for the Armstrong '517' class 0-4-2Ts and other elderly GWR tank classes. The new locomotives soon appeared in the Monmouth area, Nos. 4820, 4822 and 4823 being sent to Pontypool Road shortly after their construction, while sister engines Nos. 4802 and 4806 had been allocated to Ross-on-Wye by 1938 for service on the Ross & Monmouth branch. Another example seen on the line in the years preceding World War II was No. 4863.

Great Western saddle and pannier tank classes were employed on both passenger and freight workings at various times. The regular performers around 1920 included '1016' class 0-6-0PT No. 1062, and '1076' class 0-6-0PTs Nos. 1183, 1570 and 1609. All of these engines were double-framed locomotives.

The older GWR 0-6-0PT classes were subsequently replaced by more modern pannier tanks such as the Collett '64XX' and '74XX' class 0-6-0PTs. In 1938, Ross-on-Wye's allocation included '74XX' class 0-6-0PT No. 7416, while other members of the class seen on the Ross & Monmouth route at different times included Nos. 7412, 7420 and 7429. The visually-similar '64XX' class 0-6-0 pannier tanks were also have seen at Monmouth (Troy) on a regular basis, although these auto-fitted engines were more likely to appear on the Wye Valley or Pontypool Road routes than on the Ross & Monmouth line.

The familiar '57XX' class pannier tanks were introduced by C.B. Collett in 1929 as replacements for older 0-6-0PTs. No less than 863 examples were eventually built, the '57XX' 0-6-0PTs being the largest class on the GWR. Many former enginemen consider that, after the 'Castles', they were the best engines on the GWR! However, in Great Western days these 50 ton locomotives were classified as 'Blue' engines and, as such, they were officially barred from many branch line routes. In practice they appear to have been allowed onto certain 'Yellow' routes by special dispensation, and under BR auspices the '57XX' class engines were reclassified as 'Yellow' locomotives.

It is not entirely clear when the '57XX' class were first allowed onto the Ross-on-Wye to Pontypool Road route, though they were certainly used during the British Railways period, when they often worked the daily freight service. In exceptional circumstances they may even have worked local passenger trains if the rostered diesel car was not available, although as non-auto engines they could not be used on push-pull workings.

Tender locomotives appeared on the lines to Monmouth on a sporadic basis. They were normally employed on freight workings, particularly when through running to Hereford and Gloucester was involved. In 1921, Hereford's allocation included Armstrong 'Standard Goods' 0-6-0s Nos. 116, 500, 516, 658, 782 and 875, together with 'Dean Goods' 0-6-0s Nos. 2333, 2341 and 2355, while Armstrong 0-6-0s Nos. 792, 1083 and 1099 were stationed at Pontypool Road, together with 'Dean Goods' 0-6-0 Nos. 2446, 2562, 2568 and 2577.

Small-wheeled prairie tanks of the '45XX' class were used on the line to a limited extent during the 1930s, some random examples being Nos. 4503 and 4533, both of which were recorded at work on the Ross & Monmouth line in August 1936. There was a general easing of weight restrictions throughout the system during World War II, engines in the 'Blue' route category being allowed onto Yellow routes subject to speed restrictions or other limitations. At the same time, the western end of the Monmouth to Pontypool Road route was cleared for the operation of 'Red' locomotives, and in this context '56XX' class 0-6-2Ts often worked over the route as far as the Royal Ordnance Factory at Glascoed.

Diesel Railcar Services

Interestingly, the Ross & Monmouth, Wye Valley and Pontypool Road routes were among the relatively small number of Great Western branch lines that were worked by the company's pioneer AEC diesel railcars. The first Great Western diesel railcar was introduced in 1933, and three similar vehicles were put into service between Birmingham and Cardiff in July 1934. The original streamlined railcars were intended for use on fast, but lightly-loaded, main line services, but three further vehicles were introduced on local services in the following year. The new diesel cars were numbered in sequence from 1 to 7, the next nine vehicles to be constructed being Nos. 8 to 16.

In May 1936 *The Railway Magazine* reported that streamlined railcar No. 13 had started work in the West Wales area on 16th March, while on 23rd March sister vehicle No. 14 had 'entered service to work 17 existing steam-train services, and also to provide two new passenger services, in the Newport, Chepstow, Monmouth, Pontypool Road, Panteg and Blaenavon area'. The dieselization of the Monmouth to Pontypool Road, and Monmouth to Chepstow lines thereby commenced as early as 1936, the use of diesel railcars on local services being so successful that the Great Western continued building these vehicles until the number in service was 38.

Car No. 14 was similar to the original GWR railcars, with curved streamlining and a driving cab at each end. These earlier railcars were not fitted with buffers as they were intended to work as single units, although drawgear was fitted for emergency use. In October 1938 *The Railway Observer* reported that orders had been placed for 20 more railcars to supplement the 18 vehicles that had already been placed in service. The new diesel cars would be used on various routes throughout the GWR system, including the 'Newport, Pontypool Road, Chepstow and Monmouth' lines.

Another Great Western single unit diesel railcar used in the area was car No. 30, which was stationed at Pontypool Road for employment on the Monmouth route during the 1940s. This vehicle was one of the later examples built under Lot 1635, with angular streamlining and an overall length of 63 ft over headstocks. They were fitted with conventional buffers and draw-gear, and had a top speed of 45 mph. These later Great Western railcars were designed to convey 'tail traffic' in the form of horse boxes or cattle wagons, and on a less regular basis they sometimes hauled an additional passenger vehicle in connection with special parties or sundries traffic.

Branch passenger trains were, for many years, composed of half a dozen short-wheelbase vehicles. Photographic evidence suggests that the usual formation comprised four third class or composite coaches sandwiched between two passenger brake vans. The Great Western abolished short-wheelbase stock at a comparatively early date and, thereafter, the Ross & Monmouth, Wye Valley and Pontypool Road branches were typically worked by one or more auto-trailers, according to traffic needs. Contemporary photographs suggest that short-wheelbase stock was predominant on the Ross-on-Wye to Monmouth route until the early 1920s, after which most trains were formed of auto-cars.

Railcar No. 30 is being loaded with parcels at Monmouth (Troy) station. This view dates from February 1949, the railcar still retains its GWR livery. *John Edgington*

Railcars meet at Monmouth (Troy) on a rainy day in August 1951. The railcar on the left has arrived from Chepstow using the Wye Valley line and that on the right has passed through the tunnel (*in the background*) from Pontypool Road. *R.W.A. Jones*

Ordinary coaching stock was not entirely displaced from regular services following the introduction of auto-trains, and most of the through workings continued to be formed of conventional loco-hauled stock. Conversely, some of the through services were worked by diesel railcars or auto-trains. In 1928, for instance, two of the down workings between Ross-on-Wye and Pontypool Road were worked by conventional locomotives and rolling stock, while one up and one down through service was diagrammed for an auto-train.

Great Western Motor Bus Services

The GWR was a notable pioneer in the use of motorized road feeder services, the company's original 'road motor' route between Helston and Lizard Town being one of the very first rural bus services in the country. By 1910 the Great Western had introduced road motor services on a very large scale, Wales and the Borders being regarded as ideal areas for the employment of railway-owned motor buses.

By 1928, there were several GWR bus routes within the area bounded by Monmouth, Newport and Abergavenny. One of these routes ran from Newport to Usk, while further services extended north-eastwards to Monmouth, and north-westwards to Abergavenny, which was a nodal point for other GWR bus routes to Brecon, Pontypool Road and other destinations. A further bus route extended eastwards from Usk to the otherwise isolated village of Llansoy, this service being run on Saturdays only. Vehicles used on these diverse bus routes were based at Abergavenny, Newport and Usk - the most important omnibus depot in the district being at Abergavenny.

These extensive road services needed a relatively large allocation of motor vehicles, among the buses working from Abergavenny during the 1920s being Burford 30 cwt bus Nos. 853, Thornycroft 30 cwt vehicles Nos. 907, 927, 929, 931, 935 and 937, and Maudslay ML3 vehicles Nos. 1203, 1213, 1216 and 1219. These GWR 'road motors' carried an attractive version of the company's famous chocolate and cream passenger livery, and they worked in conjunction with the trains as useful feeders for the local railway system.

By the later 1920s the GWR was one of the largest bus operators in the country, and it seemed at the time that the company would continue to expand and develop its huge road motor fleet as an important adjunct to the rail network. Unfortunately, the undoubted success of the Great Western bus fleet led to complaints from the road transport industry to the effect that the GWR (and other railway companies) did not have Parliamentary consent to operate road services, and for this reason the railway bus routes were said to be illegal.

There was an element of truth in the allegation of illegality, and to formalize the situation whereby the GWR could operate its road services the company obtained new powers under the provisions of the Great Western (Road Transport) Act 1928. This new legislation enabled the GWR to own, work and use motor vehicles in its own right, and to enter into arrangements with other parties for the operation of road transport services. By virtue of these powers the railway company at once entered into detailed negotiations with road transport companies, and by 1933 all of the GWR motor bus services had been handed over to 'associated' bus companies.

As a result of this agreement the Monmouthshire-based road motor services were all passed to the Western Welsh Omnibus Company on the understanding that the bus company would not compete with the railway. This arrangement was supposed to lead to greater co-ordination between road and rail transport, but there is no doubt that, in many cases, the buses began to compete with the railway for what little traffic was available in rural areas. As far as the Monmouthshire area was concerned, the Great Western Railway ceased to operate road passenger services on 1st August, 1929, from which date the entire network of road feeder routes was handed over to the Western Welsh company.

Motorized Delivery Services

The demise of the Great Western motor bus services may have been an unfortunate episode, but the company continued to develop and expand its network of motorized delivery services for parcels and goods traffic. Indeed, in the short term, the end of the railway buses resulted in an increase in the number of goods delivery vehicles, as many of the older buses were rebuilt as motor lorries.

Some of the GWR motor buses based in the Monmouthshire area underwent conversions of this kind. Burford 30 cwt bus No. 853, for instance, became a lorry in January 1929 although, in this instance, its subsequent life was somewhat short, and the vehicle was scrapped around 1931. A similar conversion was carried out on former Newport-based road motor No. 930, a Thornycroft 30 cwt bus that also became a GWR lorry in January 1929, and remained in use until about 1938. It should be remarked that Great Western buses and lorries were numbered in the same consecutive fleet list, and the converted buses therefore retained their earlier numbers after their conversion to goods vehicles.

Like many other lines planned during the Victorian era, the Ross-on-Wye to Pontypool Road route was equipped with stations sited at regular intervals along the line with distances of about three miles between each station and goods yard. This distribution of stations was designed to complement a road transport system worked exclusively by horses, each station being seen as a convenient railhead for a group of villages and hamlets. With the rapid development of motorized road transport after World War I, these lavishly-equipped stations were used by less and less traffic, and to combat this situation the GWR introduced several economies.

The Great Western itself became a large scale user of motorized road transport, with railway-owned lorries being employed for local cartage work in urban areas and as 'country lorries' for collection and delivery work in rural areas. Certain stations were selected as country lorry centres while others were down-graded in various ways so that, by the later 1930s, many smaller stations were handling very little carted freight traffic. In the Monmouth area, Monmouth itself became a country lorry centre, and a large rural area was then served by road transport with GWR vehicles running on regular routes.

By 1938, Monmouth-based road vehicles were being used to serve places such as Welsh Newton (5 miles from the station) and Skenfrith (7 miles). By this means, parcels and other small consignments could be concentrated at Monmouth, while smaller stations such as Dingestow, Llandenny and Kerne Bridge were typically used for non-carted wagon load traffic such as coal and animal feed. Inevitably, this process marked the start of a period of rationalization, which would ultimately result in the total closure of hundreds of local goods yards.

So long as the GWR and the other railway companies were allowed to maintain their own fleets of wholly-owned road vehicles this did not greatly matter, as the companies concerned were able to use road transport to combat the challenge from road transport operators - the main point being that trunk hauls still took place by rail, while customers were offered a door-to-door transport service for their goods and parcels. Indeed, at a time when many road transport firms were one-man 'cowboy' operations using poorly-maintained vehicles, the efficient railway-owned road services were able to win back much traffic from rival operators.

The Great Western made use of its large fleet of motor vehicles in several ways. Most stations of moderate importance were served by cartage services within clearly defined geographical areas. In general, goods and parcels were collected or delivered free within these areas, though traders and residents on the outer fringes of urban areas were usually charged a small fee. In some instances, road vehicles were based at larger stations such as Monmouth (Troy), but worked from smaller stations in the immediate vicinity; in this way, the GWR ensured that smaller stations such as Kerne Bridge and Raglan were also served by local cartage services.

The Great Western 'country lorry services' worked on an entirely different basis. In this case, the motor vehicles assigned to particular services followed regular routes that took them well beyond the normal cartage areas. Outlying farms and villages were thereby linked to the railway system by regular collection and delivery services, every class of traffic being conveyed at reasonable rates.

The company's road delivery services were so successful that the railway was prepared to undertake the transport of non-railborne traffic such as roadstone for local authorities, or feed stuffs for farmers and agricultural merchants. Household removals became a particular speciality, demountable road-rail containers being ideal for this class of traffic. Charges were based upon a fixed hourly rate for the lorry and driver, and the estimated time that would be needed to perform the whole removal operation. If necessary, expert packers could be supplied by the GWR in return for an extra charge, while for longer distances the containers could be forwarded by fast freight trains.

The Development of Tourist Traffic

The Wye Valley district was first 'discovered' by discerning upper middle class tourists during the late 18th and early 19th centuries. The romantic poet William Wordsworth (1770-1850) was one of the first visitors to the area, and his poem *Lines Composed a Few Miles Above Tintern Abbey* (1798) did much to popularise this hitherto remote part of the country. Other famous visitors to Monmouthshire and the Wye Valley at that time included the artist J.M.W. Turner (1775-1851) and Admiral Horatio Nelson.

The growth of a national railway system during the 19th century enabled large numbers of tourists to visit the area. At first, relatively small numbers of people were able to use road transport from nearby railheads such as Chepstow and Ross-on-Wye, but the opening of the Ross & Monmouth Railway and the Wye Valley line in 1873 and 1876 respectively presented many opportunities for the development of a large scale tourist industry. At first, ordinary people came into the area as day trippers on special excursion trains, Symond's Yat, on the Ross & Monmouth line, and Tintern Abbey on the Wye Valley branch being popular destinations from the very start.

The gradual introduction of holidays with pay inevitably resulted in an increase in the numbers of working class visitors, and although it would clearly be absurd to suggest that the Wye Valley ever became a mass tourist destination such as Blackpool or Southend, there is no doubt that the various scenic and historic attractions in and around the Monmouthshire district had become very popular by the 1920s and 1930s.

This development was encouraged by a number of external factors such as improvements in the national education system, and conservation undertaken by the Office of Works. In the latter context, it is important to remember that the Ancient Monuments Act enabled sites of especial interest to be placed under state protection or 'Guardianship'. The number of 'Ancient Monuments' increased steadily during the first half of the 20th century, and as might be expected, the Welsh border castles soon formed a considerable proportion of the nation's Ancient Monuments. Goodrich Castle, for example, was placed in guardianship in 1920, while neighbouring Raglan Castle became an Ancient Monument in 1938.

The Office of Works (later the Ministry of Public Buildings & Works) carried out a great deal of work on all of these monuments, and with proper staffing arrangements, opening hours and publicity they were soon attracting an even larger number of people. The Great Western Railway was only too glad for this development to take place, as it brought extra income to the company in the form of increased leisure travel. Arguably, the Great Western did as much as the Office of Works to publicize the castles and other historic buildings which dotted Wales and the West Country in considerable numbers. Indeed, GWR publicity was particularly effective - particularly where castles were concerned.

In 1926, for instance, the company published a well-researched academic book entitled *Castles*, which described all of the major castles within the area served by the Great Western Railway. The author was Sir Charles Oman of the

University of Oxford, and this impressive volume was illustrated by line drawings, photographs, maps, plans and two full colour plates. A folding map at the back of the book showed the position of each monument in relation to the GWR network, and 'visitors contemplating a tour of the Cathedrals, Abbeys and Castles within the sphere of the Great Western Railway' were invited to write to the superintendent of the line for details of the relevant train services.

Companion volumes on *Cathedrals* (1923) and *Abbeys* (1925) were written by Martin Briggs and M.R. James respectively, while the railway company also published a wide range of county guide books and an annual holiday guide entitled *Holiday Haunts*. These publications were available at Great Western stations, in book shops or direct (post free) from the stationery superintendent at 66, Porchester Road, London W.2.

Further publicity was obtained from the company's policy of naming its largest class of express passenger locomotives after castles on the Great Western system. As one might expect, Monmouthshire castles were well-represented, No. 4077 *Chepstow Castle* being built in 1924, followed by No. 5008 *Raglan Castle* in 1927, and Nos. 5013 *Abergavenny Castle*, 5014 *Goodrich Castle*, and 5032 *Usk Castle* in 1932-35. The theme was continued by 'Castle' No. 5087 *Tintern Abbey*, 'Hall' class locomotive No. 4929 *Goytray Hall* and 'Grange' class 4-6-0s Nos. 6825 *Llanvair Grange*, 6827 *Llanfrechfa Grange* and 6828 *Trellech Grange*, all of which carried the names of local historic buildings.

The 1930s saw an upsurge in the growth of 'low cost' holidays such as hiking, camping and youth hostelling. In an inspired attempt to attract this new type of holidaymaker, the London & North Eastern Railway (LNER) converted some of its obsolete short-wheelbase coaches into holiday camping coaches. The first LNER camping coaches were in service by 1933, and the concept was so successful that the GWR immediately copied the idea.

In March 1934 *The Railway Magazine* reported that the Great Western Railway had 'decided to provide 20 old coaches specially adapted for use at certain selected camping sites'. These vehicles would be let at a weekly rental, and it was suggested that they would 'prove to be very popular with the ever-increasing number of camping holidaymakers'. In a further report, in May 1934, the same magazine stated that 19 Great Western camping coaches had been brought into use at sites in Devon, Somerset, Cornwall and Wales. Elderly four- and six-wheeled rolling stock was thereby 'diverted into a profitable old age as holiday caravans for the holiday camper'.

The Great Western camping coaches were as successful as their LNER counterparts, and the company was encouraged to place further vehicles into use at a range of new locations. In 1935, Kerne Bridge joined the growing list of GWR camping coach sites, a suitable reconditioned six-wheeler being advertised for rent in that year. This vehicle followed the usual pattern for camping coaches, two of its five compartments being gutted to form a combined living and dining room, while the remaining compartments became a kitchen and two bedrooms sleeping six people.

WYE VALLEY

KERNE BRIDGE (Type " B "). The tree-shaded village of Kerne Bridge lies between Lydbrook and Ross, within a few miles of Symond's Yat. Goodrich Castle is within half a mile and the bridge from which the village takes its name links it with the Forest of Dean. Many delightful walks may be enjoyed through the magnificent scenery of the Wye Valley. Fishing and bathing are available in the River Wye, and golf at Ross.

See page 22 for particulars of Holiday Season Tickets embracing this district (Areas Nos. 9 and 10).

PLANS OF G.W.R. CAMP COACHES—SEASON 1936.

Type " A "—6 Berths.

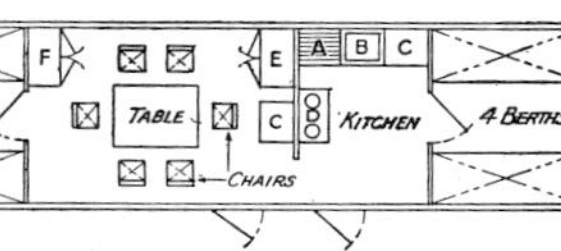

Type " B "—6 Berths.

2 BERTHS 4 BERTHS F TABLE E KITCHEN C C A B CHAIRS

Type " C "—8 Berths.

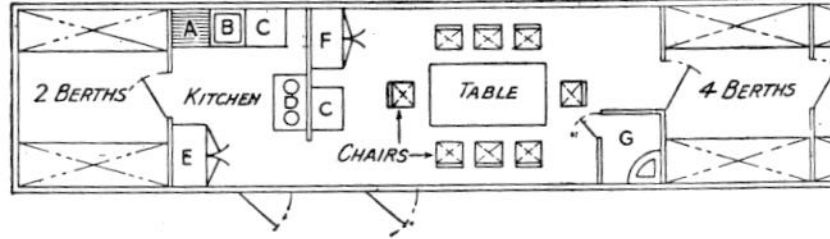

Type " D "—10 Berths. The same as Type " B," with an additional 4 Berth Sleeping Compartment.

NOTE.—Each of the 4 Berth Cabins is fitted with a moveable bed which can, if desired, be transferred to the Cabin fitted with 2 Berths.

A ... Draining Board.
B ... Sink.
C ... Table.
D ... Stove, with Oven.
E ... Cupboard.
F ... Wardrobe.
G ... Cloakroom, with Wash Basin.

CAMPING IN COMFORT AT SELECTED BEAUTY SPOTS

NOVEL & INEXPENSIVE

Extracts from the *Camp Coach Holidays* booklet of 1935.

Other Developments in the 1920s and 1930s

Until World War I, railway companies such as the GWR had enjoyed a virtual monopoly of land transport, and in these circumstances they were able to operate a large number of rural branch lines that were never more than marginally profitable. Some lines may have even lost money, but this situation was tolerated because of the 'system effect', whereby short, local lines could feed profitable traffic onto the main line network. In the changing economic conditions after World War I, the growth of road transport, rising wage bills and other factors made it increasingly difficult for lightly-used branch lines to survive, and the GWR was obliged to seek a number of economies.

In the mid-1920s the company carried out a thorough review of its entire branch line operations, and as a result a programme of economies was put into effect. In a very few cases it was reluctantly agreed that closures would have to take place, but in general the GWR branch line review recommended the introduction of operating economies such as track rationalization or staff cuts. In the latter context, smaller stations such as Llandenny and Dingestow lost their station masters, the stations concerned being placed under the control of larger stations such as Monmouth or Ross-on-Wye.

In another attempt to introduce more efficient methods of operation on the Ross-on-Wye to Pontypool Road line the GWR introduced mechanized methods of line maintenance, with reduced numbers of Permanent Way (PW) men using PW trolleys for inspection and maintenance work. In earlier days, work of this kind had been carried out by gangers who patrolled their sections of line on foot, but the introduction of manual or petrol-driven PW vehicles enabled each permanent way gang to cover a much greater length of track.

To facilitate this mode of operation the Ross-on-Wye to Little Mill Junction line was fitted with a Gangers' Occupation Key system, so that permanent way gangs could have complete possession of the single line sections upon which they were working. This system worked in conjunction with the normal single line signalling system, the idea being that, when an occupation key was withdrawn by the ganger, no trains could enter the section of line upon which work was taking place.

There were, in all, 27 occupation key boxes between Ross-on-Wye and Little Mill Junction, while other occupation key instruments were installed in signal boxes or other convenient locations. In general, the instruments were sited at intervals of a little under one mile, Box No. 24, for example, being positioned at 25 miles 77 chains, just 59 chains to the west of Usk signal box and 69 chains to the east of the next occupation key instrument in Box No. 25. Each occupation key box was equipped with an occupation key instrument, and a telephone link to the signalman responsible for the section concerned.

Under the motor trolley system, the maintenance of the line between Ross and Little Mill was carried out by three mechanized PW gangs. At the eastern end of the route, gang No. 70 looked after the line between 0 miles 40 chains and 12 miles 35 chains, while gang No. 71 was responsible for the Monmouth to Llandenny section between 12 miles 35 chains and 21 miles 65 chains. The western end of the route between Llandenny and Little Mill Junction (21 miles 65 chains to 29 miles 28 chains) was the responsibility of permanent way gang No. 72.

The introduction of road delivery vehicles for goods and parcels traffic resulted in the decline of many smaller intermediate goods yards, but there was no immediate thought of line closures. On the other hand, the little-used Monmouth to Coleford line had been closed as a wartime economy measure on 31st December, 1916, and the track was later removed between its junction with the Wye Valley branch at Wyesham Junction and Whitecliffe, to the west of Coleford. Perhaps inevitably, the next closure victim was the Severn & Wye Joint Railway, although in this case the lines concerned were retained in connection with coal and other freight traffic.

It was agreed that passenger services on the Severn & Wye Joint lines in the Forest of Dean would be discontinued with effect from Monday 8th July, 1929, and as there were no Sunday services, the last trains ran on Saturday 6th July. The sections affected extended from Lydney Town to Cinderford and Lydbrook Junction (exclusive), though it was decided that push-pull services would be maintained between at the southern end of the Severn & Wye Joint line between Lydney Town and Berkeley Road.

At the same time, in an effort to attract new sources of passenger traffic, the railway company opened new halts at various places between Ross-on-Wye and Pontypool Road, the first of these new stopping places being opened at Glascoed, between Usk and Little Mill Junction, in 1927, followed by Raglan Road Crossing in 1930 and Elms Bridge Halt, between Dingestow and Raglan, in 1933. On the Ross & Monmouth section, Walford Halt was brought into use between Ross-on-Wye and Kerne Bridge in 1931.

Some Tales and Anecdotes

The line from Ross-on-Wye to Little Mill Junction was an integral part of everyday life for many years, and it is hardly surprising that, in time, it became the subject of jokes, legends and local folk lore. The railway was, in a very real sense, a 'family' affair - many railwaymen being related to each other. Regular travellers might be addressed by their first names, while it was not unknown for trains to make special stops, so that people could alight at isolated farms and cottages; this took place more frequently on market days, when female shoppers, some of whom might be quite elderly, were burdened with heavy baggage.

Some of the regular drivers were gardening enthusiasts, and if they needed any bean sticks they would occasionally stop the train to collect a bundle of likely saplings. Permanent way men would sometimes cut down some sticks for unofficial collection, and these would later be taken back to Ross or other destinations stacked in the coal bunker or piled-up in the guard's van! In practice, station masters and other officials probably tolerated this fairly widespread activity because it helped to keep the line clear of rampant vegetation that might otherwise constitute a fire risk.

Rabbits, pheasants or other edible wildlife could also be found along the line, and it is said that some train crews were in the habit of setting traps in the hope of obtaining an extra ingredient for their cooking pots. Alternatively, pheasants might occasionally be killed by passing trains - in which case the dead birds would be eagerly retrieved. It was even suggested that certain individuals sometimes secreted a small-calibre .22 'rat gun' on the train in the hope of bagging some unfortunate bird or animal!

The tiny refreshment room at Monmouth (Troy) station was a source of local pride insofar as few branch lines could boast of such an amenity. As a privately-run establishment, the refreshment room had an informal, welcoming atmosphere, and it would sometimes remain open after the last trains had departed. There was a certain amount of friction between chapel-going teetotallers and the rank-and-file GWR railwaymen (who, in earlier years at least, tended to be Anglicans). Bill Vaughan, a teetotal signalman, would sometimes berate his work mates for drinking alcohol in the refreshment room, which he said would lead to ruin and penury.

Other stories relate to the school trains that conveyed scholars to and from Monmouth during term time. Local children attended village schools until they were old enough to leave school and start work. In the 1930s, the school leaving age was 14, but parents wishing to give their children a decent education were able to send them to Monmouth's endowed grammar school, which had been founded in Tudor times by a member of the Haberdashers' Company; a Girls' High School was subsequently built, so that able children of both sexes could work towards university entrance and a professional career.

School trains were provided on all three lines converging on Monmouth, and this brought a welcome source of regular traffic to the lines concerned. Like elite groups, the small bands of youthful commuters evolved several initiation ceremonies - such as throwing girls' hats out of the window or hiding exercise books under the seat cushions.

In the days when most journeys were made by train, and nearly all goods traffic was conveyed by rail, the railway carried a huge variety of parcels and freight traffic. Coal, stone, timber, fertilizers, livestock and milk were perhaps the main sources of traffic on the line between Ross-on-Wye and Pontypool Road, but stations such as Ross and Monmouth (Troy) handled many other items. Small boats and skiffs, for instance, were often sent by train by private boat owners, or by specialized firms such as Salters of Oxford.

In the early years of the 20th century, professional gentlemen such as the pioneering inland waterways enthusiast P. Bonthron relied on the GWR, and other railway companies, to provide convenient transport for their boats. In his book *My Holidays on Inland Waterways* (1916) Bonthron furnished details of a trip made downstream from Hay-on-Wye to Chepstow in a boat sent from Oxford to Hay. In more recent years, canoes became quite widely used on the Wye, and these too were sent by train to convenient riverside stations such as Ross or Monmouth.

Although Bonthron did not make direct use of the Ross & Monmouth branch during his Wye Valley expedition, he provided a useful glimpse of the area in Edwardian days. He recalled that the river became somewhat wider in the vicinity of Ross, and his party was able to hoist a sail in order to proceed under canvas in pleasant conditions for many miles. He noted several game fishermen - the Wye having 'a famous reputation as a salmon river', while Symond's Yat was 'a town or village of . . . quaint and straggling character on the hill-side', that was 'not unlike a Swiss town'. Interestingly, Bonthron also noted a 'small excursion steamer, built locally, with stern paddle wheels' near Ross-on-Wye.

The trains themselves had more than one local nickname. On the Ross & Monmouth section, for instance, the push-pull service provided in later years was generally known as 'The Monmouth Bullet' - presumably an ironic reference to its slow speed. Alternatively, some local people called the train 'The Coffee Pot'. Strictly speaking, this appellation applied to the engine rather than the train, and it may have been prompted by the archaic appearance of the Armstrong '517' class 0-4-2Ts and the Collett '14XX' class 0-4-2Ts which succeeded them - both classes being distinguished by tall chimneys and prominent domes.

The lines from Ross-on-Wye and Pontypool Road were traversed by several royal specials, notably on 18th and 19th November, 1936, when King Edward VIII carried out a morale-boosting tour of South Wales. The effects of the Great Depression had been severely felt in many parts of the Welsh coal mining area, and the uncrowned King was keen to see the effects of the depression at first hand. For all his faults, Edward had a social conscience, and in his short reign he displayed an active interest in the plight of the unemployed. This was a source of concern for Prime Minister Stanley Baldwin, who distrusted the young King's progressive views.

Unfortunately, Edward had fallen in love with Mrs Wallis Simpson, an American lady, who had divorced two husbands. For this reason she was regarded as an unsuitable consort for a monarch who would also be the Supreme Head of the Church of England. The Prime Minister, the church establishment and the ruling Conservative Party were all openly hostile towards Edward and Mrs Simpson, and Baldwin seems to have decided that the King would have to abdicate. Meanwhile, Edward continued to undertake his official duties, including his tour of the designated 'South Wales Special Area'.

The royal party arrived by train at Usk on 18th November, the Great Western royal train being berthed in Usk station. As usual in such circumstances, the arrangements for working the royal special were surrounded in secrecy, although the elaborate preparations served only to draw attention to the unusual proceedings on this otherwise quiet branch line. Several people claimed to have spotted the controversial Mrs Simpson at the windows of the royal train, and when the Chairman of Usk council paid an official visit to the train, local humorists claimed that he had tried to sell the King a bottle of milk so that he could hang a 'By Royal Appointment' sign above his shop window!

As usual, the royal special was composed of a mixture of special saloons, sleeping cars and brake firsts, the two special saloons being Nos. 9004 and 9005 - both of which were self-contained 'brake saloons' suitable for VIP use; both vehicles contained kitchen and pantry facilities. Speculation surrounding the whereabouts of Mrs Simpson added extra *frisson* to the occasion, but the royal visit was otherwise uneventful. Sadly, just a few weeks later, Stanley Baldwin brought the constitutional crisis to its inevitable conclusion, and on 10th December the Prime Minister announced the King's abdication. It was, commented Winston Churchill, 'the acme of tragedy'.

WORKING OF EMPTY ROYAL TRAIN FROM HEREFORD TO MONMOUTH.

WEDNESDAY, OCTOBER 22nd.

All points which become facing points and which are not bolt locked or detected must be clipped and padlocked for the passing of the empty Royal Train.

THE TRAIN TO CARRY "A" HEADLAMPS AND BE GIVEN A CLEAR RUN.

		p.m.	
HEREFORD (BARRS COURT)	.. **dep.**	**4 † 0**	For detailed arrangements for dealing with the Royal Train at Hereford, see page 15. Engines Nos. 5532 and 5516 forward.
ROTHERWAS JUNCTION	.. pass	**C**4 3**S**	
HOLME LACY	.. ,,	CS	
FAWLEY	.. ,,	CS	
ROSS-ON-WYE	.. ,,	**C**4 30**S**	**CR**
LYDBROOK JUNCTION ..	.. ,,	C**X**S	The 3.51 p.m. Monmouth (Troy) to Ross-on-Wye to be held at Lydbrook Junction to cross the empty Royal Train.
SYMONDS YAT	.. ,,	CS	
MONMOUTH (MAY HILL)	.. ,,	**C**5 0**S**	
MONMOUTH (TROY) .. **(Up Platform)**	.. arr.	**5 † 3**	For detailed arrangements for dealing with the Royal Train at Monmouth, see page 15.

A further 'royal' working took place on 22nd and 23rd October, 1941, when the LMS royal train was worked empty from Hereford to Monmouth (Troy) for overnight stabling. The formation on this occasion comprised brake first No. 5155, royal saloon No. 800, dining saloon No. 76, saloon No. 807, sleeping saloon No. 477, saloon No. 806, dining saloon No. 77 and brake first No. 5154. The train was hauled to Monmouth along the Ross & Monmouth line by Collett '45XX' class 2-6-2Ts Nos. 5516 and 5532, while on the following morning these same locomotives worked the empty royal vehicles back to Ross-on-Wye.

JOURNEY—MONMOUTH (TROY) TO KINGHAM.

WEDNESDAY, OCTOBER 22nd.

WORKING AT MONMOUTH (TROY).

The empty Royal Train from Hereford will run direct to the Up Platform for gassing and watering and any exterior cleaning which may be required.

Station Master to arrange for the Station Approach and Platforms to be cleared from 5.30 p.m. until the Royal Train has left, and for Mr. Nicholls, Gloucester; Station Master, Ross-on-Wye; Mr. J. E. Potter, Worcester; and Station Master, Kingham, to be advised the time the Train leaves.

WORKING AT ROSS-ON-WYE.

Engines Nos. 6921 and 6917 to work the Royal Train from Ross-on-Wye to Kingham will run light from Gloucester tender first at the following times :—

		p.m.
Gloucester	dep.	4 30
Grange Court	pass	**C**4 45**3**
Longhope	,,	CS
Mitcheldean Road	,,	CS
Ross-on-Wye	arr.	5 30

On arrival from Monmouth (Troy) the Royal Train will run via the Down Loop on to the Single Line at the Hereford end of the station, and be brought to a stand with the footplate of the leading engine at a point 50 yards in advance of the Down Advanced Starting Signal for the direction of Hereford, which will be lowered for the movement. The point will be indicated by a Handsignalman who will exhibit a red hand signal. Engines Nos. 6917 and 6921 to work the Train forward to Kingham will stand in the Up Siding and when the Train has come to a stand these engines will back slowly on to it and be coupled. When this has been done Engines Nos. 5516 and 5532 which worked the Train to Ross-on-Wye will be detached for disposal after the Royal Train has left. The person in charge of changing the engines must advise the Signalman by means of the telephone near the Up Main Home Signal when the Train is ready to leave.

Station Master to arrange for Mr. J. E. Potter, Worcester, and Station Master, Kingham, to be advised the distance from the footplate of the leading engine leaving Ross-on-Wye to the rear of the Train.

WORKING AT KINGHAM.

The Royal Train must run direct to the Up Cheltenham Branch Line between Kingham West Box and Kingham Station Box. A Handsignalman exhibiting a red hand signal will be stationed on the Driver's side at the exact point where the footplate of the leading engine, No. 6917, is to come to a stand.

As soon as the Royal Train has come to a stand at the appointed place and points No. 13 worked from Kingham West Box have been set for the direction of Kingham East Box and clipped and padlocked in that position, the Inspector in charge must advise the Signalman at Kingham West Box in order that "Train out of Section" may be sent to the rear, and Kingham Station Box in order that the normal acceptance of trains over the lines not affected may be resumed.

Immediately after the arrival of the Royal Train, the leading engine, No. 6917, will be detached and sent to take water, and thence to turn via Kingham East Box, after attaching a battery van at Kingham Station and propelling it to the East Box, proceeding thence to Kingham West Box, where the battery van and engine will be attached to the rear of the Royal Train, the engine remaining on the train throughout the night for steam-heating purposes. When the movement to the rear of the train has been completed, the second engine, No 6921, at the Kingham Station end of the train, must be released and sent to Kingham Station where it will be employed throughout the night.

After the passing of the 9.0 p.m. Passenger train Kingham to Cheltenham, and when the steam-heating engine with battery van has been attached to the rear of the Royal Train at Kingham West, points Nos. 11 and 13 (released for the above movement) worked from Kingham West Box must be set for the Kingham East Box direction and clipped and padlocked in that position until required to be released by the Inspector in charge.

TIME TABLE OF ROYAL TRAIN FROM MONMOUTH TO KINGHAM.

WEDNESDAY, OCTOBER 22nd.

FORMATION OF ROYAL TRAIN LEAVING MONMOUTH (TROY) :—

ENGINES (Nos. 5516 and 5532)

BRAKE FIRST	No. 5154	336 tons.
DINING SALOON	„ 77	
SALOON	„ 806	
SLEEPING SALOON	„ 477	
SALOON	„ 807	
DINING SALOON	„ 76	
H.M. THE KING'S SALOON	„ 800	
BRAKE FIRST	„ 5155	

The formation of the Royal Train arriving Kingham will be the reverse of that shewn above, and it will be worked from Ross-on-Wye by Engines Nos. 6917 and 6921.

The Train will run on the Main Line throughout the journey, via the Up Middle Line at Gloucester and via the Loop Line from Hatherley Junction to Gloucester Loop Junction.

The speed restrictions shewn apply to the Main Line and should the train be diverted to the Relief or other Line, the permanent and temporary restrictions applicable to such lines must be observed. It must be understood that additional emergency restrictions may have to be imposed, details of which will not appear in this Notice.

The Engine Headlamps and the Tail Lamps must be lighted before leaving Monmouth (Troy) and Ross-on-Wye.

Distances from Monmouth (Troy). Miles	Ch'ns	PRINCIPAL STATIONS AND INTERMEDIATE SIGNAL BOXES.	TIMES. p.m.	REMARKS.
—	—	**MONMOUTH (Troy) .. dep. (Up Platform)**	**6. 5**	For detailed arrangements for dealing with the Royal Train at Monmouth see page 15. **Speed not to exceed 15 miles per hour when passing from the Up platform to the Ross-on-Wye line at Monmouth (Troy).** **Speed not to exceed 45 miles per hour at any point between Monmouth (Troy) and Ross-on-Wye.** The 5.10 p.m. Ross-on-Wye to Monmouth (Troy) to terminate at Monmouth (May Hill), and run empty thence to Monmouth (Troy). The 6.5 p.m. Monmouth (Troy) to Ross-on-Wye to start at 6.15 p.m. The 5.1 p.m. Severn Tunnel Junction to Monmouth (Troy) to be held at Monmouth (Troy) Wye Valley Line Home Signal until the Royal Train has cleared.
—	59	Monmouth (May Hill) .. pass	**C**6. 8**S**	**Speed not to exceed 30 miles per hour between Monmouth (May Hill) and Symonds Yat from 10 miles 55 chains to 10 miles 40 chains.** **Speed not to exceed 35 miles per hour between Monmouth (May Hill) and Symonds Yat from 9 miles 40 chains to 8 miles 65 chains.** **Speed not to exceed 30 miles per hour between Monmouth (May Hill) and Symonds Yat from 8 miles 55 chains to 8 miles 45 chains**
5	40	Symonds Yat .. .. „	**C**6.17**S**	**Speed not to exceed 10 miles per hour at Symonds Yat.**
5	48	Symonds Yat Tunnel .. „	—	General Instructions (Clause 16, page 20) in regard to the examination and protection of Tunnels must be observed. **Speed not to exceed 35 miles per hour between Symonds Yat and Lydbrook Junction from 7 miles 40 chains to 6 miles 60 chains.**
7	49	Lydbrook Jct. .. .. „	**C**6.21**S**	**Speed not to exceed 10 miles per hour at Lydbrook Junction.**

Extract from Notice of Royal Trains, 22nd and 23rd October, 1941.

TIME TABLE OF ROYAL TRAIN FROM MONMOUTH TO KINGHAM—*continued.*

WEDNESDAY, OCTOBER 22nd—*continued.*

Distances from Monmouth (Troy). Miles	Ch'ns	PRINCIPAL STATIONS AND INTERMEDIATE SIGNAL BOXES.		TIMES. p.m.	REMARKS.
7	78	Lydbrook Tunnel	.. pass	—	General Instructions (Clause 16, Page 20) in regard to the examination and protection of Tunnels must be observed. **Speed not to exceed 30 miles per hour between Lydbrook Junction and Kerne Bridge from 4 miles 72 chains to 4 miles 54 chains. Speed not to exceed 30 miles per hour between Lydbrook Junction and Kerne Bridge from 4 miles 45 chains to 4 miles 5 chains.**
8	79	Kerne Bridge	,,	—	**Speed not to exceed 30 miles per hour at Kerne Bridge. Speed not to exceed 10 miles per hour when passing from the Monmouth Branch to the Down Hereford Line at Ross-on-Wye.**
13	9	Ross-on-Wye ..	arr. dep.	6.35 6.45	Change engines. For detailed instructions see Page 15. **Speed not to exceed 10 miles per hour at Ross-on-Wye. Speed not to exceed 20 miles per hour at any point between Ross-on-Wye and Grange Court.**
17	17	Mitcheldean Road	.. pass	CS	**Speed not to exceed 15 miles per hour at Mitcheldean Road.**
19	17	Mitcheldean Tunnel ..	,,	—	General Instructions (Clause 16, Page 20) in regard to the examination and protection of Tunnels must be observed.
20	3	Longhope	,,	CS	**Speed not to exceed 10 miles per hour at Longhope.**
23	52	Grange Court	,,	**C**7**X**25**S**	**Speed not to exceed 15 miles per hour at Grange Court.** The 6.20 p.m. Gloucester to Hereford to be held on the Hereford Down Branch Loop at Grange Court until the Royal Train has passed. (Paragraph 5, Clause (*h*), Page 19, must be carefully observed.)
29	52	Over Jct.	,,	—	**Speed not to exceed 30 miles per hour between Over Junction Signal Box and 115¼ mile post.**
31	8	Gloucester	,,	7.38	Via Up Middle Line.
31	39	Tramway Jct.	,,	—	**Speed not to exceed 10 miles per hour at Tramway Junction from 113 miles 59 chains to 113 miles 49 chains.**
34	43	Churchdown	,,	—	
36	65	Hatherley Jct. ..	,,	7. 49	**Speed not to exceed 20 miles per hour when passing through junction. Speed not to exceed 20 miles per hour at any point between Hatherley Junction and Kingham Station.**
37	24	Gloucester Loop Jct. ..	,,	7.51	**Speed not to exceed 15 miles per hour between Gloucester Loop Junction and Cheltenham South & Leckhampton from 106 miles 60 chains to 106 miles 40 chains.**
38	54	Cheltenham South & L.	,,	—	
42	62	Andoversford Tunnel ..	,,	—	General Instructions (Clause 16, Page 20) in regard to the examination and protection of Tunnels must be observed.
43	46	Andoversford Jct. ..	,,	**C**8.14**S**	
48	24	Notgrove	,,	**C**8.29**S**	
53	30	Bourton-on-the-Water	,,	**C**8.44**S**	
55	39	Stow-on-the-Wold ..	,,	**C**8.51**S**	
59	36	Kingham (West Jct.) ..	,,	**C**9.3**S**	**Speed not to exceed 15 miles per hour between 85½ mile post and Kingham West Box.**
59	**63**	**Stabling Point (between Kingham West and Kingham Station)** ..	**arr.**	**9. 8**	For detailed arrangements for dealing with the Royal Train at Kingham see pages 15 and 16.

Extract from Notice of Royal Trains, 22nd and 23rd October, 1941.

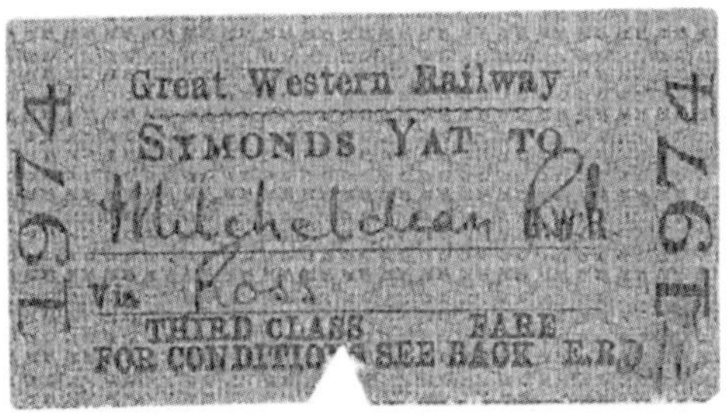

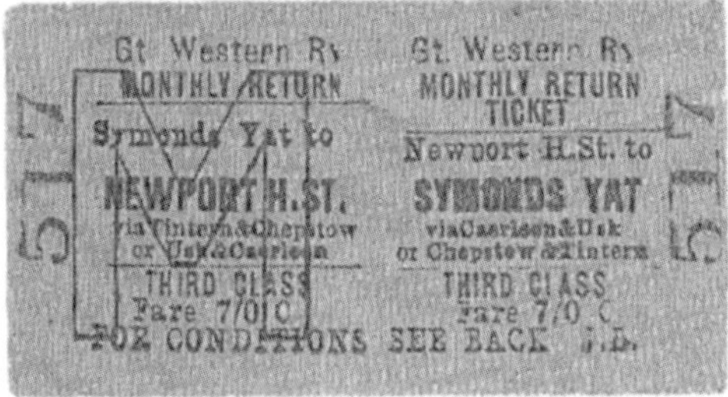

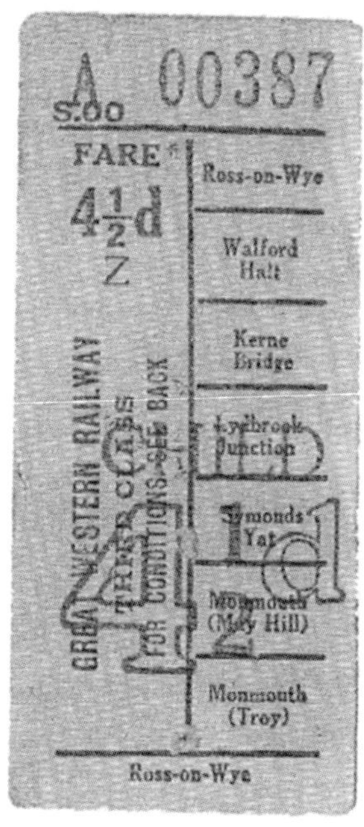

A selection of tickets used on the line.
Stephen J. Berry

A Note on Tickets

There was, in the Pre-Grouping period, an astounding range of GWR tickets, and even small stations such as Raglan or Kerne Bridge would have stocked a large range of Edmondson card tickets. These were printed in various colours to denote different types of ticket, and all were printed on standard cards measuring 57 mm x 30 mm; they carried the names of issuing stations and destinations, together with details of fares, class designations, company names and other data.

The Great Western used a complex colour-coded system, dog tickets, for example, being multi-coloured red, buff and blue issues, while government rate tickets for military personnel were printed on green cards with a broad yellowish-buff horizontal strip. The company's colour-coded system had been much simplified by the 1930s, but there were still many different types of booking, each category being distinguished by a strict colour-coded system. First class tickets from Ross to Monmouth, for instance, were white, while corresponding third class issues were printed on buff (later green) cards.

Other distinguishing colours used in the early 1930s were as follows: children's tickets - blue; government rate tickets - green or mauve; workmen's tickets - grey or pink; bicycle tickets - brown; dog tickets - deep red; third class excursions - yellowish buff. Return tickets were further distinguished by the addition of 'skeleton letters', some typical examples being R = ordinary returns; C = cheap day returns; CD circular day trips; GR = government rate; O = officer on leave; D = dog ticket; W = waiter; A = angler; CT = commercial traveller; PC = poor child; TS = training ship boy; A = American; E = excursion ticket; F = fishworker; PN = picnic party and RR = rail & river combined trip.

Great Western tickets remained in use for several years after Nationalization, but as stocks became exhausted Monmouth (Troy) and the other stations received new BR tickets. These were generally similar to those used during the Great Western period in that first class tickets were printed on white Edmondson cards, ordinary tickets were green, excursions were buff and bicycle or dog tickets were red. Small changes included the abolition of third class bookings and the introduction of second class facilities.

Another change introduced under British Railways' auspices was the introduction of bright red overprints instead of the less-conspicuous 'skeleton' letters favoured by the GWR - a BR second class return ticket from Monmouth to Ross-on-Wye would thus have been a light green Edmondson card bearing a large red 'R' on the return half. Children under 14 were issued with similar green tickets, bearing a bright red 'CHILD' overprint on each side. The study of tickets is an interesting aspect of local railway history, and it is interesting to reflect that many of these small pieces of coloured card have survived in private collections as reminders of long-vanished railways.

World War II

On Sunday 3rd September, 1939 a deteriorating international situation culminated in the outbreak of World War II. With horrific memories of the 1914-18 conflict still fresh in many minds, many people expected that the United Kingdom would soon

Collett '48XX' class 0-4-2T No. 4860 crosses the River Wye as it travels between Monmouth (Troy) to Monmouth (May Hill) with a Ross-on-Wye train on 8th April, 1945. The viaduct to the left is on the Wye Valley line for train services from Monmouth (Troy) to Chepstow.
V.R. Webster/Kidderminster Railway Museum

'48XX' class 0-4-2T No. 4822 stands at Lydbrook Junction station with a Pontypool Road-Ross train on Sunday 18th June, 1939. '45XX' class 2-6-2T No. 4588 approaches the station working a London to Monmouth excursion. *V.R. Webster/Kidderminster Railway Museum*

be devastated by fleets of massed Nazi bombers, but in reality the first months of the war were so uneventful that cynics spoke derisively of a 'Phoney War'.

The sudden and unexpected Fall of France in May 1940 heralded an altogether more serious phase of the conflict, and with the British Empire standing alone against an armed and largely hostile Europe, London, Bristol, Belfast and other large cities were, for a short time, subjected to nightly air attacks of varying severity. These raids did not affect rural branch lines such as the Ross-on-Wye to Pontypool Road route, though if enemy action caused disruption on the main lines there were inevitable delays for harassed travellers.

A nightly 'blackout' was imposed as an air raid precaution measure while, in an attempt to confuse Nazi parachutists or 'fifth columnists', station nameboards were removed or obscured in the summer of 1940. Although the war resulted in a diminution in the number of tourists and leisure travellers, petrol rationing and the restrictions placed on road transport ensured that rail traffic increased considerably, and like most British railways, the Ross-on-Wye to Pontypool Road line was soon playing a full part in the war effort.

The Monmouthshire area was not regarded as a particular target by the Luftwaffe, although the important dock installations at Cardiff and Newport attracted the attention of enemy bombers on several occasions. Newport was bombed for the first time on 26th June, 1940, and there was a relatively heavy raid on 1st July, 1941. To combat these attacks, Newport and other strategic centres were protected by anti-aircraft batteries and other defences, which were typically deployed in a defensive ring around the threatened urban area.

By the end of 1942, Newport's heavy anti-aircraft defences consisted of a sophisticated system of fixed batteries, each of which mounted four 3.7 in. high angle guns. These new defence positions incorporated command posts, magazines, barrack huts, guardrooms and other necessary infrastructure, their normal garrisons being as many as 200 men.

Installations of this kind produced considerable activity in terms of troop movements, while the anti-aircraft batteries, search light batteries and other components of the local defence system needed a constant supply of spare parts and ammunition. All of this activity brought extra traffic to the local railways, but creation of a large, rail-connected Royal Ordnance Factory (ROF) at Glascoed, between Little Mill Junction and Usk, was a wartime development of immeasurably greater importance to the Ross-on-Wye to Pontypool Road line. Construction work commenced several months before the war, and from 24th May, 1938 building workers were being taken to the site by rail. The ROF station opened on 6th October, 1940 (*see Chapter Five*).

Glascoed Royal Ordnance Factory was in full production by 1941, large numbers of workers being conveyed to and from this new facility by means of special through trains from the populous areas of the Welsh valleys. These workmen's trains ran from the Rhymney, Western and Eastern valleys, running to and from special ROF platforms within the works area. Locomotives used on these workings included '56XX' class 0-6-2Ts, double-heading being necessary in view of the length of the trains and some of the gradients encountered *en route* from Llanhilleth Junction and Crumlin Junction, and Fleur-de-Lis to Maesycwmmer Junction.

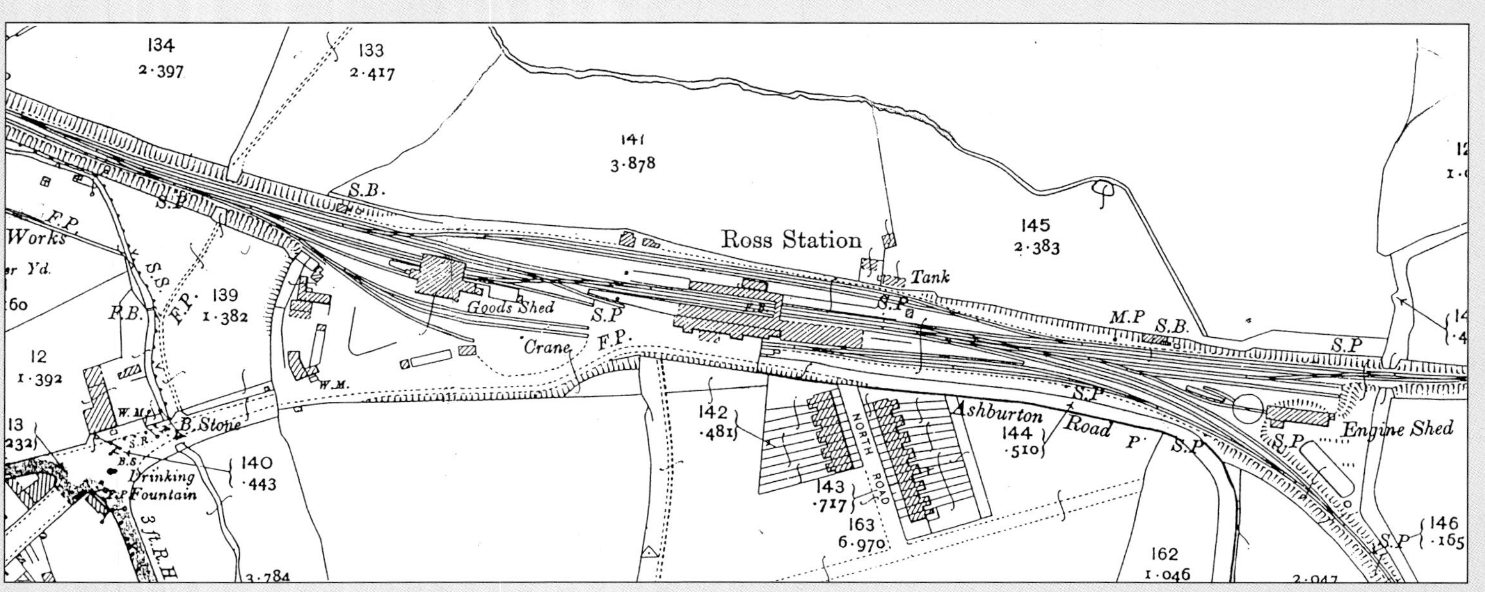

Ross-on-Wye station.

Reproduced from the 25", 1903 Ordnance Survey Map

Chapter Four

The Route from Ross-on-Wye to Monmouth

Having described the origins and history of the Ross to Pontypool Road line, it would now be appropriate to examine the stations and infrastructure of this picturesque route in greater detail. The following section will therefore take readers on an imaginary guided tour along the railway, from its eastern terminus at Ross-on-Wye to the western end of the route at Pontypool Road. In general, the topographical details that follow will be correct for the early British Railways period around 1948-1958, while the datum point for the calculation of mileages will be Ross Junction, three chains south of the station datum points.

Ross-on-Wye

Ross-on-Wye station had been opened by the Hereford, Ross & Gloucester Railway on 1st June, 1855 - at which time it had been known simply as 'Ross'. The name of the town was officially changed to 'Ross-on-Wye' in 1931 and the station was, accordingly, re-named in 1933 - a useful change of nomenclature, which helped to prevent confusion with the 'other' Ross station on the Clifden branch of the former Midland Great Western Railway in County Galway.

The original Ross station had been a crossing place on the broad gauge single line. Conversion to standard gauge took place in 1869, and the station became a junction with the opening of the Ross & Monmouth branch in 1873. Ross-on-Wye had three platforms, and in addition to the main up and down platform lines, a terminal bay was provided for Monmouth branch services at the eastern end of the down platform.

The main station building was situated on the down side, and like its counterpart at Monmouth, this standard Great Western red brick structure was of comparatively late construction, having been erected as part of a programme of improvements carried out at the end of the 19th century. (These improvements included an extensively remodelled layout and new South signal box in 1890 and extension of the bay platform line in 1896.) The building was in effect a 'de luxe' version of the usual GWR design, its most distinctive architectural features being two French style turret roofs which were graced with a profusion of ornamental ironwork; the roof was covered with grey Welsh slate.

Other details included tall chimney stacks, projecting canopies at the front and at the rear, and shallow-arched lintels above the window and door apertures. As usual on this type of Great Western building, the windows and doors were arranged in double or triple groupings beneath their lintels, while bands of different-coloured bricks were used to relieve the otherwise uniform red brickwork. The platform canopies were supported on a mixture of fluted and multi-angular metal columns, the fluted uprights being further distinguished by classical *fasces* ornamentation which recalled the splendours of ancient Rome.

The main, down side buildings at Ross-on-Wye, seen from the station approach *c*.1900. The buildings shown here were typical of those erected by the GWR at stations of intermediate importance; the building was completed around 1892. *Lens of Sutton Collection*

An 0-6-0 tender locomotive enters the down platform at Ross-on-Wye with a Gloucester to Hereford passenger working. The Monmouth branch bay can be glimpsed behind the engine; the period is *circa* 1912. *Lens of Sutton Collection*

The internal arrangements provided a range of accommodation for both staff and passengers, including a booking office, waiting room, ladies' waiting room, a refreshment room, parcels office, toilets and cloak room. Viewed from the platforms, the general waiting room was situated towards the left- hand end of the building, while (from left to right) the next section contained a ladies' waiting room; in Victorian days, this facility had been reserved for the use of first and second class female travellers. Moving westwards, the accommodation comprised the refreshment room, booking office, and finally a parcels office and cloakroom at the extreme west end of the building.

The up and down platforms were linked by a fully-enclosed footbridge, its stairways and horizontal bridge section being protected by matchboard panelling and continuous glazing. The up platform was equipped with waiting room accommodation and extensive awnings, while at night the station was illuminated by gas lighting, hemispherical lamps having replaced most of the earlier tapered glass lanterns by the 1930s.

Ross-on-Wye was, from 1873 to 1938, signalled from two signal boxes, North and South, the latter being situated near the junction at the eastern end of the station. On 12th November, 1938, these two boxes were replaced by a new cabin, of standard Great Western hip-roofed design, with 76 levers. The new signal box was of brick and timber construction, and it was sited at the east end of the down platform. Unusually, the signal box was built in an aperture which effectively severed the down platform face, although the branch platform on the south side of the box was unaffected. The crossing loop was significantly shortened at the west (Hereford) end in connection with this work.

As the box was in effect a double-sided cabin, its operating floor was glazed on all four sides - the rear wall being fitted with two generously-proportioned windows, so that signalmen could obtain a good view of the branch bay and its associated run-round loop. The signal box was heated by a coal-fired stove, while a sinuous metal chimney protruded through the slated roof. Access to the locking room was arranged via a short flight of steps that occupied a shallow stairwell in the branch platform.

The goods facilities at Ross-on-Wye included a compact goods yard on the down side, together with an array of sidings behind the up platform on the opposite side of the station. The yard contained a characteristic broad gauge-type goods shed with an internal loading platform and separate entrances for road and rail vehicles in each gable end. The shed was an enlarged design that spanned two lines, one of which served the loading platform while the other, or 'outer' road may have been intended for transhipment between railway vehicles.

There was a single-road engine shed on the down side at the east end of the station. This was originally a broad gauge shed, but it was later rebuilt and enlarged to accommodate two small standard gauge locomotives. In its rebuilt form the shed measured approximately 100 ft x 28 ft, and it contained an 84½ ft line. The shed was of stone construction, and its main doorway showed clear evidence of the modifications carried out when the building was adapted for use by standard gauge engines. The shed contained an inspection pit with a length of 80 ft 6 in., while its gable roof was surmounted by a raised clerestory of the usual kind.

The Hereford end of Ross-on-Wye station in the 1960s. The crossovers (*left foreground*) gave access to the goods shed. *S. Apperley/Courtesy C.G. Maggs*

A view along the platform at Ross-on-Wye station looking towards Hereford on 11th September, 1955. The goods shed can be seen in the distance. *R.M. Casserley*

Locomotives shedded at Ross were used on the Ross & Monmouth branch, and for local shunting duties around the station. In 1921, the local allocation comprised '517' class 0-4-2Ts No. 536, 1422 and 1465, together with '1016' class 0-6-0ST No. 1062. At the very end of the Great Western period the allocation at Ross included '2021' class 0-6-0PT No. 2102, '74XX' class 0-6-0PT No. 7420, and Collett '14XX' class 0-4-2Ts Nos. 1404 and 1405.

The shed was, since 1879, equipped with a small turntable, but on 24th November, 1938 the GWR Locomotive Committee authorized the removal of 'turntable No. 226' from Ross at an estimated cost of £10. The turntable, which had a diameter of 44 ft 7 in., had been situated in front of the shed building; old maps depict a short spur, which probably served as a coaling road for a primitive wooden coaling stage. Watering facilities were available at the west end of the down platform, and the east end of the up platform.

Ross was a small, but busy town with a population of around 5,000 in the first half of the 20th century. Its passenger bookings were always fairly healthy, 77,343 tickets being issued in 1903. This figure remained constant during the Edwardian era, though after World War I the number of ordinary bookings dropped somewhat to around 60,000 per annum. At the same time, the number of season tickets issued rose steadily, from around 200 per year during the 1920s, to 405 by 1938.

As Great Western season tickets were generally issued for periods of one, two, three, six, or even 12 months, season ticket sales may have amounted to around 24,000 return journeys (assuming that most customers had purchased three-month tickets). On this basis, it would appear that Ross-on-Wye was busier at the end of the 1930s than it had been in the Edwardian period. Similarly, in terms of parcels traffic, Ross dealt with 39,703 parcels in 1903, rising to 50,379 in 1935 and 47,126 by 1938.

The station handled about 40,000 tons of goods traffic during the early 1900s, roughly half of this traffic being in the form of inwards and outwards general merchandise traffic, while approximately 12,500 tons was coal and coke class traffic. Goods traffic reached a peak of 54,132 tons in 1930, but there was thereafter a steady decline as road transport competition and the effects of the Great Depression took their toll; by the later 1930s Ross was handling a little over 30,000 tons of freight per annum, the figures for 1937 and 1938 being 32,573 tons and 30,007 tons respectively.

At the end of the Victorian period, Ross-on-Wye station had a staff of 23, rising to 36 by the mid-1930s and 37 at the end of that decade. This increase can be attributed to the growing importance of Ross as a GWR Country Lorry Centre. In the early 1920s the station was supervised by a class one station master, who controlled two booking clerks, three goods clerks, one ticket collector, one parcels porter, two passenger guards, five porters, one working foreman, three goods checkers, two goods porters, two goods shunters, four signalmen and two goods guards. Two motor drivers had been added to the local staff establishment by the early 1930s.

Those employed at Ross-on-Wye during the BR period around 1958 included senior checker Charlie James, station foreman Les Roberts, checker Reg Perkins, porter Bert Ballinger, porter Tony Jenkins, goods porter Peter East, leading

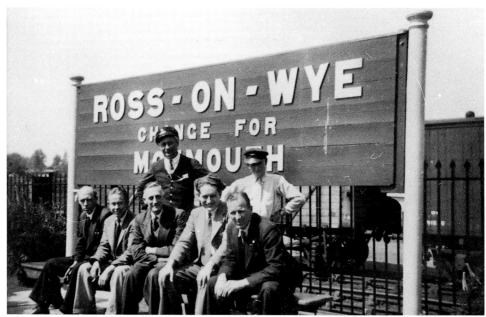

A 1950s view of the station staff posing beneath the station nameboard, which proudly proclaims 'Ross-on-Wye change for Monmouth'. *A.J. Stait/Courtesy C.G. Maggs*

Mrs Stait, the booking clerk, poses next to British Railways Bedford 'O' flatbed lorry No. JUV 385 in Ross goods yard. *A.J. Stait/Courtesy C.G. Maggs*

porter George Wood, chief goods clerk Pen Hughes, junior booking clerk Patricia Wheeler, signalman Fred Browning, motor driver Bill Cushing, and clerks Jack Foster and H. Jeremy. The station master at that time was Mr R.H. Underhill.

Traffic dealt with at Ross-on-Wye

Year	*Staff*	*Receipts (£)*	*Tickets*	*Parcels*	*Goods tonnage*
1903	23	27,360	77,343	39,703	42,478
1913	30	28,890	76,280	58,864	46,501
1923	34	42,204	63,374	46,053	43,081
1929	32	37,237	59.305	49.651	44,733
1931	32	34,288	63,532	47,455	47,731
1933	36	29,369	59,388	47,138	38,841
1935	36	26,591	60,290	50,379	38,317
1936	36	25,546	63,570	49,145	34,143
1937	37	23,765	62,932	47,838	32,573
1938	37	23,805	59,631	47,126	30,007

Walford Halt

Leaving Ross-on-Wye, down branch trains immediately diverged south-eastwards onto the single track Monmouth branch, and with the engine shed visible on the left-hand side, the branch continued curving towards the right. Having taken up a south-westerly heading, the route then continued in that direction for about three miles. Emerging from a short cutting that was spanned by a minor road bridge, trains crossed an underline occupation bridge, beyond which the line traversed a length of embankment.

Walford Halt, the first stopping place, was a simple unstaffed halt with no sidings or other connections. It was opened by the Great Western on 23rd February, 1931. Walford was 3 miles 12 chains from Ross-on-Wye, and its modest facilities consisted of a 120 ft platform on the down (east) side of the line. The halt was sited on a 1 in 100 gradient, falling towards Kerne Bridge.

Walford Halt on 10th July, 1959 looking towards Ross-on-Wye. *R.M. Casserley*

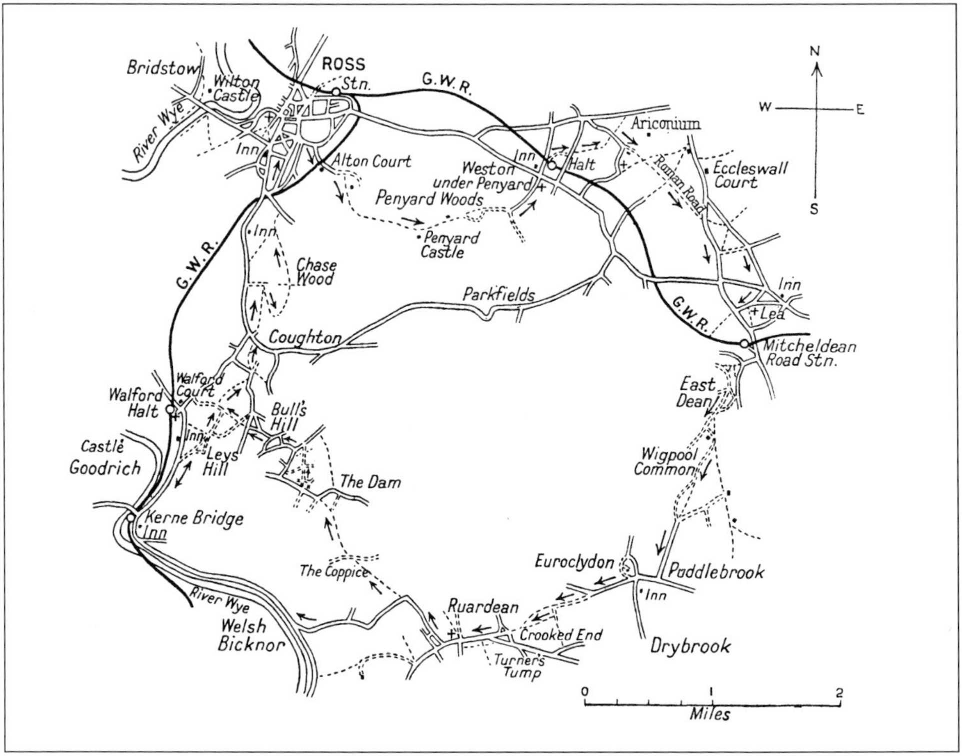

A postcard view of Kerne Bridge looking down into the Wye Valley with the road bridge over the river prominent and the station to the right of it. *P.G. Barnes Collection*

For administrative purposes, Walford was under the control of the Kerne Bridge station master, though its traffic receipts were included with those from Ross-on-Wye. Tickets were collected and issued by guards on the trains, while the platform lights were lit, cleaned and trimmed by staff from Kerne Bridge. Goods and parcels were collected and delivered in the immediate locality by Great Western delivery lorries from neighbouring Ross-on-Wye - though the halt itself was unable to deal with this form of traffic.

Kerne Bridge

From Walford Halt, down trains proceeded southwards for a further mile to Kerne Bridge (4 miles 10 chains), where a small station was provided on the east bank of the River Wye. When first opened in 1873, Kerne Bridge had been equipped with a conventional track layout incorporating an 18-chain crossing loop with a signal box and a single goods siding, the latter facility being linked to the up and down running lines by trailing connections. These arrangements were modified by 1901, when the connection at the north end of the crossing loop was removed, the signal box closed and the former down platform line was transformed into a terminal road, entered from the south. In later years, the shortened crossing loop functioned as a second goods siding, the connections at each end being worked from ground frames.

The station boasted a small, but solidly built station building, while the nearby goods yard provided the usual range of accommodation for coal, livestock and general merchandise traffic. The station building was situated on the up (northbound) platform, while the goods yard occupied a somewhat restricted site on the opposite side of the running line. A minor road was carried across the railway on a single-span overbridge immediately to the north of the platforms, the bridge being of stone and girder construction, with stone parapets and abutments.

On a minor point of detail it is interesting to note that the attractive, cottage-style station building at Kerne Bridge was very similar to its counterparts on the Northampton & Banbury Junction (N&BJ) line. As mentioned earlier, there were historic links between the N&BJ route and the Ross & Monmouth line, both lines having been built around the same time by the same engineer. In this context it seems likely that Edward Richards may have used the same plans during the construction of both lines - this theory being further strengthened by the appearance of substantially-similar station buildings on the East Gloucestershire line between Witney and Fairford, which was also built by Edward Richards.

Viewed from the platform, these small rectangular structures were of neat and symmetrical appearance with centrally-placed doors giving access to a combined booking hall and waiting room; at Kerne Bridge, the ticket office was sited to the left of the waiting room, while the ladies' waiting room was situated to the right. The gentlemen's toilets were housed in a small extension on the extreme right. Internally, the basic shell was sub-divided by transverse walling, and these dividing walls provided a firm support for two squat chimney stacks that extended through the gabled roof. The building was substantially built of local stone, the masonry being laid in 'snecked', or interrupted courses.

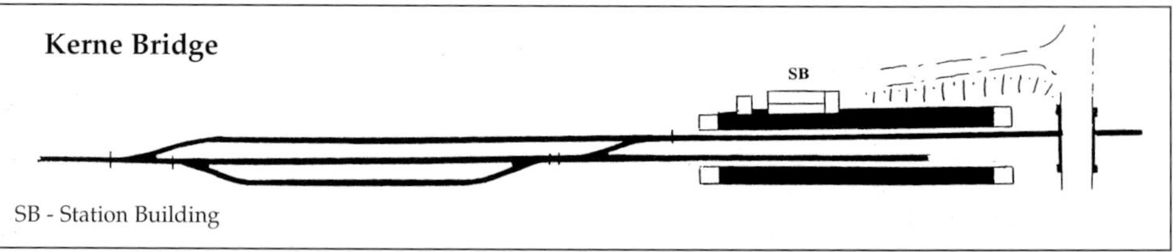

Kerne Bridge station, looking south-west towards Monmouth *c.*1912. The North ground frame can be glimpsed beyond the station building; this controlled access to the goods yard from the running line. The crossing loop was taken out of use around 1900. *Lens of Sutton Collection*

Kerne Bridge, facing Monmouth on 10th July, 1959; the abandoned down platform became a site for a camping coach in the 1930s. *H.C. Casserley*

Although the station had rarely been used for crossing up and down trains, the old down platform was an ideal location for one of the Great Western's camping coaches. Photographic evidence reveals that the first such vehicle to be stationed at Kerne Bridge was an elderly six-wheeler, though in British Railways' days a Dean bogie coach was substituted. These vehicles could be hired throughout the summer from April to October, priority being given to holidaymakers who travelled by train and purchased ordinary tickets in advance of their stay. Towels, bed linen and other essentials were provided, but people staying in the coach had to use the nearby station building for their water and 'ablution' facilities.

Kerne Bridge was not, by any stretch of the imagination, a busy station. In 1903 it issued 14,812 tickets, rising to 18,033 ordinary tickets and 22 seasons in 1923. From then onwards, there was a gradual decline in the level of passenger usage, only 7,147 tickets and 55 seasons being issued in 1937. There was an even greater decline in terms of goods traffic, and whereas around 6,000 tons of freight had been handled per annum during the early 1900s, the station dealt with only 2,550 tons of freight traffic in 1937, falling to 2,362 tons in the following year.

In part, this alarming drop in traffic can be explained by the development of GWR lorry services, which benefited larger traffic centres such as Monmouth and Ross-on-Wye. At the same time, however, Kerne Bridge lost much of its wagon load traffic, only about 1,000 tons of coal being received in the 1930s, whereas in the Edwardian period around 3,000 tons had been received in an average year. There was a similar decline in the numbers of cattle wagons handled each year, 70 wagon loads of livestock being received or dispatched in 1913, while only 16 wagons were dealt with in 1937.

Timber traffic was of considerable importance at Kerne Bridge, and when consignments of round timber were loaded at the station, handsignalmen were provided to ensure that loading operations did not foul the running line. The 1943 Appendix to the Working Timetable stipulated that, before loading could take place, the foreman loader had to obtain the permission from 'the person in charge of the station', who would in turn make sure that the necessary handsignalmen were at their posts. The handsignalmen were in contact with the signalmen at Ross-on-Wye and Lydbrook Junction, and by this means they were able to instruct the foreman loader when to stop loading for the passage of a train.

Kerne Bridge employed three people in 1903, at which time the station's wage expenses were £123, and its total receipts were £2,437. The staffing establishment was cut to just two men in 1932, but despite this efficiency saving, costs continued to rise. By 1938, paybill expenses had risen to £346, while total receipts had fallen to £1,190. To put these figures into their true perspective, it is a sobering thought that wages were five per cent of total receipts in 1903, whereas in 1938 the station's wage bill had reached 29 per cent of the total receipts. When the costs of maintenance, working expenses and rates are added, it seems quite clear that Kerne Bridge was no longer paying its way.

The station was situated in an attractive setting on the banks of the River Wye, in convenient proximity to Goodrich, which was half a mile to the west.

Another view of Kerne Bridge on 10th July, 1959. The waiting shelter seen beside the station building was formerly sited on the opposite platform, which later became a horse-loading dock (note the gated access from the road). *H.C. Casserley*

A view along the platform at Kerne Bridge looking towards Ross-on-Wye in August 1964 and the road overbridge.

Goodrich was the site of Herefordshire's most interesting castle, which had originated in the 12th century as an Anglo-Norman stronghold with a rectangular keep of typical Norman appearance. The keep was surrounded by curtain walls, mural towers, a barbican and other works of the 13th and 14th centuries. The castle was held by local cavaliers during the Civil War, as a result of which it was slighted by Parliament in 1646. In later years the ruins became a tourist attraction, and they were placed in guardianship as an Ancient Monument in 1920.

It is indicative of the importance placed on tourist traffic by the Great Western Railway that Kerne Bridge appeared in the company's public timetables as 'Kerne Bridge (for Goodrich Castle)', this information also being displayed on the station nameboards for the benefit of visiting tourists or holidaymakers.

Traffic dealt with at Kerne Bridge

Year	*Staff*	*Receipts (£)*	*Tickets*	*Parcels*	*Goods tonnage*
1903	3	2,437	14,812	4,003	6,340
1913	3	3,223	16,891	6,247	6,920
1923	3	3,926	18,033	3,574	4,419
1931	3	2,835	11,872	3,105	4,663
1933	2	2,355	8,919	3,830	4,466
1936	2	1,756	7,936	905	3,488
1937	2	1,278	7,147	2,443	2,550
1938	2	1,190	5,779	2,271	2,362

215 c Railway Bridge over River Wye at Kerne Bridge.

The bridge across the River Wye just south of Kerne Bridge.

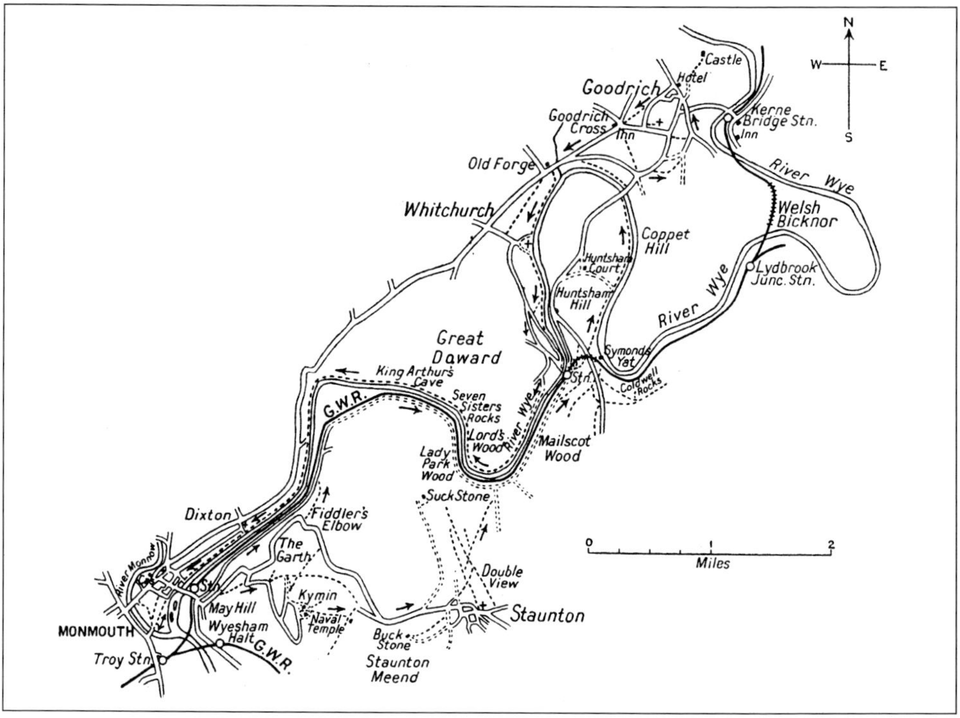

A view along the up platform at Lydbrook Junction looking towards Ross-on-Wye on 11th April, 1955. *R.M. Casserley*

Lydbrook Junction

Beyond Kerne Bridge, the single line crossed to the opposite bank of the river on Kerne Bridge viaduct (4 miles 34 chains). This girder structure was 145 yards long, and it was supported on cylindrical piers. Heading first south-eastwards and then southwards, the route passed through the 630 yds-long Lydbrook tunnel before trains recrossed the River Wye on Lydbrook viaduct and passed from Herefordshire and into Gloucestershire. Lydbrook viaduct was slightly shorter than the neighbouring Kerne Bridge viaduct, with a length of just 102 yards.

Lydbrook ('Junction' from 1st January, 1899), the next stopping place, was 5 miles 40 chains from Ross-on-Wye. Here, the Ross & Monmouth line was joined by a branch of the Severn & Wye Joint Railway, which converged from the left as trains entered the station. As mentioned above, the Severn & Wye Railway had opened its branch from Serridge Junction to Lydbrook in August 1874, but passenger services did not commence until 1875. The Severn & Wye Railway was at that time an independent concern, but in 1894 the company was acquired jointly by the Great Western and Midland Railway companies.

There were, for several years, four trains each way over the Severn & Wye Joint line between Berkeley Road and Lydbrook Junction, most services being worked by GWR locomotives and rolling stock; there were, however, one or two purely Midland (later LMS) freight workings between Sharpness and Lydbrook Junction. Although Severn & Wye passenger services were withdrawn between Lydney, Cinderford and Lydbrook Junction with effect from 8th July, 1929, the Lydbrook Junction to Serridge Junction branch continued to carry significant amounts of coal and mineral traffic.

The track layout at Lydbrook Junction incorporated a crossing loop for Ross & Monmouth workings, with two additional platforms on the down side for Lydbrook branch trains. The Lydbrook line converged with the Ross & Monmouth route at the south end of the station, a number of loop sidings being available for interchange traffic. The goods yard was sited to the north of the platforms on the down side, and its two dead-end sidings were able to handle coal, livestock and general merchandise traffic. The goods shed was merely a small lock-up at the north end of the down platform, this relatively small structure being suitable for small consignments and packages.

The solid stone station building was similar to the building at nearby Kerne Bridge, being another cottage-style structure. This distinctive building was situated on the down platform in the 'V' of the junction between the down main line and the Coleford branch. At a later stage, a brick-built extension wing had been added at the east end of the building, thereby turning it into an L-plan structure.

The only building on the up platform was an open-fronted, timber-built waiting shelter, with a single pitched roof that swept boldly out across the platform to form a small canopy. The signal box, which was sited to the west of the up platform, was a standard Great Western hipped-roof cabin on a brick base that dated from 1908 and replaced an 1874-built box.

In addition to its importance as an interchange point with the Forest of Dean lines, Lydbrook Junction was the site of a small cable factory that generated

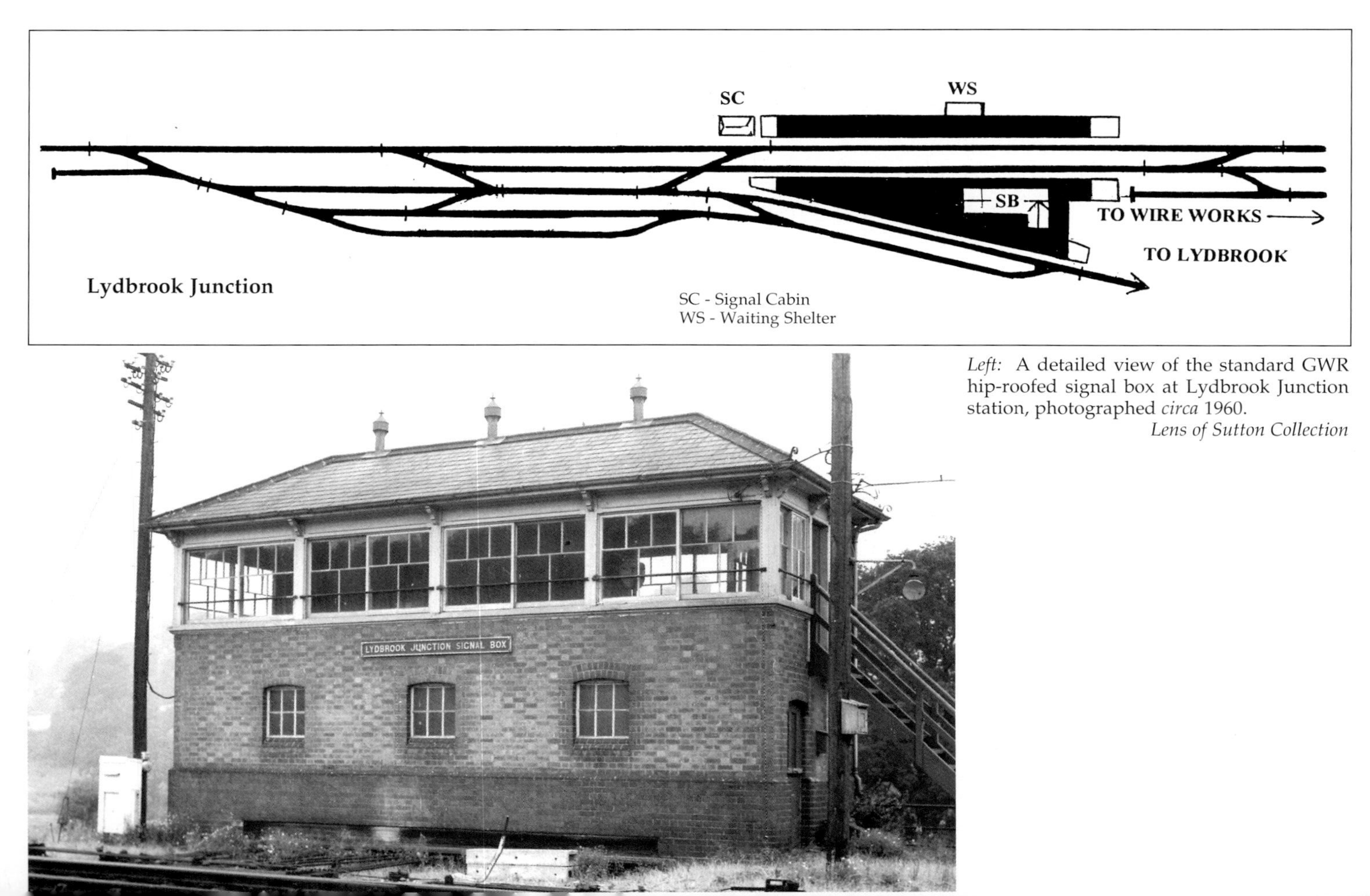

Left: A detailed view of the standard GWR hip-roofed signal box at Lydbrook Junction station, photographed *circa* 1960.

Lens of Sutton Collection

Lydbrook Junction station, looking north towards Ross-on-Wye *c*.1908. The main building, on the down side, was similar to those found elsewhere on the Ross-Monmouth line.

Lens of Sutton Collection

'14XX' class 0-4-2T No. 1445 propelling an auto-train is seen in the down platform at Lydbrook Junction on 2nd June, 1951. Railcar No. W7 stands in the Lydbrook branch platform with a Gloucester Railway Society railtour. *W. Potter/Kidderminster Railway Museum*

A general view of Lydbrook Junction station, looking south towards Monmouth.
Lens of Sutton Collection

Lydbrook Junction station, looking north towards Ross-on-Wye, *circa* 1960s.
Lens of Sutton Collection

significant amounts of freight traffic for the railway. This facility was conveniently-sited to the east of the station on the down side, and in later years the closed Severn & Wye platforms were used for cable traffic. Successive editions of the Railway Clearing House *Handbook of Stations* reveal that the wire works was being used by H.W. Smith & Co. from 1916, the private siding agreement passing to Edison Swan Cables in 1926.

The wire works siding was installed under the terms of a private siding agreement dated 5th September, 1916, and in its original form the siding was simply an extension of the goods sidings at the north end of the station. The works siding was subsequently altered and extended in connection with various developments within the Edison Swan premises. A stop-board was provided at the entrance to the private siding to stop Great Western engines from entering the works.

Lydbrook Junction had a staff of half a dozen during the 1920s, under a class four station master; by 1932 the staffing establishment had been increased from six to seven, while eight people were employed at the station by 1938. In that year Lydbrook Junction handled 19,363 tons of freight, much of this being generated by the Edison Swan cable works; in earlier years, around 1913, only about 1,000 tons of freight had been dealt with per annum. Passenger traffic was

Lydbrook Junction station from the south, with the former branch platform visible to the right of the picture. *Lens of Sutton Collection*

A view along the track to the northern portal of the 433 yds-long tunnel just north of Symond's Yat station on 15th September, 1956, with the River Wye in close attendance. *R.M. Casserley*

The railway and river at Symond's Yat were the subject of a number of commercial postcards through the years. Here we see the 'classic' view of the location, looking towards Monmouth. *The Nelson Museum, Monmouth*

fairly constant in the 1920s and 1930s, with around 5,000 bookings each year. In 1932, for instance, Lydbrook Junction issued 5,217 tickets and 15 seasons, while in 1937 5,197 tickets and 41 season tickets were issued.

Traffic dealt with at Lydbrook Junction

Year	*Staff*	*Receipts (£)*	*Tickets*	*Parcels*	*Goods tonnage*
1903	4	1,210	10,253	2,209	454
1913	4	1,299	9,552	2,002	1,038
1923	6	4,487	13,756	2,373	2,186
1930	6	14,397	6,470	2,821	9,562
1932	7	15,704	5,217	2,892	10,062
1936	7	25,190	5,070	7,036	17,800
1937	8	27,915	5,197	7,411	19,771
1938	8	27,223	4,307	5,885	19,363

Symond's Yat

From Lydbrook Junction, Monmouth trains continued south-westwards alongside the River Wye. Nearing Symond's Yat, the river turned northwards as it made a three mile detour around an intervening ridge of high land, but the railway took a more direct course as it plunged through a 433 yard tunnel. Having crossed the end of a narrow isthmus formed at the neck of a huge meander, the line soon rejoined the river, and trains ran along the water's edge towards their next stopping place at Symond's Yat, some 7 miles 50 chains from Ross-on-Wye.

Symond's Yat was a two platform station, with a 16 chain crossing loop, and a small wooden station building on the down side. Although of timber construction, this gable roofed building was another 'Edward Richards' design, that closely resembled the stone buildings at Kerne Bridge, Lydbrook Junction, and on other lines engineered by Edward Richards and his associate Charles Liddell.

A diminutive wooden shelter was provided for travellers waiting on the up platform, and because of the extremely restricted space available between the railway and the River Wye this small structure was cantilevered out over the river bank. Waiting shelters of identical design and construction could be seen at Witney and Bampton on the East Gloucestershire branch, the family likeness discernible between these attractive structures being very striking.

The track layout at Symond's Yat was simple in the extreme; there were no sidings, and the station consisted of little more than a crossing loop with a short siding at the south end of the up platform line. This modest place was, nevertheless, used as a block post and passing station on the single line, and it was for this reason fully signalled, with up and down home, starting and distant signals, the fish-tailed distant arms being permanently fixed at caution.

The signals were originally worked from a primitive, open ground frame that was sited alongside the station building on the down side. A small, single-storey signal box was subsequently erected. This modest structure was, in truth, little bigger than a ground frame hut, although it functioned as a signal cabin,

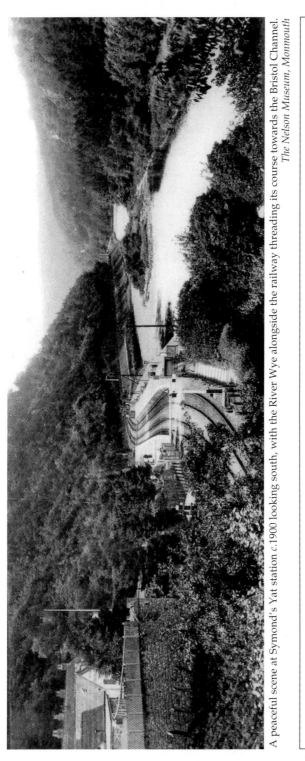

A peaceful scene at Symond's Yat station *c.*1900 looking south, with the River Wye alongside the railway threading its course towards the Bristol Channel.
The Nelson Museum, Monmouth

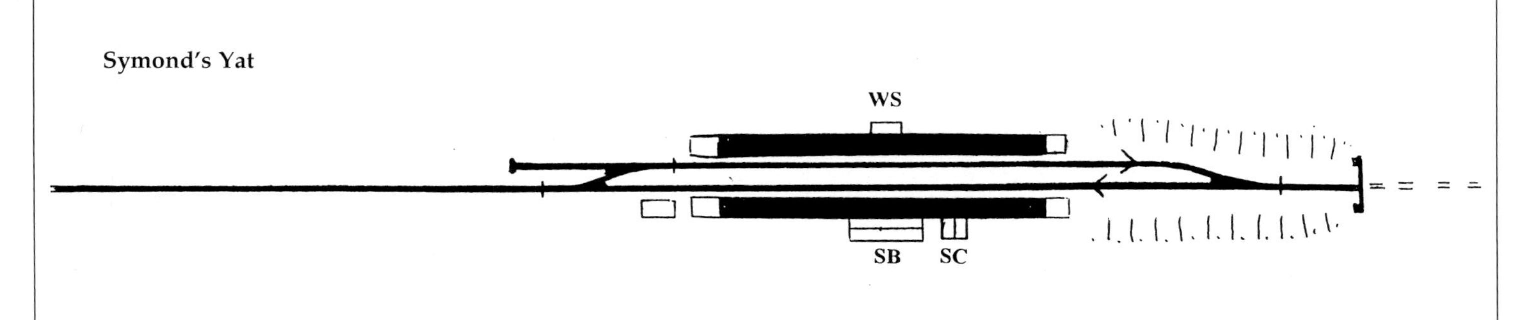

and displayed the words 'SYMOND'S YAT SIGNAL BOX' on a cast metal plate affixed to the front of the building. The signal box was of timber construction, with a slated, gable roof. Somewhat unusually, the cabin was sited at right angles to the track, with its gable end facing the platform.

The platforms were fenced with traditional pale-and-space fencing, while at night illumination was provided by oil lamps in traditional tapered glass lanterns. These were later replaced by hurricane lamps on simple upright posts. Other platform furniture included a number of park-type slatted seats which, from their appearance, were probably former Ross & Monmouth fittings that pre-dated the Great Western takeover. The two platforms were linked by a barrow crossing at the north end of the station, there being no requirement for a footbridge at such a small station.

The crossing loop at Symond's Yat served a useful purpose during the Edwardian period, when it was regularly used for passing purposes. In May 1914, for example, the 1.55 pm goods working from Hereford reached the station at 3.40 pm, and it then waited for the 2.20 pm ex-Pontypool Road passenger service in the down loop line. The latter working was booked to leave Symond's Yat at 3.53 pm, and the pick-up freight was then able to continue on its own journey at 3.55 pm. On its return journey the Monmouth to Hereford goods working crossed the 5.00 pm down passenger service in the loop at Symond's Yat, while one or two 'as required' goods services also used the station for crossing purposes.

This situation pertained for many years, but with the general run-down of the Ross & Monmouth branch during the 1950s, British Railways decided that the loop and signal box would be abolished. Accordingly, in March 1953 the loop was turned into a dead-end siding, the connection at the Ross-on-Wye end being removed. The connection at the Monmouth end of the station was retained, the siding points being worked from a two-lever ground frame. The northern half of the former loop was lifted, and a buffer stop was erected at a point roughly opposite the station building; in its new form, the old up platform line then became an ideal place for another camping coach.

The camping coach provided at Symond's Yat was an elliptical-roofed bogie vehicle, and like its counterpart at Kerne Bridge, the coach could be hired throughout the summer months. Arguably, Symond's Yat was one of the best camping coach sites on the former Great Western system, its position in a picturesque, heavily-wooded gorge beside the sparkling River Wye being idyllic.

The station was used mainly for passenger traffic, although the 1938 Railway Clearing House *Handbook of Stations* shows that basic goods facilities were available for wagon load traffic at nearby private sidings, which were under the control of the Symond's Yat station master. Parcels and small goods consignments could also be dealt with at that time, but by the 1950s this form of traffic was normally sent to or from the nearby station at Lydbrook Junction - road vehicles being employed for the intervening four miles between Lydbrook Junction and Symond's Yat.

Great Western Railway traffic statistics reveal that Symond's Yat dealt with considerable amounts of goods traffic via its private sidings, but in practice most of this traffic was in the form of stone or timber. In 1930, for instance, the

A general view of Symond's Yat station, looking towards Ross-on-Wye, probably around 1928. The brick building at the end of the platform was used as a store, while the wooden structure beside it was a permanent way hut. *Lens of Sutton Collection*

A detailed view of the timber-framed station building *c.*1912. The small signal box was erected around 1902, prior to which the signals had been worked from an open frame. The 'modesty screen' alongside the gentlemen's urinal was subsequently removed. *Lens of Sutton Collection*

Symond's Yat facing Monmouth, on 14th September, 1956. Collett '14XX' class 0-4-2T No. 1445 heads its train. Note the wooden station building, that was otherwise similar to the buildings at Lydbrook and Kerne Bridge. *R.M. Casserley*

Another '14XX' class, No. 1406, departs from Symond's Yat with a train for Ross-on-Wye in the 1950s. By this time the passing loop had been turned into a dead-end siding, which then made an ideal site for the camping coach as seen here. *R.W.A. Jones*

A view across the platform at Symond's Yat, with the signal box to the right. In the background is the Royal Hotel. The hotel was built in 1876 as a royal hunting lodge and was converted to a hotel in the 1920s. *R. Dingwall Collection*

A snowy scene from a train approaching Symond's Yat station from Monmouth on 4th January, 1959. *D.K. Jones Collection*

station dealt with 33,429 tons of freight, of which no less than 31,222 tons was mineral traffic.

Interestingly, the station (as opposed to the private sidings) also handled small amounts of parcels and sundries traffic, 1,636 parcels being dealt with in 1930, rising to 2,109 parcels and small packages in 1935.

It should be explained that the term 'parcels' was applied by the GWR to a wide range of miscellaneous traffic, including passengers' luggage in advance, poultry and pigeons in hampers. Such traffic was conveyed by passenger trains, and paid-for by weight in quantities of less than 2 cwt.

In 1922 Symond's Yat was supervised by a class five station master, who controlled two porter-signalmen. Great Western documents suggest that the station was later placed under the Lydbrook Junction station master, although Symond's Yat retained a staff of three throughout the 1930s.

Traffic dealt with at Symond's Yat

Year	*Staff*	*Receipts (£)*	*Tickets*	*Parcels*	*Goods tonnage*
1903	3	1,558	10,430	1,542	1,114
1913	3	1,036	11,804	2,146	514
1923	3	3,285	12,861	1,768	12,063
1931	3	5,887	6,767	1,463	36,204
1933	3	2,269	6,324	1,873	14,414
1936	3	3,013	5,884	1,575	17,730
1937	3	1,816	5,852	1,191	12,595
1938	3	1,669	5,233	998	5,863

Almost all the way from Symond's Yat to Monmouth the railway ran along the river's bank, this is a view from the train on 15th September, 1956. *R.M. Casserley*

Slaughter Siding

From Symond's Yat station, trains continued south-westwards as they followed the River Wye. Running alongside the turbulent river, the railway hugged the river bank, and after about one mile the route curved northwards through a 170 degree curve, as it followed the winding river downstream towards Monmouth. After about one mile, at a point 8 miles 41 chains from Ross-on-Wye, down trains reached a private siding known as Slaughter Siding.

Slaughter Siding was situated on the down side of the line, and it was provided to serve the High Meadow Iron Ore Company, and an associated coal mine. The 1938 Railway Clearing House *Handbook of Stations* shows that the siding was, by that time, being used by the Ministry of Agriculture & Fisheries. The siding was arranged as a loop, with connections to the running line at both ends. A spur at the north end of the loop branched out to reach the High Meadow Colliery, while a similar siding at the south end diverged south-eastwards to reach the High Meadow Iron Mine; both of these connecting lines were protected by locked gates, the keys for which were kept at Symond's Yat station.

The siding was worked from a 9-lever ground frame on the up side of the line, and this also controlled home and distant signals in each direction. A small wooden hut near the open lever frame contained telephone equipment, by means of which the person in charge of the siding could maintain contact with the signalmen at Symond's Yat and Monmouth (May Hill). When not in use, the signals were kept in the 'off' position, and they were only brought into use when timber or other traffic was being loaded; on such occasions, a porter-signalman was sent out from nearby Symond's Yat to assist with the operation. The connection at the north end of the siding was removed in 1944.

Slaughter Siding was initially provided at the request of the Commissioner of Woods & Forests, a private siding agreement being made as early as May 1870, some three years before the opening of the Ross & Monmouth line. The connection to High Meadow Colliery was in use by the late 1870s, while the High Meadow Iron Company siding at the south end of the main loop siding was opened under a private siding agreement dated 5th November, 1888. These sidings had fallen out of use by the early 1900s, although Slaughter Siding had evidently been brought back into use by May 1914 and it remained in use until the British Railways era, the siding connection at the southern end being taken out of use on 9th January, 1955.

Slaughter Siding took its curious name from an area of the Wye Valley known as 'The Slaughter'. This was alleged to have been the site of an encounter between the Romans and the Silures, a Roman force being ambushed by Caractacus as it attempted to ford the river at this picturesque spot.

High Meadow Siding

Continuing towards Monmouth, trains quickly reached High Meadow Siding, which, at 8 miles 66 chains, was barely a quarter of a mile from Slaughter Siding. This siding was situated on the up side of the line and, in contrast to Slaughter

Siding, it was linked to the running line by a single connection. For this reason, the siding could only be shunted by up trains - which were able to enter the siding by a reverse shunting manoeuvre. The siding connection was worked from a ground frame that was released by a key on the Electric Train Staff for the Symond's Yat to Monmouth (May Hill) single line section.

The siding was brought into use in February 1919, although the relevant private siding agreement between the GWR and the Commissioner of Woods & Forests was not signed until 1st July, 1920. As High Meadow Siding was sited on a gradient, loose shunting was prohibited, and when traffic was picked-up or dropped-off, wagons had to remain coupled to the train until they had been safely brought to a stand in the siding. The 1943 Appendix to the Working Timetable reveals that there were no signals at this siding. The siding and its ground frame were recovered on 28th July, 1946.

Roberts & Lewis' Siding

Still following the river as it meandered first west, and then northwards, the railway snaked along the river bank towards a third private siding known as Roberts & Lewis' Siding (9 miles 60 chains). This was another loop siding with connections at each end, the siding points being worked from a ground frame that was released by a key on the Electric Train Staff. When timber or other traffic was loaded at this siding, guards, shunters and other persons were warned that they were 'not to attempt to pass between the loading bank' and wagons standing in the siding, as clearances here were particularly limited. The siding was not protected by signals, though a locked gate was provided.

Roberts & Lewis' Siding was brought into use on 17th February, 1922, under the terms of a private siding agreement dated 4th November, 1921. The siding, which was situated on the down side of the line, was lengthened in 1924 - by which time a new private siding agreement had been made with Hadnock Quarries Ltd. This was terminated mid-1956, the loop siding connection at the north end having been taken out of use on 2nd January, 1955.

Beyond Roberts & Lewis' Siding, the route followed the serpentine course of the River Wye through spectacular woodland scenery, the turbulent river being visible on the right-hand side of the line for several miles.

Hadnock Halt and Siding

Hadnock Halt, the next stopping place, was a simple request stop, which had been opened by British Railways as recently as 7th May, 1951. It consisted of a very short platform, just seven inches above rail level, on the down side of the line at a point 10 miles 59 chains from Ross-on-Wye. There was a further private siding less than half a mile beyond the halt at 11 miles 9 chains. This facility, also on the down side, was known as Hadnock Siding, and it predated the halt by many years, having been opened as a 'siding station' for goods traffic in 1873.

A view of the short-lived Hadnock Halt looking towards Symond's Yat. *Arthur Day*

A general view of Monmouth (May Hill) station from the south on 25th March, 1960.
R.J. Leonard/Kidderminster Railway Museum

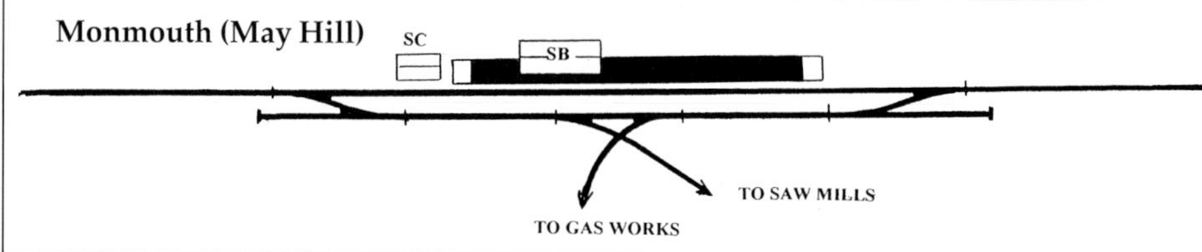

This gated siding was situated on a 1 in 132 gradient, falling towards Monmouth, and the connection to the single line at the south end of the siding was released by a key on the Electric Train Staff. There had been a connection at the north end also until 13th July, 1944 when it was removed. The siding was protected by home and distant signals which were worked only as necessary for the protection of the main line when felled timber was being loaded. When the siding was not in use the keys to the entrance gates were kept by the station master at Symond's Yat, and a duplicate set was held by the Deputy Surveyor of the Crown Woods.

Monmouth (May Hill)

On leaving Hadnock Halt, the single line continued south-westwards to the penultimate stopping place on the Ross & Monmouth section at Monmouth (May Hill), which was 12 miles 31 chains from Ross-on-Wye, and approached on a 1 in 198 falling gradient.

Monmouth (May Hill) was a passenger-only station, with a single platform on the up side of the running line. The station was better-sited in relation to the town centre than Monmouth (Troy), and this ensured that it was relatively well-used by the local community. The station had served as the original terminus of the line from its opening in August 1873 until the line was completed throughout to Monmouth (Troy) in May 1874.

The station building was a timber-framed structure clad in horizontal weather boarding. It had a low-pitched gable roof, and a small platform canopy was affixed to the front the building. Internally, this undistinguished structure contained the usual booking office and waiting room accommodation (even these had not been authorized until January 1874). The building was very basic in relation to the other intermediate station buildings on the Ross & Monmouth route, the implication being that Monmouth (May Hill) was designed as a temporary station that could be closed once the line was opened throughout to Monmouth (Troy). It was, nonetheless, retained as a passenger station after 1874, and Monmouth thereby enjoyed the benefits of two railway stations.

May Hill was a block post, but not a crossing station. Its signal box was sited to the south of the platform on the up side. This structure was a standard Great Western gable roof box, of timber construction, with the usual five-pane windows. The cabin was opened in 1905 to replace an earlier signal box that had been sited on the platform.

Although Monmouth (May Hill) had no public goods facilities, it was the site of several private sidings, the most important of which served Monmouth Gas Works; in 1912, the Gas Works Siding was used by a number of private traders. The 1938 Railway Clearing House *Handbook of Stations* lists two sidings at May Hill, these being the Monmouth Gas Works Siding and the Monmouth Steam Saw Mills Siding. The gas works closed around 1939. In April 1942 a Ministry of Food storage facility siding was set up on the down side of the line some 300 yards to the east of Monmouth (May Hill) station (12 miles 19 chains). The siding connection, which was facing to down trains, was worked from a 2-lever ground frame released by a key on the Electric Train Staff.

'14XX' class 0-4-2T No. 1456 with its train at Monmouth (May Hill). This view looks towards Monmouth (Troy) *circa* 1958. *M.D.E. Jenkins, C.G. Maggs Collection*

A branch auto-train pauses in the single platform at Monmouth (May Hill). *Lens of Sutton Collection*

The track layout at May Hill comprised a short loop siding on the down side of the single running line. The Gas Works Siding and the Steam Saw Mills Siding diverged sharply from this goods line, the curvature being so acute that shunters and other staff were warned to take 'every precaution and care' when attaching or detaching traffic. Great Western working appendices stipulated that bogie bolster wagons and long-wheelbase tube wagons were not to be worked beyond a notice board placed in the Steam Saw Mill Siding, the possibility of derailments being taken very seriously. The loop siding connection at the southern end was removed in March 1953 and the signal box closed on 5th January, 1959. Finally the loop siding northern end connection was removed by April 1960.

In 1925, May Hill station had a staff of three, including two porter-signalmen and a class four station master, but by 1929 the staffing establishment had been reduced to one general clerk and two porter-signalmen. For administrative purposes, May Hill then came under the control of the station master at neighbouring Monmouth (Troy). After a further alteration in the staffing arrangements, May Hill's labour force was cut to just two.

May Hill issued 19,696 tickets in 1903, the corresponding figures for 1913 and 1923 being 17,410 and 16,551 respectively. Thereafter, there was an apparent decline in the number of ordinary ticket sales, although the fact that up to 140 season tickets per year were sold during the 1930s would indicate that many regular travellers preferred to pay for their journeys in this convenient way. In 1935 the station issued 5,321 ordinary tickets and 149 season tickets, while in 1939 4,177 tickets and 123 seasons were issued here.

A close-up of the signal box at the south end of Monmouth (May Hill) station with the platform and station buildings visible beyond. *The Nelson Museum, Monmouth*

Collett '14XX' class 0-4-2T No. 1445 is seen approaching Monmouth (May Hill) with the 6.05 pm Monmouth to Ross train on 1st September, 1958. The bow string girder bridge crossing the River Wye is visible in the distance. *R.O. Tuck*

An aerial view of the two bridges which crossed the River Wye to the east of Monmouth (Troy) *c*.1945. The bridge near the camera carries the Ross-Monmouth line, while the bridge in the background is on the Wye Valley Railway (Monmouth to Chepstow). *The Nelson Museum, Monmouth*

Monmouth itself had a population of around 5,000 before World War II, rising to 5,432 by the early 1950s. Visitors arriving by train found themselves in a historic border town, with the remains of a Medieval castle and an interesting fortified bridge across the River Monnow. The town was associated with several famous people, including King Henry V, who was born in the castle in 1387, and Horatio Nelson, who visited the town in 1802 while touring Wales and the West Country in company with Sir William and Lady Hamilton. Aviation enthusiasts may also have been interested in the statue of Charles Rolls in Agincourt Square - the pioneer aviator being depicted with a model aeroplane.

On a footnote, it might be mentioned that when the railway was in operation Monmouthshire was administered as part of England, rather than Wales. Its anomalous position was nevertheless acknowledged in the term 'Wales and Monmouthshire', which was adopted as a cumbersome, but technically-correct description.

Traffic dealt with at Monmouth (May Hill)

Year	*Staff*	*Receipts (£)*	*Tickets*	*Parcels*
1903	4	3,775	19,696	31,284
1913	3	3,425	17,410	31,147
1923	3	4,362	16,551	30,248
1930	3	2,548	7,332	7,962
1936	2	1,656	5,033	4,032
1937	2	1,457	4,616	3,638
1938	2	1,459	4,177	3,510

Monmouth (Troy)

On departure from Monmouth (May Hill), branch trains proceeded southwards towards the River Wye, which was crossed on a bow string girder bridge (12 miles 64 chains). The Monmouth river bridge was a three-span structure, its main centre span having bow string girders, while the two subsidiary spans on each side had shorter horizontal girders. The bridge had a total length of 99 yards. Having crossed the river, trains continued south-westwards to Monmouth (Troy) station (13 miles 10 chains). Early documents refer to the station as 'Troy House'.

As their train approached Monmouth (Troy), travellers could, by glancing to the left, see the Wye Valley branch from Chepstow and Tintern, which became double as it entered the station. The Wye Valley line crossed the river on its own bridge, this impressive structure being known as the Monmouth viaduct, to distinguish it from the neighbouring Monmouth river bridge. The viaduct incorporated a girder span across the actual river, with a masonry approach section to the east, and no less than 20 arched stone spans on the western side of the river.

The track layout at Monmouth (Troy) was relatively simple, the up and down platforms being situated on each side of a 19 chain crossing loop, while the Ross, Chepstow and Pontypool lines diverged north-eastwards, eastwards and

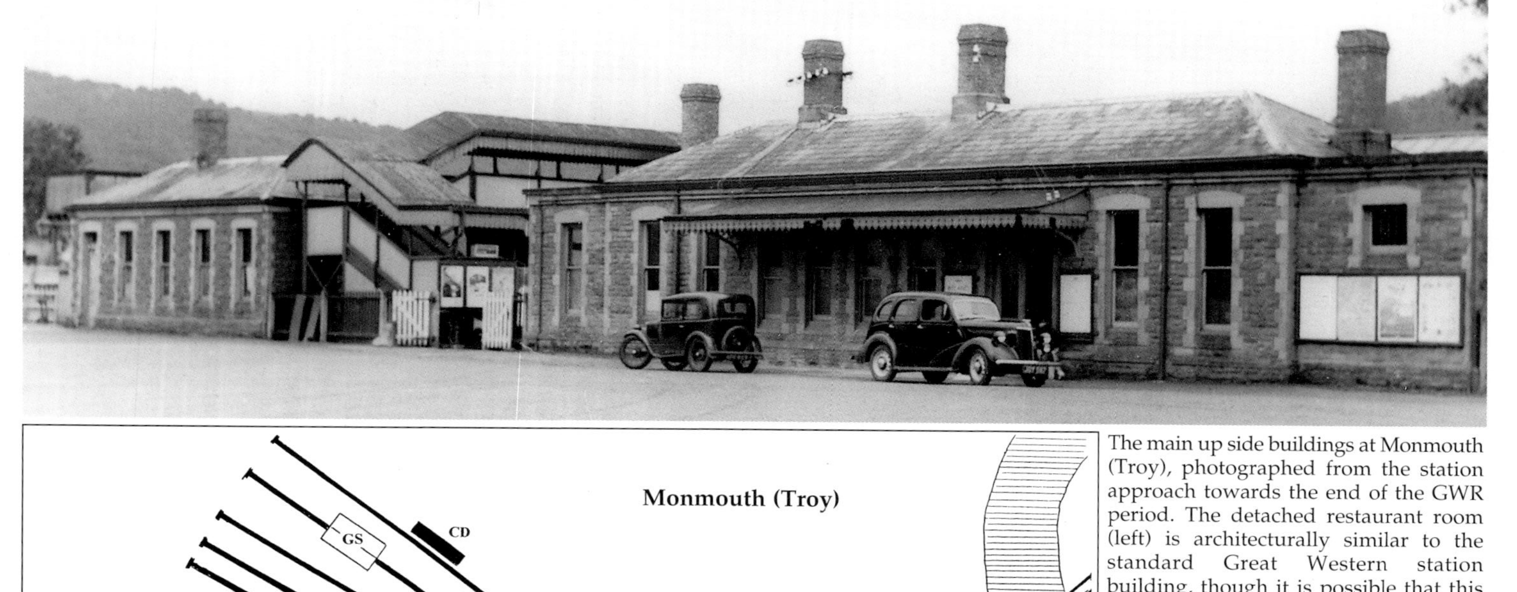

The main up side buildings at Monmouth (Troy), photographed from the station approach towards the end of the GWR period. The detached restaurant room (left) is architecturally similar to the standard Great Western station building, though it is possible that this small structure may incorporate parts of the original Coleford, Monmouth, Usk & Pontypool station building.

Lens of Sutton Collection

westwards respectively beyond the platforms. The goods yard was situated on the up, or north side of the station, and entered by means of a trailing connection from the up Ross line. There were no bay platforms or other specific junction facilities, and trains to or from Chepstow, Pontypool Road and Ross-on-Wye all shared the main up and down platforms. As briefly mentioned in Chapter Three, Monmouth to Coleford services had been withdrawn as a wartime economy measure on 1st January, 1917.

The station was extensively rebuilt towards the end of the Victorian period, when the GWR erected a range of standard hip-roofed buildings. These structures were solidly built of local stone, and the main booking office and waiting room block was sited on the up side of the running lines. There was, in addition, a detached refreshment room to the east of the main station building, this structure being another hip-roofed building that was architecturally-similar to the main booking office block. The latter building featured a projecting platform canopy, but there was no canopy in front of the refreshment room.

Facilities for passengers on the down platform consisted of a small, stone-built waiting shelter with a steeply-pitched roof that was swept forward over the platform to form a small canopy. The up and down sides of the station were linked by a typical Great Western style plate girder footbridge with a corrugated iron roof.

Monmouth (Troy) was fully equipped with a range of facilities for coal, timber, livestock, vehicles, agricultural machinery, general merchandise, and other forms of goods traffic. The goods yard contained an array of six dead-end sidings, which fanned out to serve the goods shed, coal wharves and other facilities.

The substantial stone goods shed was similar to scores of other Great Western sheds throughout Wales and the western counties of England. It was a gable-roofed structure, containing a wooden loading platform; large wooden arches inserted into each gable enabled railway vehicles to be shunted into the building for loading or unloading, while a projecting checker's office adjoined one end, its chimney being carried up to the apex of the gable.

The station was signalled from a standard GWR hip-roofed signal box on the down side of the running lines with a 38-lever frame (including five spares). This box had been built in 1916 as a replacement for an earlier one, and it was entirely typical of its period - such standardized boxes being erected all over the Great Western system after about 1900; a feature of the design were the five-pane high visibility windows, which were supposed to give signalmen a clearer view of their surroundings. The locking room and rear wall of the building were constructed of Flemish bond brickwork, while the roof was of grey Welsh slate.

Like other station of similar size and importance, Monmouth (Troy) could boast an assortment of minor buildings of various kinds. There was, for example, a weigh-house in the goods yard, while the signal box was flanked by two smaller single-storey structures, one of which was of brick construction, while the other was a timber hut on a brick base which, from its appearance, may have incorporated parts of the original signal box. There were, in addition, two sleeper-built huts, all of these ancillary buildings being used as stores or mess rooms by the engineering or signal & telegraph departments.

An Edwardian view of Monmouth (Troy) station looking towards the tunnel and Pontypool Road. *The Nelson Museum, Monmouth*

A detailed view of Monmouth (Troy) signal box, *circa* 1960s. *Lens of Sutton Collection*

A wet day at Monmouth (Troy) in this view looking from the eastern end of the station in May 1952. An ex-GWR railcar stands at the throat of the busy goods yard. The line heading straight on is for Ross-on-Wye, its curves to left shortly after passing the headshunt buffer stop, before crossing the bow string girder bridge (*seen in the distance*). The line which is seen gently curving away to the right is for Chepstow. *R.W.A. Jones*

A useful view of Monmouth (Troy), facing Ross-on-Wye on 5th April, 1931. A return half-day excursion to Paddington stands in the platform. *H.C. Casserley*

Monmouth (Troy), facing Pontypool Road on 15th September, 1956. Collett '54XX' class 0-6-0PT No. 5414 stands in the platform with a train for Chepstow via the Wye Valley line. The refreshment room can be seen to the right of the locomotive. *R.M. Casserley*

Collett '14XX' class 0-4-2T No. 1445, with auto-trailers Nos. 84 and 237, has just arrived in the down side platform at Monmouth (Troy) with the 11.00 am from Ross-on-Wye on 11th April, 1955. *R.M. Casserley*

Water columns were strategically-sited at the east end of the up platform, and the west end of the down, the down side water column being squeezed into an awkward position between the platform ramp and the east portal of the tunnel. The water supply was fed from a stilted metal tank near the signal box. At night, Monmouth (Troy) was lit by gas lamps with tapering glass lanterns, while the platforms were fenced with traditional pale-and-space fencing.

The three routes which converged at Monmouth (Troy) were all single lines, but the presence of a double-track tunnel at the west end of the platforms suggested that the line to Pontypool Road had up and down lines. In fact, the southernmost line was merely a siding which continued alongside the running line to reach a timber yard on the west side of the tunnel. The western end of the crossing loop was situated just inside the tunnel, which meant that when locomotives ran round their trains they had to draw forward into the tunnel mouth.

A further peculiarity concerned the presence of a crane in the nearby timber yard. This was situated alongside the siding in close proximity to the adjacent running line, and to prevent accidents the timber crane was normally locked out of use. When it was needed for loading timber, the mechanism was unbolted from an adjacent ground frame which was itself electrically released by lever No. 11 in Monmouth (Troy) signal box, and no trains could then pass the timber yard until the crane was relocked. As an added precaution, the crane was also secured by a padlock, the key to which was kept in Monmouth (Troy) signal box. A telephone link was provided between the signal box and the ground frame.

When the crane was needed for loading timber the loader obtained the key from the signalman, and having returned to the ground frame, he telephoned the signal box to ask permission to work the crane. If permission was granted, the signalman released the locking system so that work could begin. When the signalman required the loader to put the crane into position for being locked, he called the loader and instructed him to do so. Finally, when all work had ceased, the ground frame bolt was restored to normal, the brake mechanism on the crane was padlocked and the key was returned to the signal box.

Despite its status as a junction for the three branch services to Chepstow, Pontypool Road and Ross-on-Wye, Monmouth (Troy) had few junction facilities, and in particular the station was not equipped with any terminal bay platforms. This apparent deficiency was, perhaps, a reflection of the fact that the lines involved were lightly used branches, with no more than half a dozen passenger trains per day. Moreover, the employment of auto-trains or diesel railcars on all three routes meant that two or more workings could make use of the same platform - indeed, on some occasions as the photographs show, all three branch trains could be seen alongside the up platform, which was of ample length for the traffic involved.

Monmouth (Troy) was fully signalled, with home, starting and distant signals in each direction, together with outer homes on the Ross-on-Wye and Wye Valley lines; the fish-tailed distant arms were fixed at caution on all three routes. The up platform was provided with a bracketed starting signal controlling entry to the Ross-and-Wye and Wye Valley lines, while a similar 'two doll' assembly

'4800' class 0-4-2T No. 4831, attached to its auto-trailer, is positioned near the water column at Monmouth (Troy) station on 21st June, 1939. *V.R. Webster/Kidderminster Railway Museum*

'14XX' class No. 1422 and auto-trailer No. 188 stand at the western end of the up side platform on 11th September, 1955. The eastern portal of the 148 yds-long Monmouth tunnel at the end of the station platform takes the line on to Pontypool Road. *R.M. Casserley*

at the west end of the down platform carried two semaphore arms, the right arm of which was the down starter for Pontypool Road services, whereas the other was a subsidiary siding signal, controlling entry to the above-mentioned timber yard at the far end of the tunnel.

This arrangement allowed the station to be operated in conventional fashion, with separate up and down platforms. Trains from Pontypool Road and Ross-on-Wye generally used the up and down platforms respectively, while Wye Valley trains arrived in the down platform and departed from the up side. Terminating services from Pontypool Road ran into the up platform and, when passengers had alighted, the diesel car or auto-train would cross to the down platform in order to form the next westbound service; on occasions, however, the Pontypool Road trains would depart from the east end of the up platform - although there were no signals to formalize this practice.

An interesting minor detail at Monmouth (Troy) could be found in the station approach road, where an isolated length of tunnel served as a store. This was an abandoned relic of one of the abortive extension schemes of the 1860s, which would have resulted in Monmouth becoming a junction at the centre of several radiating cross country branch lines - one of which would have extended along the Monnow Valley to Pontrilas.

In staffing terms, Monmouth (Troy) was a relatively important centre of employment in an otherwise mainly rural area. The station itself employed around 20 people, and in the mid-1920s these included one class two station master, one booking clerk, three goods clerks, one porter-signalman, two porters, one foreman, four goods porters, one goods shunter, two signalmen, one goods guard and three carters. There were, additionally, a number of locally-based permanent way men, Permanent Way Gang No. 71 being responsible for the section of line between Monmouth and Usk.

The station was poorly-sited in relation to the main residential and commercial areas of the town, although this problem was mitigated, to some extent, by the presence of Monmouth (May Hill) station on the opposite side of the river. For this reason, Monmouth (Troy) was probably more important as an interchange station between the Ross, Pontypool Road and Wye Valley (and one time Coleford) lines, whereas May Hill was busier in terms of originating passenger traffic.

Traffic dealt with at Monmouth (Troy)

Year	*Staff*	*Receipts (£)*	*Tickets*	*Parcels*	*Goods tonnage*
1903	13	17,914	48,287	10,422	32,559
1913	14	19,038	44,122	17,198	40,554
1923	22	27,435	32,335	12,551	37,359
1929	20	20,964	11,659	10.637	34,878
1931	19	21,216	9,891	32,224	42,284
1933	18	17,831	7,599	34,043	33,497
1935	19	16,982	7,240	35,066	38,700
1936	19	16,296	7,091	34,786	32,707
1937	21	16,815	6,064	35,079	30,498
1938	21	15,172	4,974	32,852	26,774

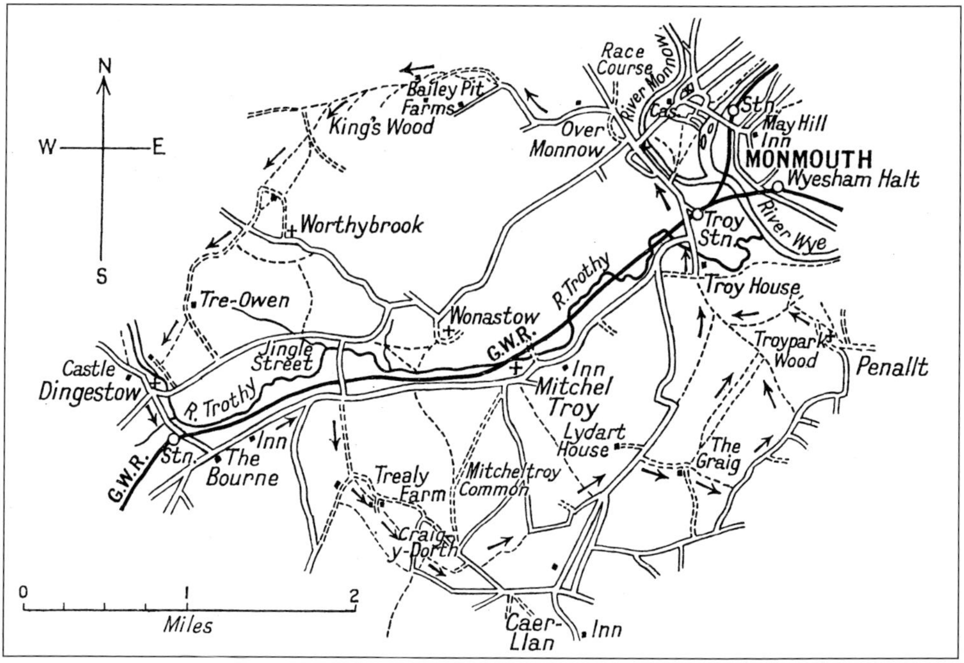

'14XX' class 0-4-2T No. 1422 at Dingestow with the 10.55 am from Pontypool Road in April 1955. *D. Chaplin*

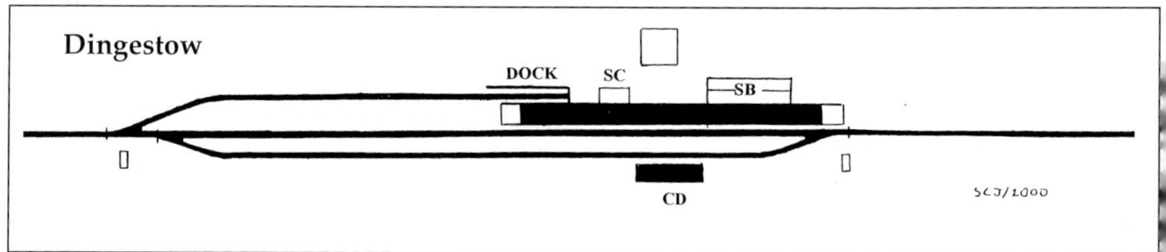

Chapter Five

The Route from Monmouth to Pontypool Road

On departure from Monmouth, Pontypool Road trains immediately entered the 148 yds-long Monmouth tunnel. Emerging from the western portal of the tunnel, down workings crossed the 320 yd Monmouth Old viaduct (13 miles 47 chains), beyond which the single line ran south-westwards beside the winding River Trothy. With the busy A40 road maintaining a parallel course to the left, the railway followed the Trothy for about three miles until, at Dingestow, the river turned away towards the north.

As their train gathered speed on its journey through rural Monmouthshire travellers could, by glancing to the left, discern the outlying hamlet of Mitchel Troy, which derived its name from the neighbouring River Trothy. Troy House, one of the Duke of Beaufort's seats, was an attractive structure that is said to have been designed by Inigo Jones; it contained several interesting fragments from the interior of Raglan Castle, while visitors were also shown an ancient sword that was supposed to have been used by Henry V at the Battle of Agincourt in 1415. In the 1850s, Troy House had been the home of Osmond Wyatt, who had been one of the promoters of the Coleford, Monmouth, Usk & Pontypool Railway and other local lines.

Dingestow

Dingestow station (at one time 'Dinastow', certainly in the 1860s), some 16 miles 42 chains from Ross-on-Wye, had a single platform on the up (north) side of the running line. A short dead-end siding on the up side served coal wharves, and there was a loop siding on the down side of the running line, the latter having a length of around 660 ft. There was formerly a signal box here (from 1892), but it was closed as an economy measure on 19th June, 1931, and the block section was then extended from Monmouth (Troy) to Usk.

The station building was a modest brick-built structure with a small canopy. A grounded van body served as a goods lock-up on the platform, and the former station master's house was sited to the rear of the station, behind the passenger platform. The siding connections were worked from two ground frames known as Dingestow East and West frames; these were brought into use in June 1931, following the abolition of the signal box. The platform was fenced with pale-and-space fencing, and the cattle loading dock was sited alongside the loop siding on the down side.

Dingestow was one of the least important intermediate stations, and in pre-Grouping days it issued only 6,000-7,000 tickets per annum. This meagre figure had dropped to 2,212 passenger bookings in 1929, in which year the station handled only 2,390 tons of goods. Much of this traffic was in the form of incoming 'minerals' or general merchandise; there was only 122 tons of coal traffic in 1929, and just 94 tons of carted traffic. A certain amount of livestock

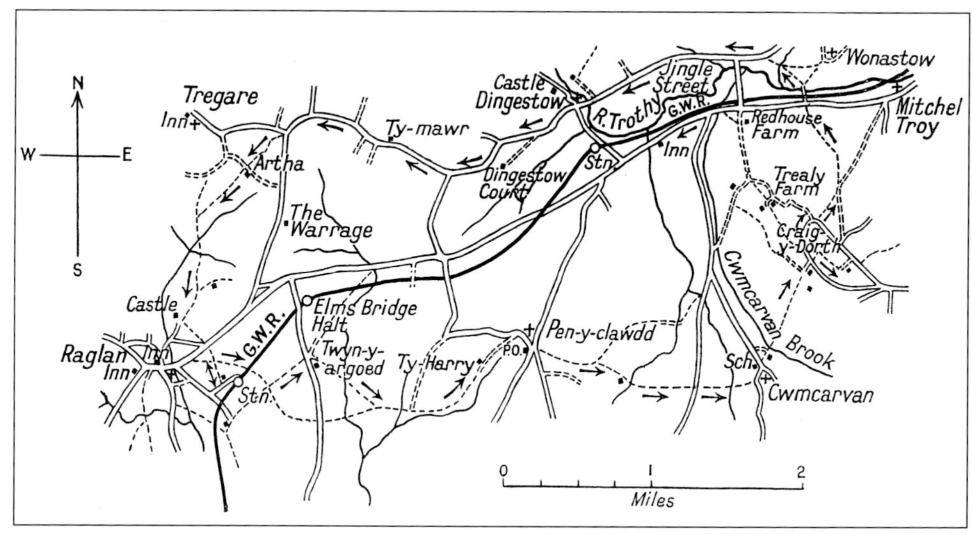

Elms Bridge Halt looking towards Pontypool Road. *Arthur Day*

was dealt with, 10 wagon loads of cattle being received or dispatched in 1932, though in 1936 the station handled 49 wagon loads.

Parcels and small goods consignments were collected or delivered by railway road vehicles from neighbouring Monmouth (Troy) station, and in practice the goods yard at Dingestow was used only for full wagon load traffic. There was one small coal wharf within the yard, and in BR days this was rented by coal merchant W.J. Wadeley. The wharf measured a little over 23 square yards, and in 1954 it received just 240 tons of coal; there was a tiny office measuring 6 ft by 5 ft.

At the beginning of the 20th century Dingestow had a staff of three, and these arrangements lasted until the 1920s. A Great Western Railway staff census dated 1925 reveals that there was, at that time, one class five station master, one signalman and one porter, though by 1929 the staff establishment had been reduced to two men. The abolition of the signal box enabled further staffing economies to be put into effect, and Dingestow had a staff of just one after 1931. By that time this remote stopping place had become little more than a halt.

Traffic dealt with at Dingestow

Year	*taff*	*Receipts (£)*	*Tickets*	*Parcels*	*Goods tonnage*
1903	3	1,041	8,143	1,380	3,069
1913	n/a	1,296	6,548	1,522	4,899
1923	3	1,604	6,742	1,211	2,140
1929	2	1,072	2,212	795	2,390
1930	2	1,307	1,671	993	2,339

Elms Bridge Halt

From Dingestow, the route continued west-south-westwards for a little over two miles to Elms Bridge Halt, the next stopping place (18 miles 66 chains). This unstaffed halt had been opened by the GWR on 27th November, 1933, and it consisted of a short platform on the up side of the line. The platform was of earth and cinder construction, with sleeper revetting. The halt was sited in a grassy cutting, public access being arranged by means of a sloping pathway from the adjacent road overbridge.

Raglan and Raglan Footpath

Beyond, the line curved onto a south-westerly heading, and with the impressive remains of Raglan Castle briefly visible away to the north, down trains descended towards Raglan station (19 miles 44 chains from Ross-on-Wye) on a 1 in 100 falling gradient. Raglan was not an original station, having been opened by the GWR on 1st July, 1876 as a replacement for two earlier stopping places known as Raglan Footpath, sited a little further to the west at 19 miles 53 chains, and Raglan Road at 20 miles 69 chains (*see below*).

On 6th September, 1863, Raglan Footpath station was the setting for a bizarre incident in which a servant girl went into an unexplained trance after being involved in brawl within the 'station house' – the incident being reported as follows by the *Bristol Mercury* on 3rd October, 1863:

GS

SB

Raglan

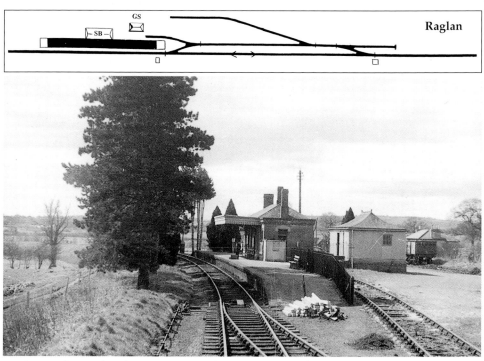

A general view of Raglan station looking towards Pontypool Road on 11th April, 1955.

H.C. Casserley

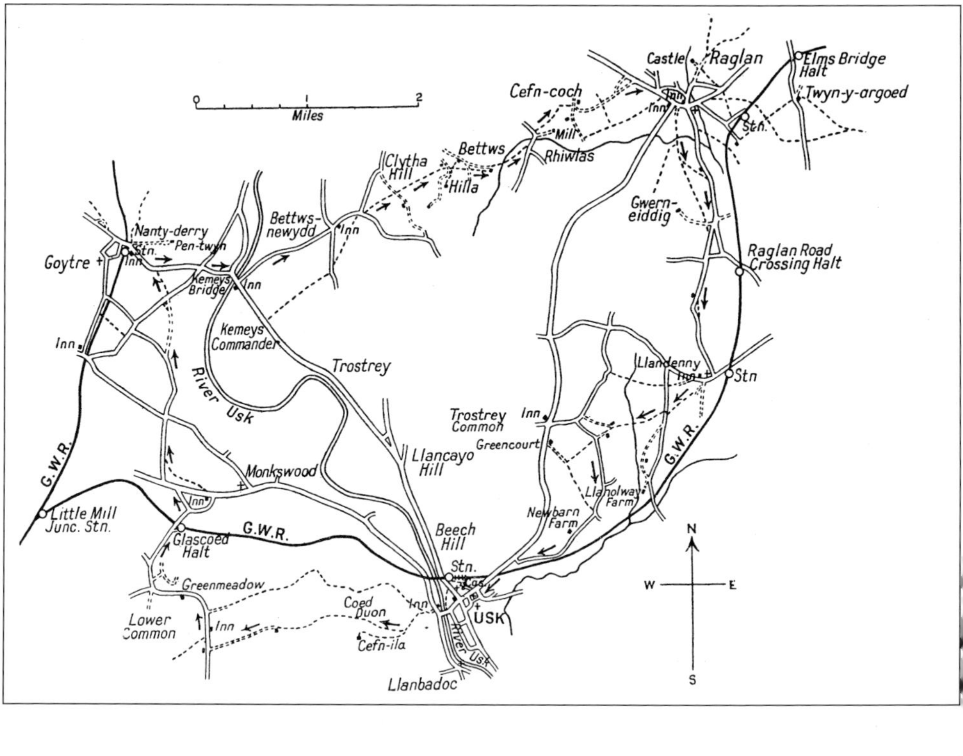

REMARKABLE CASE OF TRANCE - A most remarkable instance of stupor or trance through fright has occurred at Usk. Two servant girls went by train on Sunday the 6th inst, to Raglan Castle, and having spent the day there and taken tea at the house of some friend, the time arrived for returning home by the last train. One servant felt a little impatient to return, but the other girl, who knew that her mistress would expect her back in good time, became very impatient and anxious. This seems to have produced excitement, which was increased during a half mile walk to the station. On arriving there a party of Sunday idlers were collected, and the rain falling in torrents, all were assembled in the small station house of Raglan Footpath. A quarrel ensued in the crowded room, and then a fight, which increased the terror of the girl. At length, in the melee, the door was broken down and the fright of the girl consummated by the door falling on her and her companion; the latter fainted, but the former kept herself up till the train arrived.

When she got in she complained of her blood running cold. She came home in a chilled and half unconscious state, but on her arrival at Usk she went first to the house of the other servant to recover herself. Scarcely had she got in when an hysterical fit suddenly seized her, accompanied with violent convulsions and a state of perfect unconsciousness. Her mistress was sent for, who removed her in a carriage to her house, the Priory, Usk. She was placed in bed, and for ten days she retained a state of complete unconsciousness and of suspension of the senses of sight, hearing, touch, and taste. She neither saw, or heard, or tasted, or felt, and was proof against all attempts to awaken sensibility. Every possible attention was shown her by the kind family, and she was attended by a medical man. Food placed in her mouth in a liquid state she mechanically swallowed, but she neither ate or drank of her own accord, and took notice of no one.

The most remarkable feature of this curious incident is that the events that took place at Raglan Footpath were so vividly imprinted in the victim's mind that, even in an unconscious state, she continued to act out the whole of the evening's events in 'the most theatrical way', accompanied by manifestations of terror and anxiety:

All the conversation she has distinctly repeated - questions, answers, exclamations, expression of impatience, all cleverly given. Every action was imitated - such as eating biscuits, pinning on her shawl, trying on her bonnet, fitting on her gloves, buttoning them, beckoning her friend forward - every word and action coming consecutively in its due place - so that the whole of the evening was, on each repetition, lived over again, and her mistress and others were able to gather from her own lips every minute circumstance of that period, and all that was re-enacted, several times over, with very little variation each time. It is still more remarkable that, now that consciousness has in part returned, she forgets all about the day. The going to Raglan, and all the circumstances, which she minutely detailed, have faded from her memory. Occasional fits of terror still seize her - but in the intervals she is rational and able to converse; yet declares that not a single trace remains on her mind of any event that took place on that Sunday. The case in its detail is a curious one, psychologically and phrenomedically considered.

Raglan's simple facilities comprised a single platform on the up side of the running line, together with a small goods yard containing a coal wharf and a cattle loading dock. The red brick station building was another standard Great Western design, with the usual low-pitched, hipped roof and a projecting platform canopy. These characteristic GWR buildings followed no particular architectural style - though to modern eyes they would probably be regarded as typically Victorian structures, which were solidly and carefully built of the very best constructional materials.

Other structures at Raglan included an enlarged Great Western corrugated iron pagoda shed, provided in 1910, which served as a lock-up for parcels and small goods consignments. This distinctive building was sited behind the station building. The 1912 Railway Clearing House *Handbook of Stations* shows that Raglan then had a 4 ton 10 cwt hand crane, although by the 1930s this facility was no longer available. The track plan incorporated two goods sidings, one of which was arranged as a loop with connections at each end, while the other was a dead-end siding for coal and other 'mileage' traffic. Access to the sidings was controlled from ground frames.

In British Railways' days, the yard contained two wharves which were rented out to local traders. One of these was a coal wharf measuring 41 square yards, and used by Messrs Davies, Jones & Clench Ltd. The other wharf measured 25 square yards, this facility being leased by an agricultural implement firm.

The staffing arrangements at Raglan echoed those at Dingestow, Llandenny and the other small stations on the line, the overall picture being one of rationalization as the GWR attempted to make these isolated outposts pay their way against a background of falling traffic levels. Until the 1930s, Raglan had a staff of two porters under a class four station master, but thereafter the staff establishment was reduced to just two men.

Traffic levels here were very modest, around 10,000 tickets being issued per annum during the Edwardian period, falling to only 1,360 tickets and 30 seasons in 1929, and 1,190 tickets and 23 seasons in the following year. The amount of

Raglan station on 24th March, 1951 with railcar No. 30 working the 7.46 am Pontypool Road to Monmouth train. *Roger Carpenter/W.A. Camwell Collection*

goods traffic dealt with in 1929 was 5,323 tons, while in 1935 4,969 tons were handled. The principal source of goods traffic at Raglan appears to have been incoming minerals, which probably consisted mainly of road-building materials for the local council. In 1938, only 1,511 tons of freight were handled.

In GWR days, collections and deliveries in the Raglan area were made by a Great Western delivery vehicle that was stationed at nearby Usk. This vehicle usually made two deliveries per week, but the system was improved in August 1948, when British Railways arranged a daily collection and delivery service under the newly-introduced 'zonal' scheme.

The volume of passenger traffic at Raglan was somewhat higher than might be expected because, as a minor tourist destination, the station handled a certain amount of incoming traffic, in addition to outgoing passenger bookings. The main attraction here was of course the impressive late Medieval castle, which was sited within easy walking distance of the railway. Although it occupied the site of an earlier Anglo-Norman stronghold, Raglan was essentially a 15th century building, and as such it should really be considered as a castellated manor house - the age of military castle building having already been brought to a close by the introduction of powerful and effective artillery.

Raglan Castle was constructed on a huge scale, and although its massive towers and huge walls were built mainly for reasons of status, it was nevertheless one of the most impressive castles in the British Isles. The building was modernized during the Tudor period, but this mighty structure was finally beaten into ruins by the siege guns of the New Model Army, which forced the castle to surrender to Parliament on 19th August, 1646. The fortifications were then 'slighted', and the buildings were gradually dismantled. The ruins became a tourist attraction during the 19th century, and in 1938 the Duke of Beaufort placed the castle into state guardianship as an Ancient Monument.

Traffic dealt with at Raglan

Year	*Staff*	*Receipts (£)*	*Tickets*	*Parcels*	*Goods tonnage*
1903	3	3,275	10,857	5,627	8,544
1913	3	3,848	10,092	7,229	11,252
1923	3	4,244	8,600	3,119	8,494
1929	3	2,625	1,360	2,891	5,323
1930	3	2,305	1,190	3,054	4,808

Raglan Road and Raglan Road Crossing Halt

From Raglan, the route turned southwards, and after about one mile trains reached the unstaffed stopping place known as Raglan Road Crossing Halt (20 miles 71 chains). The halt consisted of a short platform on the down side, with a level crossing and associated crossing keeper's cottage immediately to the north. It had been opened by the Great Western on 24th November, 1930. The halt was of the usual earth and cinder construction.

Raglan Road Crossing Halt occupied the approximate site of Raglan Road which had closed on 1st July, 1876 with the opening of 'Raglan' at 19 miles 44 chains.

Raglan Road Crossing Halt looking towards Pontypool Road, 11th April, 1955. *R.M. Casserley*

Looking towards the crossing gates and Raglan along the now derelict platform at Raglan Road Crossing Halt. *R.J. Leonard/Kidderminster Railway Museum*

Llandenny

Curving imperceptibly south-westwards, the railway continued to Llandenny (21 miles 62 chains), where the facilities consisted of a single platform and small goods yard on the up side. A minor road crossed the line on the level immediately to the north of the station, and there was a single-storey signal box on the platform beside the station building. The signal box dated from 1892, and it was a typical late Victorian gable roof design.

The station building was similar to that at Dingestow, being a single-storey brick structure, with a low-pitched gable roof. The window and door apertures featured slightly-arched openings, and two chimney stacks protruded through the apex of the slated roof. Examination of the brickwork suggested that the building was of two periods of construction, the western portion being the original part, whereas the eastern end appeared to have been a later extension.

The layout at Llandenny incorporated a crossing loop, somewhat inconveniently sited on the north side of the level crossing, but as there was only one platform two passenger trains were not permitted to cross. On the other hand, two freight trains, or one passenger and one freight working were allowed to pass each other. The loop was long enough to accommodate 22 short-wheelbase goods vehicles, together with a tank engine and brake van (it had been extended in 1909).

Llandenny issued around 10,000 tickets a year during the Edwardian period, decreasing to around 5,000 per annum and around 75 seasons by the late 1920s. Freight traffic showed a similar decline from 5,557 tons in 1913 to 1,351 tons in 1931 and 1,386 tons by 1933. In the following year the station's freight traffic was placed under the control of nearby Usk. The station had a staff of four in the early 1900s. There were no formal arrangements for the cartage of goods traffic, although small parcels or packages could be collected or delivered by railway porter. In later years, 'smalls' traffic was dealt with by road delivery vehicles based at Usk station.

Llandenny had a staff of five during the 1920s, including one class four station master, two signalmen, one porter, and a female gatekeeper at nearby Raglan Road Crossing who, for management purposes, was under the control of the Llandenny station master. Staff reductions during the 1930s brought the staffing establishment down to three, these being the two signalmen and the Raglan Road Crossing gatekeeper.

Traffic dealt with at Llandenny

Year	*Staff*	*Receipts (£)*	*Tickets*	*Parcels*	*Goods tonnage*
1903	4	1,439	9,367	347	3,419
1913	4	2,092	9,335	682	5,557
1923	8	3,039	10,227	891	3,730
1929	9	1,576	4,830	945	2,905
1930	8	1,782	4,943	1,053	3,111

The distant signal on the eastern approach to Llandenny station on 11th April, 1955.
H.C. Casserley

Llandenny station, looking west towards Pontypool Road on 11th April, 1955. The cattle dock and loop can be seen to the left, while the single platform passenger station can be glimpsed on the far side of the level crossing. The layout here was altered around 1909, when the loop siding was extended west towards the level crossing. *H.C. Casserley*

Left: George William Gooch, station master at Llandenny *circa* 1915.

P. Wheeler Collection

Below: Llandenny station on 11th April, 1955, looking west towards Pontypool Road. The two goods sidings can be seen behind the standard 1890s-style GWR signal box.

R.M. Casserley

A 1958 view looking west towards the crossing gates and entrance to the goods yard at Llandenny, with the station building beyond the gates.
The Nelson Museum, Monmouth

Llandenny station building and signal box in 1958, looking east.
The Nelson Museum, Monmouth

A view along the platform at Llandenny towards Pontypool Road, 11th April, 1955.
H.C. Casserley

Cefn Tilla Halt facing Pontypool Road on 10th April, 1955; minimal facilities indeed. The bridge in the background was obviously built for double track. *H.C. Casserley*

Cefn Tilla Halt is framed within the road overbridge in this *circa* 1950s view looking east towards Ross-on-Wye. *The Nelson Museum, Monmouth*

Cefn Tilla Halt

From Llandenny, the railway curved back onto a south-westerly heading as it descended towards the River Usk along the valley of a tributary stream. The landscape visible from the windows of the gently-swaying train was still pastoral, the green fields and scattered farmsteads being typical of many Celtic areas of the British Isles. Despite the noticeable lack of towns or large villages, British Railways decided to open a new halt at a place known as Cefn Tilla, which was roughly mid-way between Raglan and Usk at 22 miles 76 chains. The halt was opened on 14th June, 1954, following an approach to British Railways by Lord Raglan, who suggested that it might attract much-needed passenger traffic to the railway.

The idea of opening the halt was first mooted in 1953, and following a site inspection by Lord Raglan and BR officials, the District Engineer estimated that a sleeper-built platform without ramps could be provided at a cost of £60. In April 1954 the Chief Regional Manager authorized an expenditure of £100, and the halt was soon completed, over 130 passengers being dealt with in the first two weeks of operation between 14th June and 30th June, 1954. In August, the halt attracted 364 inwards and outwards passengers, while in the following month 333 journeys were made to or from Cefn Tilla.

The facilities available here were primitive in the extreme, the halt being no more than a trestle platform on the down side of the line, with a length of just 12 ft. No platform ramps were provided, though the diminutive wooden platform was illuminated by an oil lamp placed in a traditional tapered glass lantern. As there was insufficient room for a nameboard on the platform itself, the name CEFNTILLA HALT was displayed on a board behind the halt. Cefn Tilla functioned as a request stop, and passengers wishing to board a train at this remote place were asked to give a hand signal on the approach of a train.

There was no village, as such, at Cefn Tilla, the name of the halt being derived from an early 17th century manor house known as Cefntilla Court, which was sited about a quarter of a mile to the west of the railway. The nearest settlements to the halt were Gwernesney, Llangeview and Llansoy, all of which were situated on the east side of the line. Cefntilla Court contained several interesting relics of the Napoleonic and Crimean wars, although railway enthusiasts of an older generation would perhaps have been more familiar with Cefn Tilla through its associations with 'Saint' class 4-6-0 No. 2936 *Cefntilla Court*.

Usk

From Cefn Tilla, the single line continued more or less due west for a little over two miles to Usk, the principal intermediate station on the Monmouth to Pontypool Road line. As down trains approached the station, they passed through the 256 yd Usk tunnel, beyond which the single line doubled to form a 16 chain crossing loop. A private siding, known as Davies' Siding, was sited about 10 chains to the east of the tunnel on the up side of the running line. It

The approach to Usk, looking westwards along the single line on 11th April, 1955.
R.M. Casserley

The eastern portal of Usk tunnel facing west towards Pontypool Road on 11th April, 1955; the railway entered this tunnel as a single line, and emerged at Usk station as double track. *H.C. Casserley*

was entered via a siding connection that was facing to the direction of up trains, though in earlier years the layout had been arranged as a loop with connections at each end. The east end connection was taken out in January 1928. The siding, which closed on 28th July, 1937, served a saw mill.

Usk passenger station was 25 miles 14 chains from Ross-on-Wye, and its layout incorporated a physically-detached goods yard, which was sited a little way beyond the passenger station on the west side of Usk viaduct. The latter structure was 60 yards in length, and formed of plate girders supported on masonry piers. The crossing loop continued westwards across the viaduct, which therefore carried a double line of rails.

The passenger station was in a very attractive setting, with steep, wooded cuttings on both sides, and the tunnel mouth immediately to the east. Restricted space meant that the pointwork at the Monmouth end of the crossing loop was actually within the tunnel, so that down trains entered the tunnel on a single line and emerged on a double track! This arrangement was unusual, though by no means unique - another example being found at Haverthwaite, on the Lakeside branch of the Furness Railway.

The main station building was sited on the down platform, and there was a subsidiary waiting room block on the opposite platform. Both of these structures were hip-roofed brick buildings of the now-familiar Great Western standard design. A full-length canopy was provided on the platform side, together with a much smaller canopy on the other side of the main building. The up side waiting room also boasted a small canopy. Architectural details included tall chimneys with 'oversailing' upper courses, and characteristic large-paned windows with slightly-arched heads.

The signal box, which was also of standard Great Western appearance, was situated to the west of the platforms on the up side. The box was similar to those at Dingestow and Llandenny, albeit considerably larger - all three boxes being typical 1890s-style gable roof cabins with small-paned window frames. A GWR-style water crane was available to the west of the platforms on the down side, and this was supplied from a stilted metal tank of the usual Great Western design. All of these structures dated from the major reconstruction that had been carried out at Usk by the GWR in the 1890s. This work was authorized in 1893 and completed by January 1897, when the remodelled station came into full use. The former engine shed and turntable no longer existed by then, but they may have been displaced earlier than this.

The reconstructed station was well-equipped by branch line standards, and in addition to its new brick buildings, Usk was equipped with one of the Great Western's distinctive covered footbridges - the only station between Ross-on-Wye and Pontypool Road to sport such an amenity (apart from Monmouth (Troy)). This feature was, however, taken down at a relatively early date, and public access between the up and down sides of the station was then effected by means of a barrow crossing at the Pontypool Road end of the platforms.

The goods yard was on the down side of the line, and it was entered via a long headshunt that extended westwards from the Pontypool Road end of the crossing loop. The yard contained coal wharves, loading docks, cattle pens and a 5 ton yard crane. It was situated below the level of the running line, and for

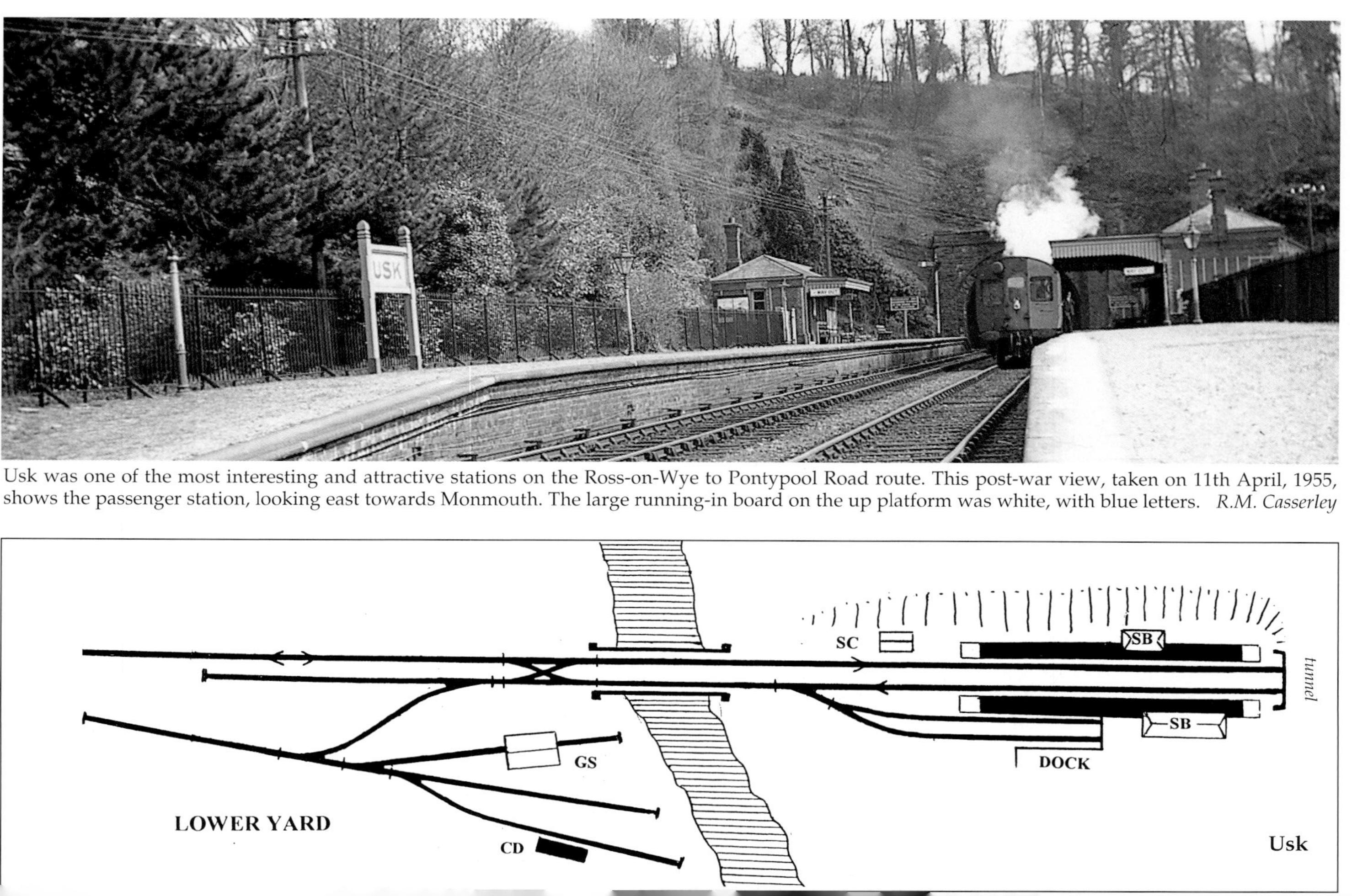

Usk was one of the most interesting and attractive stations on the Ross-on-Wye to Pontypool Road route. This post-war view, taken on 11th April, 1955, shows the passenger station, looking east towards Monmouth. The large running-in board on the up platform was white, with blue letters. *R.M. Casserley*

A fine general view of Usk station looking east towards the tunnel. At the time this photograph was taken the station was being used for goods traffic only. *R.W.A. Jones*

A 1955 view of Usk signal box looking east towards Ross-on-Wye. *Derek Chaplin*

A delightful scene at Usk in post-war years. An ex-GWR railcar has just arrived from Pontypool Road. *Oakwood Collection*

0-6-0PT No. 8461 shunts the morning goods train in the goods yard at Usk on the west bank of the River Usk on 18th April, 1962. By this date the track had been lifted beyond the tunnel at Usk station. *Derek Chaplin*

this reason it was sometimes known as the 'Lower Yard'. There were three dead-end sidings, one of which served a goods shed. Guards and drivers responsible for taking trains down the incline to Usk Lower Yard were instructed to confer in order to decide how many hand brakes should be applied to ensure a safe descent (according to the weight of the train).

Additionally, Usk's goods facilities included two dead-end sidings behind the down platform at the passenger station which were used for horse boxes, and similar forms of traffic. These short sidings were entered via a trailing connection from the down main line, and they were known as 'the bay' and 'the cattle pen' siding. In practice the inner, or bay line, was fenced-off from the adjacent platform, and this limited its usefulness; the outer cattle dock road, in contrast, served cattle pens and a short loading platform. The cattle dock occupied the approximate site of Usk's small engine shed, which had been closed in the Victorian era.

The layout at Usk, with its dispersed goods facilities, meant that the operation of the station was more complicated than would otherwise have been the case. It was usual, at various times, for freight trains to remain at the station for considerable periods of time while the engine performed shunting operations in the main Low Level Yard. It was also necessary for short distance light engine workings to take place between the Low Level Yard and the station, or between the goods yard and Davies' Siding at the east end of the tunnel.

In May 1914, for instance, the 4.10 pm goods working from Monmouth (Troy) to Pontypool Road was scheduled to reach Usk at 5.15 pm, and it did not resume its journey until 7.35 pm. Following the departure of the 5.15 pm down passenger service from Monmouth (Troy) to Pontypool Road at 5.45 pm, the goods engine carried out any shunting that might be necessary at Davies' Siding, this operation being completed before the arrival of the 6.20 pm up service from Pontypool Road at 6.34 pm. Five minutes were normally allowed for the short trip between the goods yard and Davies' Siding, while work at the siding was normally accomplished in about 15 minutes.

In traffic terms, Usk was busier than Dingestow, Raglan or Llandenny, over 30,000 tickets being issued per year during the pre-Grouping period. In 1923, the station issued 30,798 tickets and 236 seasons, though by 1929 these figures had fallen dramatically to just 5,125 tickets and 79 seasons. This catastrophic loss of passenger traffic can probably be attributed to the effects of bus competition. The situation regarding goods traffic was much healthier, 22,083 tons of freight being dealt with in 1913, and 22,752 tons in 1929. The amount of traffic dropped to around 14,000 tons per annum during the mid-1930s, but rose to 27,022 tons in 1938, much of this traffic being building materials.

Cattle traffic was also of considerable importance, 149 wagon loads of livestock being forwarded or received in 1903, rising to 212 wagons in 1913 and around 600 wagon loads per annum during the 1920s. Livestock traffic at Usk declined slightly in the following decade, though in 1931 the station handled 567 wagon loads, falling to 368 wagons in 1934, and then rising once again to 430 wagon loads of cattle in 1936. Carted traffic showed a steady increase from the mid-1930s onwards, and by 1938 the station was dealing with around 4,000 tons of carted traffic per annum.

In 1925 Usk had a staff of 11, including one class three station master, one general clerk, two porters, one working foreman, one goods porter, two signalmen, one goods clerk, one goods guard and one charwoman. Additionally Permanent Way Gang No. 72 was responsible for the section of line between Llandenny and Glascoed. The staffing arrangements at Usk were modified slightly in the 1930s, the foreman being replaced by a checker. In 1930, the payroll expenses were £1,357, against total receipts of £7,881.

Usk itself was a small market town with a population, in the 1930s, of about 1,300. As intimated in Chapter One, the history of this small Welsh town dated back to Romano-British times, Usk having originated around 47 AD as the Roman fortress of *Burrium*. The first unit stationed here was probably part of *Legio XX*, the 20th, or Valerian Legion, which was then attempting to subdue the Silures; later, the legionary fort at Usk was superseded by a more important fort that had been developed by *Legio II* at nearby Caerleon. A small town or *vicus* nevertheless remained at Usk, together with a military supply depot. Numerous Roman artefacts were discovered in and around Usk during the 18th and 19th centuries.

Usk's Medieval castle, which was situated on an eminence overlooking the town, was much smaller than those at Goodrich and Raglan, and it attracted few visitors; writing in the 1920s, Sir Charles Oman stated that the ruined stronghold was in 'in such bad order' and 'so overgrown with ivy, that is hard to get any general view, or to draw certain conclusions'. The castle was, at one time, held by Richard de Clare, the Earl of Striguil and Pembroke who, in 1170, initiated the Norman conquest of Ireland. This ruthless adventurer, better known as Strongbow, was so successful that in the following year King Henry II sailed to Dublin to received the homage of his new Irish subjects.

Other attractions in and around Usk included some delightful riverside scenery along the picturesque Usk Valley, and an interesting old church, that had once formed part of a Benedictine nunnery. In 1891, J.H. Clark recorded that the town stood 'on a considerable tract of ground', its streets forming a square pattern; the buildings were said to be 'very irregular and many of them much dilapidated', though there had been many improvements within a period of about 60 years. The town was 'well drained by means of sanitary pipes', and 'by the help of the Borough funds and Highway and Local Board rates, most of the footpaths' were 'paved or asphalted'.

Traffic dealt with at Usk

Year	*Staff*	*Receipts (£)*	*Tickets*	*Parcels*	*Goods tonnage*
1903	13	9,795	30,957	7,843	18,932
1913	n/a	8,803	31,124	7,001	22,083
1923	8	12,806	30,798	8,421	20,071
1929	9	9,709	5,125	9,614	22,752
1930	8	7,881	4,702	10,478	16,344

Glascoed Halt and Royal Ordnance Factory

From Usk, the railway ran first north-westwards and then more or less due west as it approached its junction with the Newport, Abergavenny & Hereford main line at Little Mill. After about a mile and a half, trains reached the prosaically-named 'Glascoed Factory East Access Halt', which served the eastern parts of Glascoed Royal Ordnance Factory. The halt consisted of a simple platform on the down side of the running line, some 26 miles 66 chains from Ross-on-Wye. This unadvertised stopping place was brought into use for Royal Ordnance Factory workers on 3rd January, 1943.

There was a further unadvertised stopping place at Wern Hir Halt (27 miles 10 chains) which had been opened for workers traffic in January 1939 and would therefore have been particularly useful when the Ordnance Factory was under construction. This makeshift and very temporary workmen's halt appears to have been closed in June 1941 - part of its platform having been utilized during the construction of the nearby West Access Halt, while the remaining portion was removed thereafter.

Continuing westwards, the trains soon reached Glascoed Crossing Halt (27 miles 38 chains). This was another unadvertised workers' halt, which had originally been called 'Glascoed Factory West Access Halt'. This facility was situated on the down side of the line, and there was a level crossing immediately to the west of the platform. The halt was brought into use for ROF workers on 12th June, 1941.

Just five chains beyond Glascoed Crossing Halt, the single line doubled to form a lengthy crossing loop, which extended westwards for a distance of 19 chains. A further platform, known as Glascoed Halt, was situated on the north side of the double-track section at 27 miles 58 chains, while a junction to the east of the platform on the down side gave access to the extensive ROF premises. The junction, which was facing to the direction of up trains, was laid to permit through running to and from Pontypool Road, and it was controlled from a signal box on the up side of the line.

When first opened by the GWR on 16th May, 1927, Glascoed Halt had in fact been sited on the opposite (i.e. down) side of the line, but the halt was moved to its new position in connection with the building of the Royal Ordnance Factory on 22nd April, 1938. The platform was of timber trestle construction; other facilities here included a typical Great Western corrugated iron 'pagoda' hut, together with a nameboard and electric lighting.

Although it was of comparatively recent construction, Glascoed signal box was of traditional appearance. It was sited to the south of the platform, on the up side of the line. This signal box was opened on 21st August, 1938 in connection with the newly-installed crossing loop.

The Ordnance Factory branch diverged south-eastwards into the works complex, a large passenger station being provided for the benefit of wartime ordnance workers, who travelled daily to and from their homes in the Eastern and Western valleys. The platforms at Glascoed ROF station were sited on each side of a triple-tracked layout, and they were by-passed by an array of goods exchange sidings on the north side. Trains for construction workers ran to Glascoed level crossing (no platform) from 24th May, 1938. It is believed that a temporary platform within the site was provided later that year. Royal Ordnance Factory staff began using the station on 6th October, 1940.

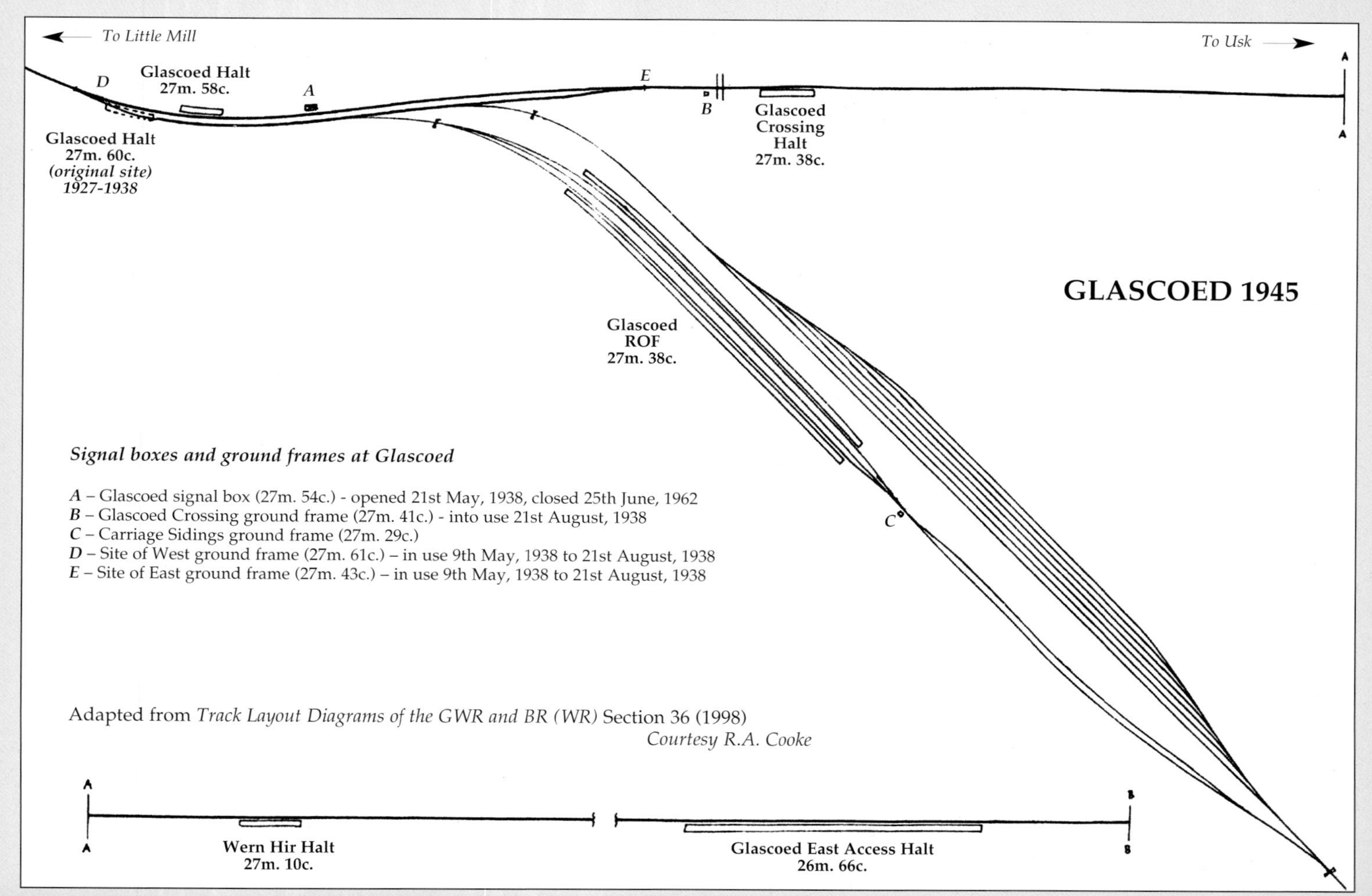
GLASCOED 1945
To Little Mill
To Usk
D
Glascoed Halt
27m. 58c.
A
E
B
Glascoed Crossing Halt
27m. 38c.
Glascoed Halt
27m. 60c.
(original site)
1927-1938
Glascoed ROF
27m. 38c.
C
Signal boxes and ground frames at Glascoed
A – Glascoed signal box (27m. 54c.) - opened 21st May, 1938, closed 25th June, 1962
B – Glascoed Crossing ground frame (27m. 41c.) - into use 21st August, 1938
C – Carriage Sidings ground frame (27m. 29c.)
D – Site of West ground frame (27m. 61c.) – in use 9th May, 1938 to 21st August, 1938
E – Site of East ground frame (27m. 43c.) – in use 9th May, 1938 to 21st August, 1938
Adapted from Track Layout Diagrams of the GWR and BR (WR) Section 36 (1998)
Courtesy R.A. Cooke
Wern Hir Halt
27m. 10c.
Glascoed East Access Halt
26m. 66c.

Glascoed East Access Halt looking towards Pontypool Road, 11th April, 1955. *R.M. Casserley*

Glascoed Crossing Halt, previously known as Glascoed Factory West Access Halt, 11th April, 1955. The crossing ground frame is behind the bracket signal. *H.C. Casserley*

Glascoed Halt, looking east towards Ross-on-Wye during the British Railways' era. The Glascoed signal box visible beyond the platform was opened by the GWR on 21st August, 1938.
Lens of Sutton Collection

Glascoed Halt looking towards Pontypool Road, 11th April, 1955. *R.M. Casserley*

A general view of Glascoed ROF station in the late 1960s.

Lens of Sutton Collection

Little Mill Junction

On departure from Glascoed, down trains proceeded north-westwards for a short distance, before the line commenced a leftwards turn. Having passed beneath two minor road overbridges, the railway crossed an unclassified woodland track on the level, and with the A472 road running parallel on the right, the line converged with the Newport, Abergavenny & Hereford route at Little Mill Junction (29 miles 22 chains).

Little Mill Junction was situated in the 'V' of the junction between the Monmouth and Hereford routes. The first three-platform station closed on 1st July, 1861 and reopened, serving the Monmouth branch only, on 1st May, 1883. A curved platform was provided for branch trains, while the up and down main lines ran through the station on the west side of the branch platform. The station building was a small stone structure of no architectural pretension, its low-pitched slated roof being swept down over the platform to create a modest canopy. Little Mill Junction had a staff of 10 in 1929, including one class four station master, two porters, four goods shunters and three signalmen. The signal box was extended by 6 ft and the 40-lever frame replaced by one of 55 levers on 20th November, 1938. This was to accommodate the additional sidings installed east of the branch line in connection with the working of Glascoed ROF.

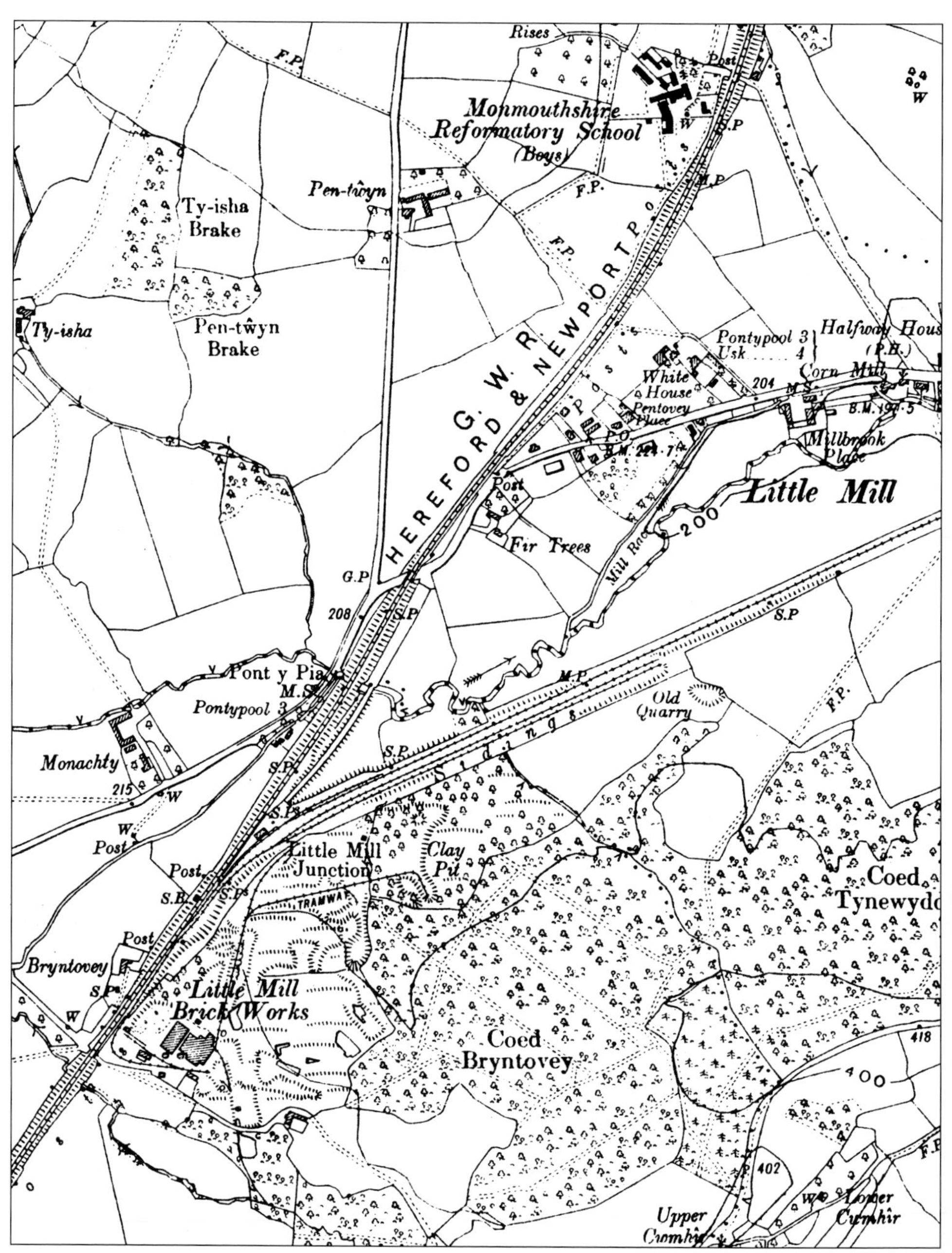

Little Mill Junction. *Reproduced from the 6", 1938 Ordnance Survey Map*

Little Mill Junction, facing Monmouth on 11th April, 1955. Trailer No. 188 stands in the single branch platform. The Newport, Abergavenny & Hereford line is to the left. *R.M. Casserley*

Little Mill Junction facing Pontypool Road on 11th April, 1955. The stone station building can be seen to the right. *R.M. Casserley*

A detailed view of the station building at Little Mill, *circa* 1960s. *Lens of Sutton Collection*

Pontypool Road

From Little Mill Junction, branch trains proceeded south-westwards along the Newport, Abergavenny & Hereford main line for nearly two miles before finally coming to rest in the platforms at Pontypool Road station. Here, the 30 mile 74 chain* journey from Ross-on-Wye came to an end in a busy main line station that served as the junction for several other local lines.

The Newport, Abergavenny & Monmouth Railway reached Pontypool Road on 2nd January, 1854, and on 20th August, 1855 the first section of the Taff Vale Extension line was opened between Pontypool Road and Crumlin Junction. This line was completed throughout to Quakers Yard on 11th January, 1858, and it later became part of an interesting cross-country route between Pontypool Road and Neath. With its connections to the Taff Vale Railway and other busy coal-carrying lines, the Neath to Pontypool Road line brought extra traffic to the Newport, Abergavenny & Hereford main line, and increased the importance of Pontypool Road station.

When first opened the Newport, Abergavenny & Hereford route had joined the Monmouthshire Railway & Canal Company at Coedygric Junction, the Monmouthshire line being used as means of access to Newport. In 1874, the opening of the Pontypool, Caerleon & Newport Railway provided an alternative route between Pontypool Road and Newport (Maindee Junction), and following this, four long distance trains per day were introduced between Cardiff, Pontypool Road, Hereford and the North of England. Meanwhile, the Monmouthshire Railway routes from Newport to Pontypool, Blaenavon and Abersychan were continuing to develop as part of a complex network of lines in the industrial area to the west of Pontypool Road.

By the end of the Victorian period the Pontypool area had become a busy railway centre, with several stations and goods yards. In addition to the main line station at Pontypool Road, there were stations at Pontypool (Clarence

* Pontypool Road station had been rebuilt some ¼ mile further north in 1909.

A postcard view showing the original station at Pontypool Road. *Lens of Sutton Collection*

A pre-1908 view of Pontypool Road, showing the original Newport, Abergavenny & Hereford station buildings and a GWR four-coupled passenger locomotive, which appears to be 'Atbara' class 4-4-0 No. 3382 *Mafeking*. This locomotive was scrapped in 1911, following an accident at Henley-in-Arden. *John Alsop Collection*

Street) on the Neath line, and at Crane Street on the Monmouthshire Railway, together with a number of smaller stations on the surrounding lines.

Pontypool Road station was rebuilt on a new site during the early years of the 20th century, the modernized station facilities being opened on 1st March, 1909. The new station incorporated a spacious island platform, with terminal bays at each end and through lines on either side. The lengthy through platforms could each accommodate two trains, this mode of operation being made possible by the presence of two scissors crossovers, which effectively divided the up and down sides of the station into four platforms. The new station buildings were of the usual Great Western standard design, with extensive canopies over the centre section of the platforms.

The station area was signalled from three signal boxes, which were known as Station North, Station Middle (reduced to a ground frame in September 1957) and Station South. There were further signal boxes at the various junctions and goods yards south of the station (*see Ordnance Survey map opposite*).

In operational terms Pontypool Road was particularly significant in that it was the site of an important motive power depot. Coded 86G by British Railways, the depot was sited to the south of the passenger station amid a complex web of sidings and trackwork. The shed building was of unusual design, being in effect two sheds placed end-to-end. The main building was a classic 'covered roundhouse' depot, with an internal turntable that fed a fan of radiating spurs. The building measured around 250 ft x 175 ft at ground level.

A view looking north of Pontypool Road during the 1908 re-modelling.
John Alsop Collection

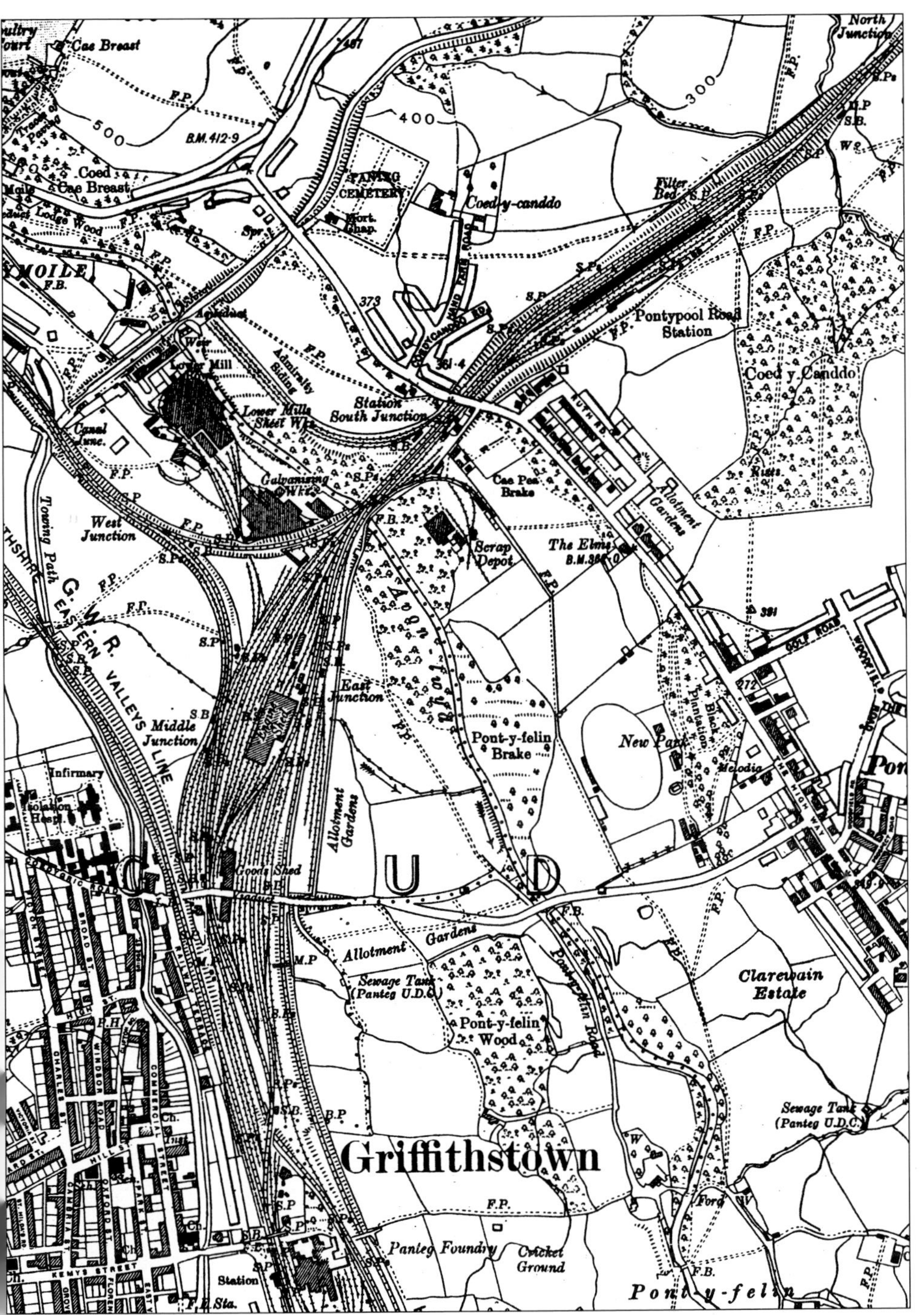

Pontypool Road station is seen top right, the engine shed and goods shed can be seen on the right-hand side of the triangle lines formed by the Newport-Hereford line and the lines heading west towards Pontypool. *Reproduced from the 6", 1938 Ordnance Survey Map*

A panoramic view of the new station at Pontypool Road, which was opened in 1909.
Lens of Sutton Collection

A busy scene on 15th May, 1936 at the south end of Pontypool Road station. Bulldog 4-4-0 No. 3372 *Sir N. Kingscote* is seen centre while to the right is 'Saint' class 4-6-0 No. 2905 *Lady Macbeth*.
V.R. Webster/Kidderminster Railway Museum

A June 1939 view towards the southern end of Pontypool Road shed with an assortment of pannier tanks, Churchward Moguls and even an 'ROD' 2-8-0 visible. *L&GRP*

'74XX' class 0-6-0PT No. 7402 takes on coal at Pontypool Road shed, September 1936. *W. Potter/Kidderminster Railway Museum*

A general view of Pontypool Road station, *circa* 1960s. *Lens of Sutton Collection*

Pontypool Road station, showing details of the signalling, *circa* 1960s. *Lens of Sutton Collection*

Collett '14XX' class 0-4-2T No. 1422 waits with the 10.55 am train to Monmouth (Troy) in the north bay at Pontypool Road station in 1955. *Derek Chaplin*

Ex-GWR railcar No. W30 in the north bay at Pontypool Road in August 1951. *R.W.A. Jones*

Adjoining this building, on the south side, was a slightly smaller, hipped roof building containing eight parallel shed roads, one of which extended northwards into the roundhouse. This smaller building measured approximately 125 ft x 175 ft, the combined length of the roundhouse and straight shed buildings being over 400 ft. There was a large coaling stage, of standard Great Western design, to the north of the roundhouse, together with a range of other facilities including a water tower, water columns, mess rooms and stores.

This large and important shed normally housed around 90 locomotives, ranging from shunting tanks to 'Halls', 'Saints' and other 4-6-0s. At the time of the Grouping Pontypool Road's allocation included 'Saint' class 4-6-0s Nos. 2903 *Lady of Lyons*, 2905 *Lady Macbeth*, 2946 *Langford Court* and 2954 *Tockenham Court*, though the majority of engines shedded there at that time were shunters or heavy freight locomotives such as 'Aberdare' class 2-6-0s Nos. 2616, 2625, 2630, 2634, 2640, 2650, 2665 and 2677, and '28XX' class 2-8-0s Nos. 2805, 2808, 2816, 2820, 2822, 2825, 2826, 2829, 2830, 2834, 2837, 2839, 2842, 2851 and 2857.

At the end of the Great Western era, this busy shed housed a similar assortment of locomotives, many of which were heavy freight locomotives of the '28XX' and '42XX' classes. There were no less than 34 0-6-0PTs, most of which belonged to the ubiquitous '57XX' class, together with 'Hall' class 4-6-0s Nos. 4912 *Berrington Hall*, 4932 *Hatherton Hall*, 4933 *Himley Hall* and 5975 *Winslow Hall*, and 'Grange' class 4-6-0s Nos. 6820 *Kingstone Grange*, 6840 *Hazeley Grange* and 6875 *Hindford Grange*.

The elevation of the main station building at Pontypool Road, *circa* 1953.

Lens of Sutton Collection

Chapter Six

The Final Years

The end of the war in Europe was followed, on 26th July, 1945, by the election of a radical Labour Government that had promised to nationalize rail transport, the coal industry and other major industries. Accordingly, at midnight on 31st December, 1947, the Ross-on-Wye to Pontypool Road line became part of the Western Region of British Railways. However, this momentous change of ownership made very little difference to the way in which the railway was operated, and the lines to Monmouth continued to serve the public as they had done during the Great Western era.

The only obvious change after 1948 concerned the liveries of locomotives and rolling stock. Until Nationalization the engines seen at Monmouth had been painted green, but in BR days they appeared in drab, unlined black (in theory, passenger locomotives such as the Collett '14XX' class 0-4-2Ts should have been painted in LNWR-style lined-black livery, but in practice this colour scheme was rarely applied to Western Region engines). A similar change of livery transformed the appearance of branch rolling stock, the traditional GWR chocolate-and-cream colour scheme being replaced by an overall maroon livery, while the GWR diesel railcars were adorned in a new carmine-and-cream livery scheme.

Post-War Train Services

The Ross-on-Wye to Pontypool Road route was still worked as two sections, with a connecting service on the Wye Valley branch between Monmouth (Troy) and Severn Tunnel Junction. There was little attempt to provide through workings, though some services from Pontypool Road ran through to Monmouth (May Hill) for the benefit of school children during school term time only. Services were, by the early 1950s, restricted to weekdays only.

There were five trains each way on the eastern section of line between Ross-on-Wye and Monmouth (Troy), together with a limited number of short-distance shuttle workings between Ross and Lydbrook Junction. In the up direction, trains left Monmouth (Troy) for Ross at 9.36 am, 12.55, 3.51, 6.05 and 8.25 pm, while in the reverse direction Monmouth trains departed from Ross-on-Wye at 8.15, 11.08 am, 3.00, 5.10 and 7.30 pm. Freight traffic was conveyed by a pick-up service that was scheduled to leave Ross-on-Wye at 12.05 pm, and reach Monmouth at 1.40 pm. The return working departed from Monmouth (Troy) at 2.45 pm.

The train service in operation on the Pontypool Road to Monmouth (Troy) line provided four passenger workings and one pick-up freight service each way. In the up, or eastbound direction, the first train of the day departed from Pontypool Road at 7.46 am and reached Monmouth (Troy) at 8.30 am; this service then ran through to Monmouth (May Hill), where it terminated. The

ROSS-ON-WYE, MONMOUTH, and PONTYPOOL ROAD.
(Third class only).

Miles	Down	Week Days only.																				
		mrn		mrn		mrn		mrn X		mrn		non X	aft		aft		aft X	aft		aft X	aft	
	Ross-on-Wye ¶ .... dep	7 5	..	..	..	8 22	..	..	..	1110	..	..	2 5	..	3 12	..	..	5 10	..	..	7 30	..
4	Kerne Bridge A..............	7 15	..	..	..	8 32	..	..	..	1120	..	..	2 15	..	3 22	..	..	5 20	..	..	7 40	..
5¾	Lydbrook Junction..........	7 18	..	..	..	8 36	..	..	..	1125	..	..	2 19	..	3 26	..	..	5 24	..	..	7 46	..
[illegible]	Symonds Yat..................	..	..	..	..	8 41	..	..	..	1130	..	..	2 23	..	3 31	..	..	5 29	..	..	7 51	..
12¾	Monmouth (May Hill).......	..	..	..	..	8 50	..	..	..	1143	..	..	..	..	3 42	..	..	5 38	..	..	8 0	..
13	" (Troy) 89 .... arr	..	..	..	..	8 55	..	..	..	1145	..	..	..	..	3 44	..	..	5 42	..	..	8 8	..
	dep	..	..	..	..	..	..	9 10	..	..	..	12 0	..	..	..	..	3 51	..	..	7 5	..	..
16½	Dingestow ¶..................	..	..	..	..	..	..	9 16	..	..	..	12 6	..	..	..	..	3 57	..	..	7 11	..	..
19½	Raglan ¶.....................	..	..	..	..	..	..	9 24	..	..	..	1215	..	..	..	..	4 6	..	..	7 19	..	..
21¾	Llandenny......................	..	..	..	..	..	..	9 31	..	..	..	1222	..	..	..	..	4 13	..	..	7 26	..	..
25	Usk ¶..........................	..	..	8 50	..	..	..	9 39	..	..	..	1230	..	..	..	..	4 21	..	..	7 34	..	..
29	Little Mill Junction.[125	..	..	8 59	..	..	..	9 52	..	..	..	1242	..	..	..	..	4 32	..	..	7 45	..	..
31	Pontypool Road 8), 122, ar	..	..	9 4	..	..	..	9 57	..	..	..	1246	..	..	..	..	4 38	..	..	7 55	..	..

Miles	Up	Week Days only.																				
		mrn	mrn X		mrn	mrn	mrn X		aft	aft		aft	aft X		aft		aft	aft		aft X	aft	
	Pontypool Road......... dep	..	7 46	..	8 33	..	11 0	..	Saturdays only.	..	..	..	2 30	..	..	..	..	..	..	6 5	..	..
2	Little Mill Junction ¶.......	..	7 52	..	8 37	..	11 5	..		..	..	..	2 34	..	..	..	..	..	..	6.10	..	..
6	Usk	..	8 5	..	8 47	..	1116	..		..	..	..	2 45	..	..	..	..	..	..	6 22	..	..
9¼	Llandenny ¶.................	..	8 10	..	..	..	1123	..		..	..	..	2 52	..	..	..	..	..	..	6 29	..	..
11½	Raglan ¶......................	..	8 18	..	..	..	1128	..		..	..	..	2 58	..	..	..	..	..	..	6 37	..	..
14½	Dingestow......................	..	8 27	..	..	..	1137	..		..	..	..	3 6	..	..	..	..	..	..	6 45	..	..
18	Monmouth (Troy) 89... arr	..	8 33	..	..	..	1143	..		..	..	..	3 12	..	..	..	..	..	..	6 51	..	..
	dep	..	..	..	..	9 38	..	..		1 20	..	..	..	..	4 15	..	..	6 5	..	..	8 10	..
18½	(May Hill)	..	..	..	..	9 40	..	..		1 24	..	..	..	..	4 18	..	..	6 9	..	..	8 13	..
23½	Symonds Yat..................	..	..	..	..	9 50	..	..		1 34	..	2 30	..	..	4 28	..	..	6 19	..	..	8 23	..
25¾	Lydbrook Junction	7 40	..	..	..	9 57	..	..	1210	1 40	..	2 35	..	..	4 33	..	4 50	6 24	..	..	8 28	..
27	Kerne Bridge A ¶............	7 44	..	..	..	10 1	..	..	1214	1 44	..	2 39	..	..	..	..	4 54	6 28	..	..	8 33	..
31	Ross-on-Wye (*below*).... arr	7 53	..	..	..	1010	..	..	1223	1 53	..	2 48	..	..	..	..	5 3	6 37	..	..	8 43	..

A Station for Goodrich Castle. **X** Third class only. Limited accommodation.
¶ "**Halts**" at Walford between Ross-on-Wye and Kerne Bridge; at Elms Bridge, between Dingestow and Raglan; at Raglan Road Crossing between Raglan and Llandenny; and Glascoed between Usk and Little Mill Junction.

Ross-Monmouth-Pontypool Road services as shown in *Bradshaw's Guide* September 1945.

Ross-Monmouth-Pontypool Road timetable, 27th September, 1948.

Table 114 ROSS-ON-WYE, MONMOUTH, and PONTYPOOL ROAD—(Third class only)

Miles		Week Days only														
		a.m	a.m	a.m	a.m X	a.m		non X	p.m	p.m X	p.m E	p.m	p.m X	p.m		
	Ross-on-Wye ...... dep	7 5	..	8 15	..	11 0	..	..	3 0	..	4 30	5 15	..	7 30	..	..
3½	Walford Halt..............	7 12	..	8 22	..	11 6	..	..	3 6	..	4 37	5 22	..	7 36	..	..
4	Kerne Bridge	7 14	..	8 25	..	11 9	..	..	3 10	..	4 40	5 24	..	7 39	..	..
5½	Lydbrook Junction.........	7 18	..	8Z36	..	1114	..	..	3 14	..	4 43	5 29	..	7 45	..	..
7½	Symonds Yat...............	..	..	8 40	..	1119	..	..	3 19	..	..	5 34	..	7 50	..	..
12½	Monmouth (May Hill)..	..	..	8 55	..	1130	..	..	3 28	3 45	..	5 43	..	8 0	..	..
13	" (Troy).. arr	..	..	8 57	..	1133	..	..	3 31	3 47	..	5 47	..	8 3	..	..
	dep	..	..	..	9 10	..	..	12 0	..	3 48	..	..	7 5	..	..	..
16½	Dingestow..................	..	..	..	9 16	..	..	12 6	..	3 53	..	..	7 11	..	..	..
18¾	Elms Bridge Halt.........	..	..	..	..	..	..	1212	..	3 59	..	..	..	..	..	..
19½	Raglan ....[Halt	..	..	..	9 24	..	..	1215	..	4 1	..	...	7 19	..	..	..
20¾	Raglan Rd. Crossing	..	..	..	9 28	..	..	1219	..	4 4	..	..	7 23	..	..	..
21¾	Llandenny	..	..	..	9 31	..	..	1222	..	4 6	..	..	7 26	..	..	..
25	Usk	..	8 50	..	9 39	..	..	1230	..	4 13	..	..	7 34	..	..	..
27	Glascoed Halt	..	8 55	..	9 46	..	..	1236	..	4 18	..	..	7 40	..	..	..
29	Little Mill Junction.....	..	8 59	..	9 52	..	..	1242	..	4 22	..	..	7 45	..	..	..
31	Pontypool Road.... arr	..	9 4	..	9 57	..	..	1246	..	4 26	..	..	7 51	..	..	..

Miles		Week Days only														
		a.m	a.m X	a.m	a.m	a.m X		p.m	p.m X	p.m	p.m E	p.m	p.m X	p.m		
	Pontypool Road.... dep	..	7 46	8 33	..	11 0	..	..	2 30	..	..	..	6 10	..	..	..
2	Little Mill Junction....	..	7 50	8 37	..	11 5	..	..	2 34	..	..	..	6 14	..	..	..
5	Glascoed Halt..........	..	7 54	8 41	..	11 9	..	..	2 38	..	..	..	6 18	..	..	..
6	Usk	..	8 5	8 47	..	1116	..	..	2 45	..	..	..	6 25	..	..	..
9¼	Llandenny..............	..	8 12	..	..	1123	..	..	2 52	..	..	..	6 32	..	..	..
10¼	Raglan Rd. Crossing	..	8 15	..	..	1125	..	..	2 55	..	..	..	6 35	..	..	..
11½	Raglan ....[Halt	..	8 18	..	..	1128	..	..	2 58	..	..	..	6 38	..	..	..
12¼	Elms Bridge Halt......	..	8 21	..	..	1131	..	..	..	..	..	..	..	..	..	..
14½	Dingestow..............	..	8 27	..	..	1137	..	..	3 6	..	..	..	6 46	..	..	..
18	Monmouth (Troy) arr	..	8 33	..	..	1143	..	..	3 12	..	..	..	6 52	..	..	..
	dep	..	..	..	9 36	..	..	1250	3 35	3 51	..	6 5	..	8 25	..	..
18½	" (May Hill)..	..	..	..	9 40	..	..	1253	3 37	3 54	..	6 9	..	8 28	..	..
23½	Symonds Yat............	..	..	..	9 50	..	..	1 3	..	4 4	..	6 19	..	8 38	..	..
25½	Lydbrook Junction.....	7 40	..	..	9 55	..	..	1 8	..	4 9	4 55	6 24	..	8 43	..	..
27	Kerne Bridge	7 43	..	..	10 0	..	..	1 12	..	4 12	4 59	6 28	..	8 46	..	..
27½	Walford Halt............	7 46	..	..	10 4	..	..	1 15	..	4 15	5 2	6 30	..	8 51	..	..
31	Ross-on-Wye ....arr	7 53	..	..	1010	..	..	1 21	..	4 22	5 8	6 37	..	8 58	..	..

E Except Saturdays.

X Limited accommodation.

Z Arrive 8 28 a.m.

next up service left Pontypool Road at 11.00 am and reached Monmouth (Troy) at 11.43 am, while afternoon services departed from Pontypool Road at 2.30 and 6.10 pm, reaching Monmouth (Troy) at 3.12 and 6.52 pm respectively. The 2.30 pm ran through to May Hill in school term time, whereas the 6.10 pm terminated at Monmouth (Troy).

In the opposite direction westbound, or down, services left Monmouth (Troy) at 9.00 am, 12.00 noon, 4.06 and 7.05 pm. The first down service ran empty from Monmouth (May Hill), having earlier worked through to the latter station as a school train. Similarly, the 4.06 pm started its journey from May Hill during school term days. Freight traffic was conveyed by an up working that left Pontypool Road at 8.50 am, and returned from Monmouth (Troy) at 5.00 pm - the engine having been used for local shunting and trip work during the interim.

Post-war train services on the Wye Valley branch comprised five passenger and one freight working each way. In the up direction, Wye Valley passenger services left Monmouth (Troy) at 9.00, 11.50 am, 3.55, 6.06 and 8.15 pm, while in the down direction trains arrived from Chepstow at 8.42, 11.29 am, 1.45, 5.00 and 8.10 pm. A freight service left Chepstow at 8.15 am and was scheduled to reach Monmouth (Troy) at 10.45 am, although in reality this working often terminated at Tintern; if the train ran through to Monmouth, it was timetabled to depart for Severn Tunnel Junction at 12.20 pm.

Fares, during the early British Railways period, were still comparatively cheap. In 1949, for example, a third class return ticket from London Paddington to Monmouth (Troy) cost only 39*s*. 6*d*., while the return fare from Monmouth to Birmingham Snow Hill was 22*s*. A third class return fare from Usk to London cost 41*s*. 10*d*., and a corresponding ticket to Birmingham cost 24*s*. 5*d*. Children's tickets cost half the adult fares, while first class tickets cost roughly 50 per cent more than ordinary third class tickets. In addition, most stations sold a wide range of reduced fare tickets including cheap day returns, excursions, and circular tour tickets.

In locomotive terms, the lines from Ross-on-Wye to Monmouth and from Monmouth to Pontypool Road remained a bastion of Great Western influence. The familiar ex-GWR diesel railcars continued to operate most of Monmouth's passenger services, the Wye Valley and Pontypool Road routes being worked by diesel cars during the early 1950s, whereas the Ross & Monmouth branch train was normally worked by a Collett '14XX' class 0-4-2T and a single auto-trailer.

Ex-Great Western diesel railcar No. 13, which had first been employed in the area during the 1930s, was noted at work on the line in September 1954, while car No. 4 appeared on local branch workings in October 1953. Two other railcars used on the Monmouth routes during the BR period included Nos. 27 and 31. On occasions, the rostered diesel railcar would fail, and push-pull sets would then appear on the Wye Valley or Pontypool routes while, in 1957, one of the diesel cars was withdrawn from service as a result of its poor condition. Meanwhile, pick-up goods services continued to be steam-worked on all three lines.

The usual passenger engines seen at Monmouth during the post-war period were '14XX' class 0-4-2Ts, Nos. 1404, 1420, 1421, 1422, 1423, 1445, 1455, 1456 and

'14XX' class 0-4-2T No. 1455 is seen with a passenger train at Symond's Yat in 1949. Note that the passing loop was still intact at this time. *R.W.A. Jones*

In this view of Symond's Yat, '57XX' class 0-6-0PT No. 8776 pauses with a passenger train of rather mixed stock. It is taken about five years later than the previous view and the passing loop has been removed and a camping coach is now *in situ*. *R.W.A. Jones*

A trio of passenger services in the up platform at Monmouth (Troy) on 1st September, 1953. Railcar No. W21 (*front*) will work a train to Chepstow, while sister railcar No. W30 is on a Pontypool Road service. At the rear is '14XX' class 0-4-2T No. 1455 with a train for Ross-on-Wye.
W. Potter/Kidderminster Railway Museum

Once again we see three passenger services at Monmouth (Troy) with railcar No. 30 ready to work the 9.10 am to Pontypool Road. In the up platform '14XX' class 0-4-2T No. 1445 and auto-trailer No. W174 will form the 9.25 am to Ross-on-Wye. Obscured by the footbridge in the up platform is Collett '64XX' class No. 6415 and auto-trailer No. W153 which will form the 9.10 am to Newport, via the Wye Valley line, 24th March, 1951. *Roger Carpenter/W.A. Camwell Collection*

Auto-trailer No. 33 has just arrived at Monmouth (Troy), accompanied by a '14XX' class 0-4-2T, with a train from Ross-on-Wye in February 1949. *John Edgington*

This 59 ft 6 in. auto-trailer, No. W207W, was photographed at Monmouth (Troy) on 11th April, 1955. It had been built by the Gloucester Carriage & Wagon Co. in 1906 as steam railmotor No. 75. It was withdrawn in December 1956. *H.C. Casserley*

1460 being among the regular performers. Collett '54XX' and '64XX' class auto-fitted panniers also appeared on local passenger workings, No. 5414 being kept on standby for about three years for service on the Wye Valley route while '64XX' class 0-6-0PTs Nos. 6412, 6426, 6430 and 6439 also turned up at Monmouth on various occasions during the 1950s.

As mentioned in Chapter Three, the Ross-on-Wye to Pontypool Road route was worked mainly by tank engines, although in pre-Grouping days small tender engines had sometimes been used on freight or excursion workings. There was a reappearance of tender locomotives in BR days in the form of Collett '2251' class 0-6-0s, and these engines continued to work on the line after the withdrawal of passenger services. One of the engines known to have appeared on the Ross & Monmouth branch was '2251' class 0-6-0 No. 2286.

Apart from the '2251' class 0-6-0s, the usual form of motive power on branch freight workings during the 1950s was the Collett '57XX' class 0-6-0PTs. Classified in the '4F' power group by BR, these hard-working locomotives were more than capable of handling local freight workings on the Ross & Monmouth, Wye Valley and Pontypool Road routes. Numerous '57XX' class panniers appeared on the line, some random examples being Nos. 3737, 3728, 3789, 5765, 7707, 7712, 8701 and 9619. A summary of the principal locomotive classes employed on the Ross-on-Wye to Pontypool Road route is given in the table below.

Some Locomotives used on the Ross to Pontypool Road Line

Class	*Type*	*Typical Numbers*
Armstrong '517'	0-4-2T	216, 222, 468, 526, 534, 536, 545, 574, 576, 845, 979, 1164, 1422, 1432, 1465, 1476
'Metro'	2-4-0T	632, 1455, 1462
'2021'	0-6-0ST	2066, 2131, 2140, 2160
'1016'	0-6-0PT	1062
'1076'	0-6-0PT	1183, 1570, 1609
Collett '14XX'	0-4-2T	1404, 1406, 1420, 1421, 1422, 1423, 1432, 1445, 1455, 1456, 1460, 1463
Collett '74XX'	0-6-0PT	7412, 7416, 7420
Collett '64XX'	0-6-0PT	6412, 6426, 6430, 6439
Collett '57XX'	0-6-0PT	3737, 3728, 3789, 5765, 7707, 7712, 8701, 8776, 9619
Collett '54XX'	0-6-0PT	5414
Collett '56XX'	0-6-2T	6693
Hawksworth '94XX'	0-6-0PT	8461
Armstrong Goods	0-6-0	116, 392, 516, 658, 782, 875, 1083
Dean Goods	0-6-0	2333, 2341, 2355, 2562, 2568, 2577
Collett '2251'	0-6-0	2286
Churchward '45XX'	2-6-2T	4503, 4533, 4588
GWR Railcar		4, 13, 14, 27, 30, 31

Closure of the Monmouth to Pontypool Road Line

In retrospect, the late 1940s and early 1950s were a time of more or less complete stagnation in which little attempt was made to run the line economically, yet few people could imagine a time when rural branch lines would finally cease to exist. The one significant innovation in early BR days was the appearance of the new halts at Cefn Tilla and Hadnock, and an improved train service, which must be seen as a final attempt to stimulate traffic growth at a time when Government policies and the insidious growth of road transport were poised to inflict massive damage upon Britain's nationalized railway system.

In 1953, BR pointed out that the four trains each way on the section of line between Monmouth and Usk were carrying very few passengers. Although the line from Little Mill Junction to Usk was still needed in connection with freight traffic, the remaining part of the route was clearly unremunerative, and it was intimated that closure was a distinct possibility. Alarmed at this threat to their transport system, farmers, local authorities and other rail users protested vigorously, and as a result it was agreed that the railway would be retained for a six month trial period. Furthermore, there would be a much enhanced train service between Pontypool Road and Monmouth (Troy).

The new timetable commenced on 14th June, 1954, from which date local travellers were given a choice of no less than 11 trains each way - this being the best train service ever provided on the bucolic Monmouth to Pontypool Road route. In the up direction, eastbound workings departed from Pontypool Road at 6.45, 7.46, 9.55, 10.50, 11.55 am, 12.50, 2.30, 3.44, 5.10, 6.10 and 7.55 pm. Balancing down services left Monmouth (Troy) at 7.35, 9.00, 10.43, 11.48 am, 12.45, 1.50, 3.48, 4.55, 6.05, 7.05 and 8.45 pm, while an additional evening train was provided in each direction on Thursdays and Saturdays only.

In connection with this ambitious new timetable, BR also introduced a comprehensive range of cheap tickets from branch stations to Newport, Cardiff, Chepstow, Hereford, Abergavenny, Gloucester, Cheltenham and other destinations, while the new halt at Cefn Tilla was brought into use in conjunction with the improved timetable. The intensified train service was, moreover, extensively advertised through the medium of local newspapers, posters and handbills which were freely distributed throughout the area served by the railway.

Sadly, the post-war years were a period of acute decline for rural railways such as the Monmouth to Pontypool Road route. With the end of petrol rationing and the increasing use of private road transport, these lines began to lose what little passenger and freight traffic still remained, and in these circumstances closures and retraction became inevitable. In the case of the Monmouth to Pontypool Road line it was clear that, despite the enhanced train service, the line was still losing money, and BR therefore decided that the branch would revert to a service of just four trains each way with effect from 7th February, 1955.

The decision to close the line between Monmouth and Usk had, in fact, been taken by BR managers in December 1954 on the basis that the experimental train service had demonstrated that the branch could never be placed in a satisfactory financial position. The original plans for closure of the line were therefore revived, and in accordance with the normal closure procedures, the Transport Users' Consultative Committee (TUCC) for Wales & Monmouthshire was asked to consider the closure proposals in the light of experience derived from the six-month period of experimental operation.

This decision caused considerable dismay among rail users, some of whom felt that BR had deliberately provided too many extra trains. Figures published at the end of 1954 revealed that the Monmouth to Pontypool Road line had carried 7,943 passengers in the six-month period between June and November 1953, whereas the railway had attracted 15,158 passengers during the experimental six-months trial period between June and November 1954. The increased number of passenger bookings had generated additional revenue, but at the same time operating costs had risen from £4,560 in 1953 to £9,120 in 1954 because the revised train service had required two diesel cars and two train crews in place of the single unit that had previously been employed.

There was a general feeling that the railway authorities had rigged the experimental train service to ensure that the line would not pay its way. One local councillor pointed out that they had asked BR for an improvement in travelling facilities, hoping merely for revised train times and perhaps one or two additional trains that would provide viable connections with main line services. Perversely, BR had virtually tripled the branch train service, thereby incurring increased operating costs that had obviously wiped out the extra income obtained from additional ticket sales for local journeys.

It was also pointed out that the diesel cars that had become such a familiar feature of the line's operation seemed to have been replaced by more expensive steam trains, while other people complained that there had been no attempt to arrange a Sunday service to encourage leisure travel in the picturesque Wye Valley area.

The TUCC inquiry was held at Cardiff on 29th March, 1955, and as might be expected, there were large numbers of objections from all sections of the community. Mr W.J. Wadeley, the Dingestow coal merchant, complained that if the railway was closed he would have to travel five miles in order to obtain his supplies in Monmouth, while the Monmouth Rural Community Council argued that replacement bus services would not be able to get people to work during periods of inclement weather. Lord Raglan asked if the line could be worked more efficiently as a light railway, although in reply BR argued that there was insufficient traffic for any form of rail service in such a sparsely populated district.

Crucially, the Chairman of the inquiry noted that, although the County and other councils had been approached by the TUCC secretary, four of the main local authorities had 'offered no opposition'. The Monmouth Borough Council and the Monmouth Rural District Council had both objected, and indeed the RDC had sent a deputation of three councillors, including S.W. Jones of Raglan and E.J. Porter of Llandenny, to oppose the closure. These local councillors were able to present a whole range of arguments against the proposed closure, but unfortunately, their case was compromised by the fact that Monmouth itself would not be losing its train service.

A special train ran during September 1956 conveying Roman Catholic pilgrims from Swansea (High Street) to Usk where they visited a shrine. The motive power provided was unusual and came in the form of Collett '56XX' class 0-6-2T No. 6693. *R.W.A. Jones*

During Autumn 1957 the Pontypool Road-Usk section was used for driver training for newly allocated Cardiff (Canton)-based diesel multiple units. A dmu is seen here parked opposite Usk signal box on 12th October, 1957. *R.W.A. Jones*

The British Railways representatives, in contrast, were able to demonstrate convincingly that the railway was unremunerative, and perhaps inevitably, the TUCC agreed to the proposed closure by 10 votes to two. This information was made known to the Monmouth Rural District Council on the following Friday, and in sombre mood Councillor E.J. Porter reported that only two members of the TUCC had shown any interest in their case; he thought that most of the committee members had come from areas to the west of Cardiff. Councillor S.W. Jones added that the Rural District Council representatives had been 'just a lone voice in the wilderness', and he regretted that none of the other local authorities had bothered to attend the TUCC meeting.

In May 1955, BR announced that the passenger service between Pontypool Road and Monmouth (Troy) (exclusive) would be withdrawn with effect from 13th June, on which date the section of line between Monmouth and Usk would be closed to all traffic. Alternative passenger services would be provided by the Western Welsh and Red & White Omnibus companies, while the existing arrangements for the collection and delivery of goods and parcels traffic in the area served by the railway would be maintained by British Railways road vehicles operating from Monmouth and Usk. Alternative arrangements for dealing with livestock, coal and other full wagon load traffic would still be available at Usk and Monmouth (Troy) stations.

In the event, external events intervened before the official closure could be implemented. Labour relations on the recently-nationalized railways deteriorated during the early 1950s, mainly because the three railway unions insisted that railwaymen's pay should reflect the growth of other industrial wages throughout the wider economy. In 1954 the Government and the employers capitulated to union demands, and granted wage increases. At this juncture, inter-union rivalry intervened, and ASLEF, the footplatemen's union insisted that drivers and firemen should receive higher pay to ensure their 'differentials'. As a result, they called a national strike on Saturday 28th May, 1955.

The strikers had very few supporters, the general consensus being that their demands were selfish and counterproductive. Around 17 per cent of the enginemen, most of whom belonged to the National Union of Railwaymen, remained at work, and this enabled a skeleton train service to be provided on some lines. A settlement was reached on 14th June, but as this was the day after the Little Mill to Monmouth route should have closed, there were no last day ceremonies. The branch had, for all intents and purposes, closed on Saturday 28th May, on which day ASLEF had ceased work.

The withdrawal of passenger services did not entail complete closure, and goods trains continued to run from Pontypool Road to Usk. There was, moreover, still a considerable amount of traffic at the western end of the line between Little Mill Junction and Glascoed Ordnance Factory, and this ensured that the signal box at Glascoed was retained for several years after the cessation of passenger traffic. The truncated section between Glascoed and Usk was reduced to one-engine-in-steam operation in May 1959, a wooden train staff lettered 'Glascoed-Usk' being kept in Glascoed signal box for that purpose.

If goods workings or light engines were required to work through to Usk when the signal box at that station was closed, there were arrangements

The SLS Centenary Special arrives at Usk hauled by '57XX' class pannier tank No. 4668 on 12th October, 1957. A dmu can be seen near the bridge over the river in the distance. *R.W.A. Jones*

Another view of the SLS Centenary Special at Usk on 12th October, 1957. This time looking towards the tunnel mouth and Monmouth. Note the passengers using the board crossing, the footbridge having been removed many years earlier. *The Nelson Museum, Monmouth*

whereby signalmen could be sent out on up workings from Glascoed. On such occasions the Glascoed signalman sent a 'Blocking Back' signal to Little Mill Junction and returned the token to the instrument. He then reversed points No. 18 in Glascoed signal box and lowered the up starting signal, so that the train could draw towards the Glascoed up advanced starting signal. After returning the up loop to up starting signal to danger and Points No. 18 to normal the signalman handed the wooden train staff to the driver and instructed him to proceed.

With the Glascoed signalman on the footplate, the up train could then pass Glascoed up advanced starting signal at danger, while on arrival at Usk the train was halted at the up home. The signalman having opened Usk signal box, it was possible for any necessary shunting operations to take place as normal. When this work was completed, the signalman at Usk conferred with his afternoon counterpart at Glascoed, and upon obtaining the latter signalman's permission the train or light engine was able to return to Glascoed.

These arrangements were subsequently modified, and with the closure of Glascoed signal box on 25th June, 1962 one-engine-in-steam operation was introduced throughout between Little Mill Junction and Usk, a wooden single line staff being kept in Little Mill Junction box. The connection to the Royal Ordnance Factory sidings at Glascoed was worked by a hand lever, the points being secured by a padlock and chain which could be unlocked by a key on the Train Staff. At Usk, up trains had to be brought to a stand at a stop board that was sited 55 yards to the west of the goods yard, the guard being responsible for all movements beyond the stop board and the safe operation of all remaining points and connections. The section of line from Glascoed to Usk was closed on 13th September, 1965.

The eastern section of line between Usk and Monmouth was not lifted for several years, and it remained in a derelict condition with a length of track removed. On 12th October, 1957 the Midland Area of the Stephenson Locomotive Society arranged an enthusiasts' special to commemorate the centenary of the Usk to Monmouth line, and as the abandoned part of the route was still in reasonably good condition BR agreed to restore the missing section of line to facilitate the running of a through train. The two-coach special left Pontypool Road at 2.00 pm and returned from Monmouth (Troy) at 4.00 pm, the return fare being five shillings. Motive power, on this occasion, was provided by '57XX' 0-6-0PT No. 4668.

2nd - SPECIAL ARRANGEMENT
STEPHENSON LOCOMOTIVE SOCIETY
(MIDLAND AREA)
Special Train in connection with
USK – MONMOUTH CENTENARY
12th OCTOBER, 1957
Pontypool Road to Glascoed, Usk, Llandenny
Raglan, Dingestow and Monmouth (Troy)
and Back
(W) (1266)
For conditions see over
0250 0250

Ticket from the Stephenson Locomotive Society railtour of 12th October, 1957.
Stephen J. Berry

No. 4668 is seen with the SLS Centenary Special as it prepares for the return journey at Monmouth (Troy) on 12th October, 1957. *R.W.A. Jones*

No. 4668 on the return trip with the SLS Centenary Special at Dingestow on 12th October, 1957. *R.W.A. Jones*

Closure of the Ross & Monmouth Branch

The withdrawal of passenger services from the Pontypool Road to Monmouth section left Monmouth with two distinct rail services, from Ross-on-Wye, and from Chepstow via the Wye Valley route. There was no attempt to work the remaining lines on a Chepstow to Ross-on-Wye axis, and the former Ross & Monmouth and Wye Valley routes continued to operate with different locomotives and train crews.

In common with many other rural lines throughout Britain, the Ross & Monmouth branch was never regarded as a particularly remunerative route. This problem was compounded by a method of accounting adopted when dealing with branch lines, which treated them in isolation from the main line British Railways system and thereby ignored the 'network effect'. It was impossible properly to ascertain the true value of local lines, and as a result the calculations of profit and loss were based purely upon the traffic receipts generated on the branch lines themselves.

Conversely, the cost of operating and maintaining local lines such as the Ross & Monmouth route were only too obvious, and viewed in this light very few branch lines were really profitable. In the case of the Ross & Monmouth line, it was abundantly clear that the branch was carrying very few passengers, and it therefore came as no real surprise when, in 1958, it was announced that BR was seeking to withdraw passenger services from the Ross & Monmouth branch between Monmouth (Troy) and Ross-on-Wye, and also from the Wye Valley branch between Chepstow and Monmouth. The proposed closure would result in a situation whereby Monmouth became completely isolated from the national railway system.

The news that BR was intending to close both of Monmouth's remaining rail links evoked a storm of protest. Numerous objections were received from organizations as diverse as the National Farmers' Union (NFU), Wesley Guild Holidays Ltd, the National Union of General & Municipal Workers, Monmouthshire County Council, Monmouth Rural District Council, and private individuals such as Mrs Mary Hartill of Newent, who was 'shattered at the news of the intended closure of that superb stretch of line along the Wye Valley'.

The Herefordshire branch of the NFU claimed that the proposed closure would strike a severe blow at the rural community, and 'perhaps lead to the withdrawal of freight facilities', which would have very adverse effects on the agricultural industry. With admirable perspicacity, the NFU objectors argued that the methods of accounting adopted by the British Transport Commission in seeking to prove that the line was 'unremunerative' could be used to prove that whole sections of the railway system were uneconomic. The farmers' representatives suggested that the threatened lines should be regarded as useful feeders to the main line, and worked as cheaply as possible with diesel cars and unstaffed stations.

The reference to diesel units is significant in that the Ross & Monmouth and Wye Valley branch lines had reverted to push-pull operation at the end of 1957, most trains being formed of steam locomotives and auto-cars. This was clearly

Table 114

ROSS-ON-WYE and MONMOUTH

WEEK DAYS ONLY—(Second class only)

Mls		am			am			am		pm Will not run after 6th Sept.		pm			pm		pm		pm Will not run after 6th Sept.	
—	**Ross-on-Wye** ¶ dep	7 5	..	..	8 15	..	..	11 0	..	1 50	..	3 0	..	..	4E30	..	5 15	..	7 0	..
3¼	Walford Halt	7 12	..	..	8 22	..	..	11 6	..	1 56	..	3 6	..	..	4E37	..	5 21	..	7 6	..
4	Kerne Bridge	7 14	..	..	8 25	..	..	11 9	..	2 0	..	3 9	..	..	4E40	..	5 24	..	7 9	..
5½	Lydbrook Junction	7 18	..	..	8 30	..	..	11 13	..	2 3	..	3 13	..	..	4E43	..	5 28	..	7 13	..
7¼	Symonds Yat	..	..	..	8 34	..	..	11 18	..	2 8	..	3 18	..	..	..	..	5 33	..	7 18	..
10¾	Hadnock Halt	..	..	..	8A39	..	..	11A24	..	..	..	3A24	..	..	..	..	5A39	..	7A24	..
12½	**Monmouth** (May Hill)	..	..	..	8 45	..	..	11 29	..	..	..	3B40	..	..	..	..	5 44	..	7 29	..
13	" (Troy) ¶ arr	..	..	..	8 48	..	..	11 33	..	..	..	3 42	..	..	..	..	5 47	..	7 32	..

Mls		am			am			pm		pm Will not run after 6th Sept.		pm		pm			pm		pm Will not run after 6th Sept.	
—	**Monmouth** (Troy) ¶ dep	..	..	..	9 36	..	..	12 45	..	..	..	3 51	..	..	..	..	6 5	..	8 37	..
½	" (May Hill)	..	..	..	9 39	..	..	12 48	..	..	..	3 54	..	..	..	..	6 8	..	8 40	..
2¼	Hadnock Halt	..	..	..	9A43	..	..	12A51	..	..	..	3A57	..	..	..	..	6A11	..	8A42	..
5¾	Symonds Yat	..	..	..	9 50	..	..	12 58	..	2 25	..	4 4	..	..	..	..	6 18	..	8 50	..
7½	Lydbrook Junction	7 35	..	..	9 55	..	..	1 3	..	2 30	..	4 9	..	4E55	..	..	6 24	..	8 55	..
9	Kerne Bridge	7 38	..	..	10 0	..	..	1 7	..	2 33	..	4 13	..	4E59	..	..	6 28	..	8 59	..
9¾	Walford Halt	7 41	..	..	10 3	..	..	1 10	..	2 36	..	4 16	..	5E 2	..	..	6 32	..	9 3	..
13	**Ross-on-Wye** ¶ arr	7 48	..	..	1010	..	..	1 17	..	2 43	..	4 23	..	5E 8	..	..	6 39	..	9 9	..

A Calls to take up or set down. Passengers wishing to alight must give notice to the Guard at the previous *stopping* station and those desiring to join should give the necessary hand signal to the Driver.   B Arrive Monmouth (May Hill) 3 29 pm

E Except Saturdays

¶ Bus services operate between: **Ross-on-Wye and Coleford; Coleford and Lydney; Coleford and Monmouth; and Coleford and Lydbrook.**

BR public timetable for Ross and Monmouth services, 1958.

a retrogressive step, particularly in view of the long tradition of railcar operation on Monmouth's branch lines. Opponents of closure also pointed out that there had been little attempt to introduce more efficient methods of operation on the threatened lines - which had continued to be worked on the Victorian system with fully-staffed stations, mechanical signalling, and manned level crossings. It seemed that BR was determined to close the Ross & Monmouth and Wye Valley lines at any cost.

Several of the objectors referred to what appeared to be a progressive deterioration in terms of timetables and the poor reliability of locomotives and rolling stock. There was a perceived lack of co-ordination between the Wye Valley and Ross & Monmouth branches, and little attempt was made to provide connections with main line trains to and from London. Moreover, many people felt that the two branch lines could have been worked as one continuous cross-country route between Chepstow and Ross-on-Wye, an added benefit from this mode of operation being the opportunity for BR to develop May Hill as Monmouth's main station, so that travellers from Chepstow and the Wye Valley route would no longer have to change trains at Troy in order to reach the town centre.

On a more generalized level, there were widespread fears that the closure of the railway would impede the development of tourism in the Wye Valley area, which would be detrimental to the economy of the entire district. Several isolated villages would be completely cut-off, causing obvious hardship to the villagers concerned. A further objection concerned the needs of workers who travelled daily by train to the Edison Swan wire works at Lydbrook.

A particular complication arose as a result of the 'cross-border' nature of the Ross & Monmouth branch, which meant that the closure would have to be considered by both Welsh and English areas of the TUCC. Strictly speaking, no less than three committees would be involved, but it was agreed that to expedite the closure process, the Wales & Monmouthshire committee would act on behalf of the other two committees.

The closure was discussed at length by the TUCC at a meeting held at the Beaufort Arms in Monmouth on Thursday 25th September, 1958. At that meeting, it was agreed that the objectors had made a very good case for retention of the rail links, although the TUCC chairman pointed out that if the two threatened lines were retained for a period of three years the accumulated loss would be 'at least £60,000'. This loss might be reduced by the reintroduction of diesel railcars, though even then, there was 'every prospect of a substantial loss continuing'. At that point, the chairman closed the meeting, and said that the proceedings would be resumed in the Angel Hotel Cardiff, on the following day.

The resumed meeting opened with a discussion on the costs of providing a replacement bus service, and there was considerable debate in respect of the expenses quoted by BR for the replacement of two '14XX' class locomotives for the Wye Valley line and one '14XX' class engine for the Ross & Monmouth route. To many critics, these figures simply did not add up, although the BR representatives present at the meeting were able to produce some baffling explanations in relation to the renewal and depreciation costs for a 40-year-old tank engine.

MONMOUTH
and its
RAILWAYS

Photographic Souvenir
and
Historical Notes

in connection with the

LAST PASSENGER TRAIN

on the

MONMOUTH - ROSS and
MONMOUTH - CHEPSTOW

branches of the Western Region
of British Railways

(formerly Great Western Railway)

SUNDAY, 4th JANUARY, 1959

Organised by

THE STEPHENSON LOCOMOTIVE SOCIETY
(Midland Area)

being the first Rail-Tour of the Golden Jubilee Year of the Society

---

The sincerest thanks of the Society are made to Mr. M. D. Greville (*Railway World*, July, 1958), and Rev. W. J. P. Shireh... (*Memorials of Monmouth* No. 6—Railway... to quote historical matter from their article...

037

STEPHENSON LOCOMOTIVE SOCIETY
(MIDLAND AREA)
SPECIAL LAST TRAIN TOUR of former
ROSS and MONMOUTH RAILWAY
and former WYE VALLEY RAILWAY
(latterly Great Western Railway)
SUNDAY, 4th JANUARY, 1959
Birmingham (Snow Hill), Chepstow, Tintern, Redbrook-on-Wye, Monmouth Troy, Symonds Yat, Lydbrook Jct., Ross, Monmouth Troy, Chepstow, Sudbrook Branch, Severn Tunnel Jct. and Birmingham (Snow Hill).
(W) (8228)
For conditions see over

037

Souvenir programme and ticket issued for the Stephenson Locomotive Society's special on 4th January, 1959. *John Debens*

The chairman conceded that 'it was a very serious matter that a county town should be isolated from the passenger rail network', but he felt that the traffic potential of the Wye Valley area was very small. Other committee members agreed that the prospect of increasing traffic by the introduction of new diesel units was extremely remote, although they were reluctant to recommend outright closure.

It was eventually decided that the British Transport Commission should be allowed to carry their closure plans into effect, with the proviso that the trackwork and other infrastructure between Chepstow, Monmouth and Ross-on-Wye should be left *in situ* for a period of three years 'to facilitate a possible restoration of passenger train services, for which diesel units may then be available and the cost of operating the same be covered to a sufficient extent to justify their introduction'.

Following this compromise decision, BR was able to proceed with the closure of the two lines concerned, and it was announced that passenger services would be withdrawn between Monmouth (Troy) and Ross-on-Wye, and between Chepstow and Monmouth, with effect from 5th January, 1959. As this was a Monday, the doomed branch lines would be closed on Saturday 3rd January, which would be the last day of regular operation.

As usual on such occasions, the lines carried many extra travellers on their final day of operation, while large numbers of people turned out to see and photograph the last trains. One of the locomotives in service on the last day of regular operation was Collett '14XX' class 0-4-2T No. 1455, while the final train was strengthened to five coaches to accommodate large numbers of extra travellers. Before the last up train left Monmouth (Troy), veteran traveller Mrs Olive Tate presented the driver, William Soule, with a Union Flag and a card inscribed 'Au revoir, old push and pull. Thank you'; Mrs Tate had used the line for 40 years.

At Symond's Yat, station master E.J. Bartlett, who had worked at the station for 13 years, was presented with an inscribed clock in recognition of his services to the travelling public, while the historic nature of the occasion was underlined by the drinking of champagne that had been given by a local hotelier who was sorry to see the demise of the railway. On arrival at Ross-on-Wye, the last up train was welcomed by the Ross Town Band playing *Auld Lang Syne*, while champagne was offered to the train crew.

A special last train was arranged by the Midland Area of the Stephenson Locomotive Society on Sunday 4th January, 1959. This working left Chepstow at 11.20 am and, travelling via Tintern and Monmouth, it worked through to Ross-on-Wye. The train consisted of eight coaches, with '64XX' class 0-6-0PT No. 6412 at one end and sister engine No. 6439 at the other, both locomotives being turned out in spotless green livery. No. 6412 was driven by driver A. Bowen and fired by J.M. Thomas, while No. 6439 was driven by C. Barratt and fired by O.J. Williams. Both crews had been provided by Newport Ebbw Junction shed. The guard was Frank Jones of Newport.

The special left Chepstow at 11.30 am, bearing a headboard proclaiming that it was the 'LAST TRAIN MONMOUTH - ROSS'. On arrival at Monmouth, a pilot driver boarded the leading engine, and the eight-coach excursion then proceeded along the Ross & Monmouth branch, with an intermediate stop at

The SLS 'Last Train' pauses at Ross-on-Wye on Sunday 4th January, 1959; No. 6412 has just brought the eight-coach special into the station.

Sister engine No. 6439, coupled at the other end of the train, prepares to depart from Ross on the final down working to Monmouth on 4th January, 1959.

Two views of Symond's Yat taken from the roof of the last train! *Above:* View looking north on 4th January, 1959, enthusiasts record the historic occasion as they photograph No. 6412. *Below:* View looking south with, at the other end of the eight-coach train, No. 6439 in the distance.

(Both) D.K. Jones

Symond's Yat. A large crowd awaited the arrival of the train at Ross-on-Wye, where the locomotives were able to take water. The special left Ross-on-Wye at 1.55 pm, and having returned to Chepstow, the railtour concluded with a visit to the Sudbrook branch; the fare for this historic last day special was 10*s*. 6*d*. from Chepstow or 22*s*. 6*d*. inclusive of a cheap day return from Birmingham.

As it had been agreed that the Ross & Monmouth route would be left *in situ* for a period of three years, there were hopes that the railway might be re-opened with a service of diesel railcars. At one stage, the local council expressed an interest in purchasing the line so that it could be worked as a tourist amenity during the summer months, although in the event this idea was never seriously pursued. In the interim, the booking office at Monmouth (Troy) remained open for the sale of tickets, while the privately-run refreshment room continued to serve the public!

Hadnock Halt and siding and Symond's Yat station were closed completely, and the line was abandoned between east of Monmouth (May Hill) and Lydbrook Junction, though goods facilities were retained elsewhere on the route. In this truncated form, the surviving sections of the line might have found a role in the modern railway network, but sadly, the 1960s were the Beeching era, when the Government of the day seemed more interested in closing railways than in developing them. Perhaps inevitably, the remaining sections of line were slowly whittled away, although the final closures were a protracted process.

The Final Years

The subsequent history of the lines from Ross-on-Wye to Monmouth, and from Monmouth to Pontypool Road is a sorry tale of piecemeal closure and abandonment. As usual in the case of freight-only lines, it is by no means easy to identify the precise dates at which the last movements of rolling stock actually took place, but the sequence of official closures was as follows.

Monmouth (Troy) signal box closed on 27th March, 1960 and the layout was rationalized, what remained being controlled from a new ground frame. The section between Monmouth (Troy) and east of Monmouth (May Hill) (12 miles 15 chains) was retained for the Ministry of Food siding traffic until 6th January, 1964, while public freight traffic survived at Kerne Bridge and Lydbrook Junction until 10th August, 1964 and 2nd November, 1964 respectively. Thereafter, Lydbrook Junction continued to be used for private siding traffic until 1st November, 1965, when the final section of line between Lydbrook Junction, Ross-on-Wye and Grange Court was closed to all traffic. Monmouth (Troy), meanwhile, lost its goods facilities with effect from 6th January, 1964 when the Wye Valley branch was closed north of Tintern quarry.

As the pace of closure and rationalization gathered momentum throughout the 1960s it became increasingly clear that every railway in the area was threatened with total extinction. The demise of the Ross & Monmouth branch left the former Hereford, Ross & Gloucester line in splendid isolation as the only passenger line for miles around. Local travellers hoped that rationalisation had gone far enough, but in 1963 the line from Grange Court to Hereford was listed for closure in the notorious Beeching report on 'The Reshaping of British Railways'.

The Beeching proposals were rushed into effect, and despite the usual protests, the railway from Ross-on-Wye to Hereford, Rotherwas Junction was closed with effect from Monday 2nd November, 1964. This deletion did not entail the complete closure of Ross-on-Wye station because the line from Grange Court was still needed in connection with remaining freight traffic to Lydbrook Junction. Sadly, even this residual fragment of the erstwhile Ross & Monmouth Railway succumbed to closure on 1st November, 1965, and with its demise the final section of the railway network around Ross-on-Wye passed into oblivion.

The fate of the remaining section of line between Little Mill Junction and Glascoed was somewhat happier in that this truncated fragment of the Coleford, Monmouth, Usk & Pontypool Railway continued to carry military stores and equipment to and from the ordnance factory, which has remained in operation as a defence-related establishment.

Pontypool Road became one of the very few stations left in the area, although its facilities were much reduced. The long cross-country route to Crumlin, Aberdare and Neath was closed to passengers from Monday 15th June, 1964, the last trains being run on Saturday 13th June. Pontypool Road motive power depot was closed in May 1965, and in the next few months the station was itself reduced to local status. The number of trains calling at Pontypool Road was reduced from 14 each way in May 1965 to eight northbound and six southbound by May 1968. The train service was later improved, though the infrastructure at this once-busy junction was reduced to little more than a bare island platform.

The abandoned stations and goods yards between Ross-on-Wye and Little Mill Junction were left to their various fates, some stations and halts being demolished, while others were adapted for new roles. At Raglan, for example, the station became a council depot, while Monmouth (Troy) station found a new lease of life as a road haulage depot and coal yard.

In 1992 the corrugated iron pagoda shed at Raglan was purchased by the Dean Forest Railway for use as a workshop at Norchard. This was a comparatively easy task, as GWR pagodas were designed as lightweight pre-fabricated structures that could be assembled at any site. The removal of a permanent building to a new site obviously entails much greater effort, but this is what eventually happened to the standard GWR station building at Monmouth (Troy). In this instance, the building was dismantled and then painstakingly reassembled, stone-by-stone, at Winchcombe on the Gloucestershire Warwickshire Railway.

This somewhat drastic action was deemed necessary because the original brick station building at Winchcombe had been demolished. Although Monmouth (Troy) was of stone construction, this characteristic Great Western building was seen as an ideal replacement for the original Winchcombe building, which had been a standard GWR station building of a slightly later design. The reconstruction took place in 1990, and in this way a historic Victorian building was put back into use on a preserved railway.

Ross-on-Wye station was demolished in the mid-1970s, and its site is now occupied by an industrial estate. Revival, in a sense, nevertheless took place in the following decade when the Severn Valley Railway (SVR) constructed a standard GWR station building at Kidderminster, using plans of the Ross-on-Wye building. The reconstructed station features a lengthened centre portion, while

Station buildings in dilapidated condition at Llandenny in January 1989. *(Both) P. Wheeler*

A class '47' diesel with a train from Glascoed's Royal Ordnance Factory is seen approaching the site of Little Mill Junction station on 8th May, 1989. *P.G. Barnes*

A Newport-bound unidentified class '156' 'Sprinter' passes Little Mill Junction signal box as class '47' No. 47330 waits at the home signal with a train from Glascoed Royal Ordnance Factory on 8th May, 1989. *P.G. Barnes*

Two views of Monmouth (Troy) station during its preparation for removal to Winchcombe. *Above:* Platform canopy detail. *Below:* The stone work is marked up prior to dismantling.
(Both) L.W. Knott

A general view of the station building at Monmouth (Troy) with work in hand for dismantling and removal to Winchcombe. *L.W. Knott*

Looking splendid in its new location, the former Monmouth (Troy) station building renders useful service as the Gloucestershire Warwickshire Railway's replacement station at Winchcombe, 14th August, 1997. *P.G. Barnes*

A general view of the derelict remains at Monmouth (Troy) goods yard in 2001. *J. Kennedy*

A close up of Monmouth (Troy) goods shed in 2001. *J. Kennedy*

A view looking along the trackbed over the bridge which carried the railway across the river at Usk in 2001. *J. Kennedy*

the long wing at the eastern end of Ross-on-Wye has been replaced by a projecting wing at right angles to the main block at Kidderminster. Otherwise, the new SVR terminal building is a very close replica of its prototype at Ross-on-Wye.

The rebuilt station building at Winchcombe and the replica structure at Kidderminster serve as two tangible memorials to the Ross-on-Wye to Pontypool Road line. The preservation movement has also managed to save some of the locomotives that once worked on the vanished route, three notable survivors being Collett '64XX' class 0-6-0PTs Nos. 6412 and 6430, and more especially Collett '14XX' class 0-4-2T No. 1420.

Conclusion

The rise and fall of the Ross-on-Wye to Pontypool Road line is, in many ways, a microcosm of British railway history. Planned during a period of unparalleled material progress, the Ross & Monmouth and Coleford, Monmouth, Usk & Pontypool railways were designed as infrastructure projects that would stimulate economic development and thereby benefit all sections of the local community. This was, in fact, what eventually took place, and although the two railways were not in themselves particularly profitable, they gave rise to several useful 'spin offs', including the development of agriculture, and the start of the modern tourist industry.

Sadly, the growth of alternative forms of transport after World War I caused irreparable damage to the railway, making it impossible for the line from Ross to Pontypool Road to survive as a purely commercial undertaking. Although the railway continued to play an important role as a social service in an isolated

The bow string girder bridge over the River Wye between Monmouth (Troy) and Monmouth (May Hill) still makes a splendid scene in this view taken in 2001. *J. Kennedy*

The plate girder bridge which carried the railway over the River Usk in 2001. Usk lower yard was situated on the western side of the river (the side on which the photographer is standing) and the station was situated on the eastern side of the river. *J. Kennedy*

Raglan station now serves as a council depot and yard. The station building is seen from the forecourt on 1st June, 2001. *P.G. Barnes*

A view from the trackbed of the platform side of Raglan station looking towards Pontypool Road, 1st June, 2001. *P.G. Barnes*

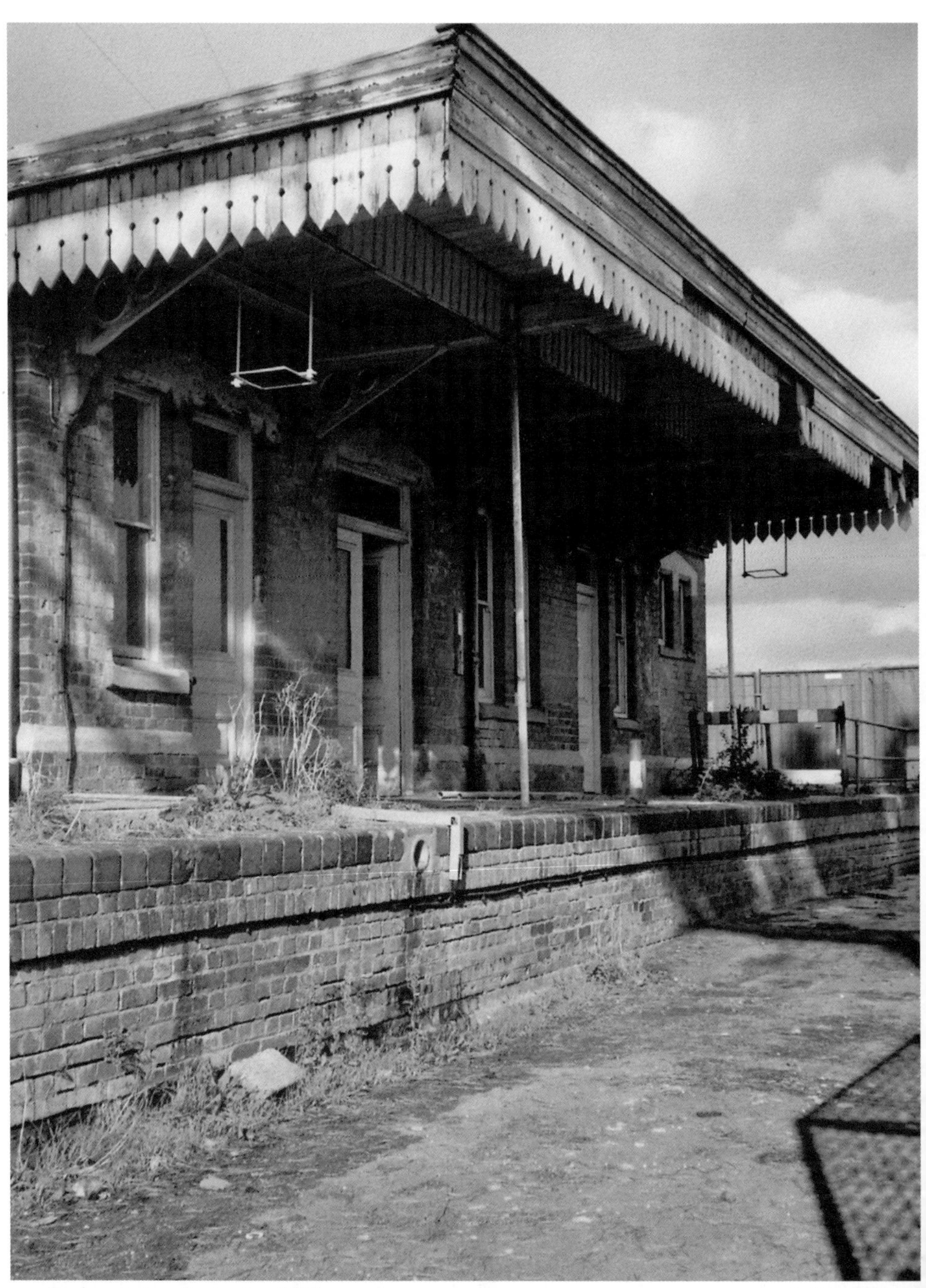

Raglan station, September 2007. *J. Kennedy*

Usk goods shed on 17th October, 2007. *(Both) P. Evans*

Usk tunnel on 17th October, 2007. *(Both) P. Evans*

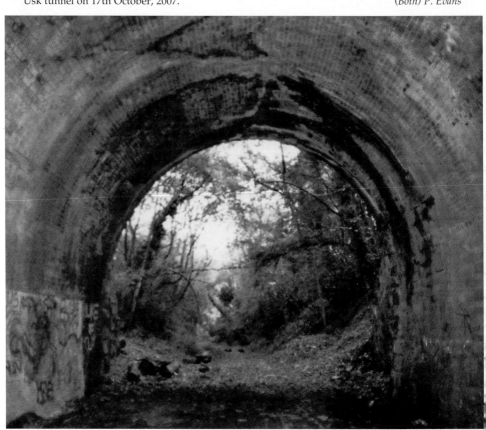

rural area, the Conservative Government of the 1950s was not prepared to use taxpayers' money to sustain this lightly-used branch line as a social amenity, and in these circumstances, closure became inevitable.

By any reasonable analysis, the decision to withdraw passenger services between Ross-on-Wye, Monmouth and Pontypool Road was probably the right one, though it was clearly regrettable that a historic county town such as Monmouth should have been deprived of its entire railway system. On a more contentious level, it could be argued that the nationalization of road, rail and air transport after World War II gave governments of all complexions a unique opportunity to co-ordinate land transport, but it is manifestly clear that this did not take place. From 1951 onwards, road transport was promoted at the expense of rail, with results that are only too obvious.

As a result, public transport facilities in rural areas were much reduced, and in this context the Monmouthshire area fared very badly. All branch lines were closed, leaving only the South Wales main line and the 'North and West' route from Newport to Hereford. Towns such as Monmouth and Ross-on-Wye were deleted from the railway network, and local travellers were left with a handful of railheads at places such as Chepstow and Lydney.

Viewed dispassionately, it is perhaps unfortunate that some remnant of the local branch line system could not have been retained in modified form as a feeder to the main lines. A single line from Chepstow to Monmouth and thence to Ross would, for example, have provided a rail link for central Monmouthshire, while serving as a useful tourist attraction in the popular Wye Valley district. Sadly, this was not to be, and one is left with the inescapable conclusion that governments of the 1960s and early 1970s were determined to transfer as much traffic as possible to the roads, with no regard for environmental issues, or the long term national interest.

The bridge over the Wye east of Monmouth (Troy) station in 2009. To the left is the masonry for the bridge which carried the railway line to Chepstow. *D. Kennedy*

Bibliography and Further Reading

The publisher wishes to thank Mr R.A. Cooke for his help and generosity, and for allowing his research on the Ross-on-Wye to Pontypool Road line to be used to enhance this Second Revised Edition of this book.

At first glance, the following list would appear to contain ample material on the Ross, Monmouth & Pontypool Road line, although on closer examination it will be seen that many of the listed books and articles relate to locomotives, rather than railway history or infrastructure. In fact, very little has ever been written on this interesting cross-country route, but it is hoped that the following bibliography of printed sources may be of interest to modellers or local historians seeking further information.

Abergavenny & Monmouth Railway, Act of Incorporation 1865
Behrend, George, *Gone with Regret* (Lambarde Press 1964)
Bolger, Paul, *BR Steam Motive Power Depots: WR* (Ian Allan 1982)
Bradshaw's Railway Shareholders' Guides, passim
Bradshaw's Railway Timetables, passim
Bristol Mercury, The
British Railways Closure Files, *passim*
British Railways Magazine, The, passim
British Railways, Public & Working Timetables, Signalling & Permanent Way Alterations, General Instructions & Working Notices, etc.
Carpenter, Roger, Symond's Yat Station, *British Railway Journal* No. 4, 1984
Clark, J.H., *Usk Past & Present* (1891)
Coleford, Monmouth Usk & Pontypool Railway, Act of Incorporation 1853
Cooke, R.A., *Track Layout Diagrams of the GWR and BR(WR)* Section 36 (1998)
Copsey, John, 48XX Auto Engines, *Great Western Railway Journal* Nos. 22 & 23, 1997
Copsey, John, '2251' Class Mixed Traffic 0-6-0s, *Great Western Railway Journal* No. 24, 1997
Fox, J. Charles, *The Little Guide to Gloucestershire* (1914)
Cummings, John, *Railway Motor Buses & Bus Services* (Oxford Publishing Co. 1980)
Davis, J.J., The Railways of Monmouth, *The Railway Magazine*, September 1952
Dictionary of National Biography, The
Freezer, Cyril J., Locomotives of the GWR: Push-Pull Panniers, *Railway Modeller*, September 1969
Freezer, Cyril J., Locomotives of the GWR: The 45XXs, *Railway Modeller* January 1969
Freezer, Cyril J., Locomotives of the GWR: 14XX Class 0-4-2T, *Railway Modeller*, October 1967
Freezer, Cyril J., Locomotives of the GWR: The Ubiquitous Pannier, *Railway Modeller*, June 1967
Gloucester & Dean Forest Railway, Act of Incorporation 1846
Glover, Mark & Celia, *The Ross & Monmouth Railway* (Brewin Books 1994)
Great Western Railway Magazine, The, passim
Great Western Railway, *Towns, Villages, Outlying Works etc* (1938)
Great Western Railway, *Holiday Haunts, passim*

Great Western Railway, *Traffic Dealt with at Stations & Goods Depots*
Great Western Railway, Station Accounts Instruction Book (1929)
Great Western Railway, Register of Private Sidings
Great Western Railway, Census of Staff (1922, 1925 & 1929)
Great Western Railway, Signalling alteration, working notices etc., Working & Public Timetables, *passim*
Grote Lewin, Henry, *The Railway Mania & its Aftermath* (1936)
Handley, B.M., & Dingwall, R., *The Wye Valley Railway* (Oakwood Press 1983)
Harrison, Ian, *Great Western Railway Locomotive Allocations for 1921* (Wild Swan Publications 1984)
Hereford, Ross & Gloucester Railway, Act of Incorporation 1851
Holcroft, Harry, *An Outline of Great Western Locomotive Practice* (Locomotive Publishing Co. 1957)
Hunter, Fred, Signalman's Day at Monmouth Troy, *Great Western Railway Journal* No. 8, 1994
Jenkins, Stanley C., *The Northampton & Banbury Junction Railway* (Oakwood Press 1990)
Jenkins, Stanley C., & Quayle, Howard, *The Oxford Worcester & Wolverhampton Railway* (Oakwood Press 1977)
Joby, R.S., Father & Son Business, *The Railway Magazine*, February 1980
Jones, P.T., *The Welsh Marches & Lower Wye Valley* (The British Publishing Co. 1931)
Journal of the House of Commons, passim
Journal of the House of Lords, passim
Kelly's Directories of Herefordshire, passim
Lyons, Eric, *An Illustrated History of Great Western Locomotive Sheds* (Oxford Publishing Co. 1972)
MacDermott, E.T., *The History of the Great Western Railway*, Vols I & II (GWR 1926 & 1931)
Monmouth & Hereford Railway, Act of Incorporation 1845
Monmouthshire Beacon, The
Northampton & Banbury Junction Railway, Acts 1863, 1865, 1866 & 1870
Oman, Charles, *Castles* (GWR 1926)
Paar, H.W., *The Great Western Railway in Dean* (David & Charles 1965)
Proceedings of the Institute of Civil Engineers, passim
Railway Clearing House, *Handbook of Stations* 1910, 1922 and 1938 editions
Railway Observer, The, passim
Railway Times, The, passim
Ross & Monmouth Railway, Acts of 1865 & 1867
Ross Gazette, The, passim
Smith, William H., Ross-on-Wye, *Great Western Railway Journal* No. 2, 1992
South Wales Railway, Act of Incorporation 1845
Taylor, A.J., *Raglan Castle* (HMSO 1950)
Times, The, passim
Wade, G.W. & Wade, J.H., *The Little Guide to Herefordshire* (1917)
Worcester, Dean Forest & Monmouth Railway, Act of Incorporation 1863

Index